INTRODUCTION to
TAGMEMIC ANALYSIS

TRANSATLANTIC SERIES in LINGUISTICS

Under the general editorship of
Samuel R. Levin
Hunter College
of the City University
of New York

ANALYTIC SYNTAX

OTTO JESPERSEN

THE STUDY OF SYNTAX
The Generative-Transformational Approach
to the Structure of American English

D. TERENCE LANGENDOEN

INTRODUCTION to TAGMEMIC ANALYSIS

WALTER A. COOK, S.J.
Georgetown University

HOLT, RINEHART AND WINSTON, INC.
New York   Chicago   San Francisco   Atlanta
Dallas   Montreal   Toronto   London   Sydney

Preface

Introduction to Tagmemic Analysis is an application of the methods of linguistic science to practical language problems at the level of grammar. It presupposes a general introduction to the science of linguistics and a knowledge of phonetics and phonemics. This introduction deals with inductive methods for analyzing real languages beginning with explicit sets of data. In the application of these methods, the beginner is encouraged to use his knowledge of traditional grammar, within the limitations imposed by a strictly formal approach to analysis.

The tagmemic system is used as the formal method for presenting the results of this inductive analysis. It is maximally taxonomic; every function and form is given a name. This system seems best suited for students beginning language analysis and for more advanced students who are analyzing an unknown language for the first time. At a later stage, more sophisticated methods for presenting the results of analysis might be attempted.

Tagmemic analysis cuts across the boundary between morphology and syntax, and presents the structures of grammar by a single method. In the present work, after an introduction dealing with method, models, and practice, the system is presented in Chapter 1, Tagmemic Analysis. Structures at the various levels of grammar are presented in the following chapters: 2, Sentence Level; 3, Clause Level; 4, Phrase Level; and 5, Word Level. Methods for determining the number of sentences generated and their underlying structural descriptions are given in Chapter 6, Morpheme Level. Finally, the basic units of the phonological, lexical, and syntactic components of the grammar are described in terms of their feature, manifestation, and distribution modes in Chapter 7, Language Description. Suggested problems and a list of tagmemic symbols for use in problem work are included at the end of the text.

At each stage of development, an attempt has been made to be as explicit as possible with regard to the sources used, and each chapter is supplemented by suggested readings with annotations. Tagmemic theory is developed from the works of Kenneth L. Pike and Robert E. Longacre. Practical tagmemic formulations are based on the work of Benjamin Elson and Velma Pickett, and the laboratory manual of William R. Merrifield. To a lesser degree, use is made of the writings of other tagmemic authors, particularly those of the Summer Institute of Linguistics, who in facing practical language problems have contributed so much to the development of the theory.

Grateful acknowledgment is made to Kenneth L. Pike, Robert E. Longacre, and William R. Merrifield for their constructive criticism of early tagmemic writings, and for materials supplied from the Summer Institute of Linguistics; also to Ruth M. Brend for comments on an earlier version of the manuscript. A debt of gratitude is also due my former teachers at the School of Languages and Linguistics and its dean, Robert Lado, for their encouragement. And then there are students, who always manage to teach us while we teach them.

WALTER A. COOK, S.J.

Washington, D.C.
May 1969

Contents

*In human speech, different sounds
have different meanings. To study this
coordination of certain sounds with
certain meanings is to study
language.*

Leonard Bloomfield, *Language*, 1933

INTRODUCTION to
TAGMEMIC ANALYSIS

INTRODUCTION: METHOD, MODELS, AND PRACTICE

Linguistics is the scientific study of language. The object of this study is language, "a purely human and noninstinctive method of communicating ideas, emotions and desires by means of a system of voluntarily produced symbols." (Sapir, 1921:8).[1] The particular viewpoint adopted by the linguist in this study of language is the search for language structure. The methods he uses to discover and describe language structure are scientific.

The central problem in language analysis is the problem of the inaccessible machinery in the mind of man which produces the utterances of language in a regular and systematic way. It is the problem of fundamental grammar. In the early history of linguistic science, Ferdinand DeSaussure (1916:14) distinguished between language and speaking. Speaking is willful, individual and accidental; language is systematic, conventional and belongs to the psychological order. It is language, not speaking, that is the object of linguistic study. More recently Noam Chomsky (1965:4) distinguished competence from performance. Competence is "the speaker-hearer's knowledge of his language," and performance is "the actual use of language in concrete situations." It is competence, not performance, that is the object of our study. The problem of language analysis is to discover and describe the language competence of the speaker.

Grammar in this fundamental state, the competence of the speaker, is largely unconscious. People use language unconsciously, without being aware of the shift in grammatical structures as they use the language for communication. Whether

---

[1]This refers to the author, date, and page number of the reading in the Selected Bibliography at the end of the text.

language is learned in early childhood, or at an advanced age, the processes rapidly become habitual. In order to analyze language, one must work backward from performance, which can be observed, to a competence that is not accessible by any direct approach. The analyst then attempts to construct a model of grammar, which is a formal statement of competence, based upon the objective evidence that is presented to him in the actual performance of the speaker.

The Scientific Method

As in most physical and some behavioral sciences, the method used in the analysis of languages is primarily an inductive one. This method is not a matter of free choice; it is forced upon us by the nature of the language problem.

The Little Black Box. To illustrate how inductive science works, John G. Kemeny (1959:131) gives the example of the box with inaccessible machinery. Suppose you have a locked box, which cannot be opened without destroying its contents. One can observe how the box works, and predict how it will act. We can form a theory as to what kind of machinery is in the box, and we will maintain that theory as long as our predictions concerning the box are verified.

The problem of the box is similar to the problem which faces the linguistic analyst. He can note the performance of the native speaker of a language, but the competence of the speaker is not accessible to him. Therefore he constructs a formal grammar, a statement of competence, and maintains his theory as long as it continues to predict accurately the performance of native speakers. But this formal grammar has only a relation of equivalence, not a relation of identity, with the fundamental grammar in the mind of the speaker. The grammatical model generates language utterances *as if* it were a native speaker.

The Search for Competence. The linguistic analyst has competence as the object of his study, yet this is not directly accessible. He can only approach competence through: (1) the input, the material which goes into the mind of man to form a grammar; (2) reflection on his own language competence; or (3) the output, the performance of the speaker.

No one has ever completely measured the material which goes into the mind of the child to form a grammar, nor do we know how this material is assimilated and organized. Reflection also seems to be a poor tool, since language is largely unconscious. Although the analyst is clearly capable of editing his own language to make it grammatical, he is wary of subjectivism; and if he analyzes his own language at all, he prefers to work from some objective evidence of actual performance.

The result is that the only really objective evidence available to the linguistic analyst is the performance of native speakers of the language. In the search for competence, the goal of the analyst is to catch the unconscious competence of the native speaker in the actual performance, to work backward from what is factual and evident to the structures underlying this systematic behavior.

The Inductive Cycle. The inductive method is a cyclic method which goes from facts to theory to new facts. It consists of four steps: (1) observation of the data, (2) insight into the structure of the data, (3) formulation of a hypothesis, and (4) verification of the hypothesis. In the first two steps we observe and guess, a regressive argument from consequent to antecedent. In the next two steps we formulate and check, a progressive argument from antecedent to consequent. The process is described by Bochenski (1965:92) and Kemeny (1959:86).

Applying this theory to language, we first observe the performance of the native speaker and guess at the underlying language competence. We then formulate a statement of competence and check this against the known performance of the native speaker. The observe and guess steps are called *discovery;* the formulate and check steps are called *verification.* The four steps may be represented in the following schematic diagram:

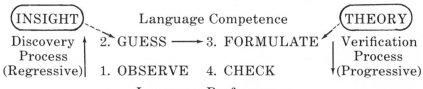

The Four Steps. The steps of the inductive method characterize this scientific method as empirical, intelligent, exact and objective.

> *Step 1: Observation of the data* is an empirical step in which the linguist records language performance in protocol statements—statements in a form recognizable and readable by other analysts. In problems at the grammatical level, the given data is assumed to be in phonemic script.
>
> *Step 2: Insight into the structure of the data* is an intelligent step and prevents the process from being

mechanical. It is intuitive, based upon the data, but aided by the background, training and intelligence of the analyst, who must be able to generalize, to compare, to see regularity.

Step 3: Formulation of the hypothesis is an exact step in which the results of discovery are formulated in an exact way according to some given theory. The theory provides new terms, general ways of speaking about language, and must be used in a consistent way by the analyst.

Step 4: Verification of the hypothesis is an objective step in which the formulated results are mechanically verified. Assuming the investigation has been empirical (Step 1) and exact (Step 3), the results should be independent of the subjective attitudes of the analyst, and publicly verifiable by any other analyst using the same data and methods.

Discovery Process. The tagmemic theory of language analysis has traditionally emphasized the discovery process. According to the author of the theory, Kenneth L. Pike, the discovery procedures are not mechanical, but contain elements of intuition (1967:225, fn. 6). In any discovery process there are "analytic leaps" (1967:493) which, in the study of language, are based on the facts of proportion and analogy, substitution and expansion. The intuitive, nonmechanical nature of the discovery process, however, does not prevent the formal presentation of results from being exact. Analytic procedures require reference to meaning and intuitive judgment, but presentation does not (1967:493).

Robert E. Longacre openly calls the procedures guess-and-check, but states that they "need not be mechanical to be useful" (1964:12). The guesses contain "elements of creative thinking," and are based on the facts of "closure" and "choice." Speakers are aware when a construction is closed, and often backtrack to reword a construction. The element of choice is evident in the hesitation of a speaker, as he attempts to find the right word or expression (1964:14). The guesses made by the analyst are then formulated in an exact way and subjected to a series of checks, which call for revision of the formal statement and allow the analyst to come up with some better guesses along the way.

Verification Process. With the advent of transformational models, attention has been focused upon mechanical verification procedures. Although traditionally the tagmemic theory has been more concerned with the discovery process, the language generated from tagmemic models has been tested with native speakers in extensive translations. The impact of this new emphasis on verification has, however, caused a reevaluation of the theory in terms of explicit generative power.

Longacre (1964:32) develops the power of a tagmemic grammar through four steps: (1) readings (combinations), (2) permutations, (3) manifestations, and (4) substitution of lexical and phonological material. By these steps, tagmemic grammars can be formalized as devices which generate the grammatical sentences of the language. "Provided the grammar has been carefully constructed," says Longacre (1964:31), the analyst will "end up with the grammatically possible, and never with the grammatically impossible."

Following the suggestion of Longacre, it can be demonstrated that the tagmemic model is an exact model which is capable of (1) generating the original data, (2) generating trial utterances at random which are acceptable to native speakers, and (3) generating, given a finite grammar and lexicon, the entire grammatical output of the grammar together with the underlying structural description of each sentence.

Models of Grammar

The result of the discovery process in language analysis is a model of grammar ready for verification. Most language models consider both the forms of language and the function of these forms in the language. Models which emphasize the functional aspect are functional models.

Functional Models. In the analysis of language, three questions must be asked about each linguistic form: (1) What is it? (2) What does it do? and (3) Where does it occur? The answer to the first question identifies the form as a member of a definite form class. The answer to the second question identifies how this form functions within the language. The answer to the third question gives the distribution of the functioning form unit.

The concept of function is not new in the study of language. As Chomsky has pointed out (1965:63), even traditional grammars gave us information about grammatical categories (which we call "form") and grammatical relationships (which we call "function"), and grammatical models must account for both in language description. In practice, however, he advocates a strictly formal model of grammar, in which grammatical functions, or relationships, are implicit (1965:69).

Functions by Levels. Function is present at all levels of the grammar. Function may be distinguished from form in phonology, in lexicon and in grammar. In phonology, the phonemes of a language have a differential function. They do not carry meaning; they are sound units which differentiate the meaningful forms of language. They are "points in the pattern" to which the native speaker reacts (Sapir, 1921:56). In the lexicon, the morphemes, or form units of the language, have a referential function. Within the communication system of language, the function of the morpheme is simply to refer to an area of meaning. This association is purely conventional, and independent of the shape of the forms which are used. For example, vowel replacement is used in such forms as *goose/geese* to represent plural, and in such forms as *take/took* to represent past. "Wherever we go," says Sapir (1921:59), "we are impressed by the fact that pattern is one thing, the utilization of pattern quite another." Further research in languages other than the English language, he suggests, might further emphasize "this relative independence of function and form" (1921:59). In grammar, the units have a grammatical function, and add a grammatical meaning to forms, over and above the meaning they have as lexical items (Fries, 1962:70). Total linguistic meaning equals lexical plus grammatical meaning.

Word Functions. The form of words in isolation is distinct from the function of words in syntax. The form, or category, of a word is defined by the inflectional paradigm of the word. A noun is a word that takes noun inflections. The function of a word in syntax is defined by the usage of the word; a nominal is a word that "acts like" (hence – AL) a noun in syntax. In *The Structure of English* (1952), Fries presented a model of English structure based upon functional usage. The groups that he isolates are called Class 1 (nominal), Class 2 (verbal), Class 3 (adjectival) and Class 4 (adverbial). In addition, the groups of functional words A through O, fifteen groups in all, are isolated by the same procedures.

The results of the slot and filler technique employed by Fries are really function, not form, classes. This analysis could be followed by subanalysis, a technique in which the forms which act like nouns and fill noun slots in the structure are sorted. Among these forms will be found nouns – forms that take noun inflections – and other forms that appear in cross-functional usage with nouns. For example, in the sentence, *Barking is noisy*, the form *barking* is used as a noun. But this is a verb form, marked by the verbal inflection *-ing*. The same form may appear in adjectival use in *The barking dog*, and in verbal use as a main verb in sentences such as *The dog is barking*.

Group Functions. Groups may be named by the head word of the construction, as *noun phrase, verb phrase,* and so on.

These are categorical labels. The same groups, as they are used in syntax, may be given functional labels, such as *nominal phrase*, to indicate what function they have in syntactic usage. Extending Fries' technique to include word groups is a type of superanalysis that labels group functions. Listing word form, word function, and group function shows three levels of structure. Applied to the sentence given by Longacre (1960), these levels are:

Group Function	1(S)	$\longleftrightarrow$	2(P)	1(O)
Word Function	(D + 3 + 3 + 3 + 1)		(2)	(D + 1)
Word Form	(D + 3 + 2-ing + 2-d + 1)		2-d	(D + 1)
Sentence	The slow, lumbering covered wagon pulled the family.			

Phrase structures emerge at the word function level, and clause patterns at the group level. Function words tend to disappear at higher levels, and the resulting grammatical patterns can be expressed in terms of four basic functions as nominal, verbal, adjectival, and adverbial groups.

Function-Form Units. Subsequent to the development of the model using functional word classes, Kenneth L. Pike introduced the tagmemic model, which uses a function-form unit. While working with artificial languages, Pike found that the basic units of grammar could neither be expressed in terms of function alone, in such strings as $S + P + O$, nor in terms of form alone, in such strings as $N + V + N$, but demanded that both function and form be expressed, in such strings as $S:N + P:V + O:N$ which is read as "subject slot filled by a noun phrase, predicate slot filled by a verb phrase, and object slot filled by a noun phrase." He then concluded that the basic unit of grammar must be a correlation of function and form, the correlation of a grammatical function or slot with the list of mutually substitutable fillers that fill that slot.

This unit was labeled the tagmeme, from the Greek word *tagma* meaning "arrangement," and posited as the fundamental unit of grammatical arrangement, corresponding to the units of sound in phonology, and the units of meaningful form in morphology. The tagmeme unit is a slot-class correlative. The functional slot gives the grammatical relation, the filler class gives the grammatical categories involved, but neither exists without the other. Function is manifested by forms, and forms do not occur in grammar without having identifiable function.

String Constituents. The emphasis that the tagmemic model placed upon the functional aspect of grammar caused a radical change in the analysis of language. If function is primary, then the analysis of any construction is going to result in as many functional parts as can be identified within the construction. This results in the cutting of the construction string into many functional parts simultaneously. Other grammatical models current at the time used the principle of immediate constituent analysis, which required that the construction string, with rare exceptions, always be cut into two parts. This binary cutting operation was repeated successively until the morphemes, or ultimate constituents of the string, were reached.

In tagmemic string-type analysis, the construction is viewed as a set of multiple relations. The tagmeme units are points in the pattern, and are related to each other within that pattern. The functional points are not rigidly defined. They are largely intuitive, and correspond to traditional notions of subject and predicate, head and modifier. But this laxness of definition in the early stages of analysis helps to provide flexibility in separating functions within the construction string. Further refinements of this analysis permit a pinpointing of more exact grammatical meanings attached to each functional slot, such as subject-as-actor in active sentences, and subject-as-goal in passive sentences.

Grammatical Levels. The concept of the tagmemic model was further clarified by the introduction of grammatical levels. The function-form unit, or tagmeme, occurred in constructions of the string type, which, in turn, occurred as well-defined levels within the grammar. These levels are the natural levels of sentence, clause, phrase, word, and morpheme. The idea of tagmemes at various levels is attributed by Pike to Longacre (1967:432, fn. 1). Elsewhere, Pike says that the concept of levels is now widely accepted as part of tagmemic theory (1967:232, fn. 9).

The introduction of grammatical levels that are well defined allows the analyst to begin his analysis at any level of the grammar. He need not begin with the sentence; he may begin by analyzing words or phrases, and can continue analysis to levels above the sentence. But the final grammar will present a well-ordered set of rules dealing with the structures of sentences, clauses, phrases, and words down to the ultimate constituents, or morphemes, of the language.

In generating sentences from this grammatical model, the form units which are listed in the lexicon are programmed into word level structures, words into phrases, phrases into clauses, and clauses into sentences. For those who wish to carry the analysis further, sentences can be programmed into higher and more complex structures.

Tagmemic Model. The resulting tagmemic model contains a grammar, a lexicon, and a phonological component. The grammar is a series of syntactic statements concerning sentence, clause, phrase, and word level structures. Each construction at each level is formulated in terms of tagmeme units, which explicitly give both the function and the form of each element in the construction. The lexicon lists the form units of language, together with their classification and gloss, and the morphophonemic rules to account for the varying forms of morphemes. Finally, the phonological component gives the phonemic sentence a phonetic realization in the language.

The model generates all and only the grammatical sentences of the language; it assigns a structural description to each sentence generated and an explicit function to each part of each structural description. The "all and only" provision can be reduced to an exact mathematical figure for all sentences generated by a finite grammar with a limited lexical inventory. This is the generative potential of the grammar. The structural descriptions can be constructed as tree diagrams, if the grammar is properly constructed in levels from higher to lower. And in the structural descriptions, every branch of every underlying phrase structure diagram may be explicitly labeled as to its function within its own construction, thus making the branching process explicit.

Theory and Practice

The test of a linguistic model is how it stands up in practice. It is only by coming face to face with real analytic problems that one is able to judge the value, as well as the limitations, of the model. The present text is designed to be used in practical analysis.

Supplementary Exercises. On page 195, a list of supplementary exercises is suggested for use with the present text. The best laboratory manual available is William R. Merrifield's *Laboratory Manual for Morphology and Syntax*, revised 1967, Summer Institute of Linguistics. In this revision, problems #1 to #91 deal with morphology, and problems #92 to #188 deal with syntax. The list of exercises suggested here includes the first twenty problems dealing with syntax, #92 to #111, but regular use of the manual will suggest other combinations just as effective.

The syntax problems of the manual are series of sentences given in phonemic script, together with the translation of each sentence. In solving the problems, the set of sentences is accepted as the language, and solutions are based upon the data given in the problem. Where assumptions must be made about the language in question, they must be explicitly stated. All of the data is taken from real languages, so the problems encountered are real, not hypothetical problems.

Tagmemic Notation. A list of eighty tagmemic symbols, with their definitions and use, is given on page 197. It is a basic list, intended to be sufficient for simple declarative sentences, although new symbols might be needed for other sentence types. Symbols constitute a language about language. Working with a limited list of symbols, analysts are able to communicate fundamental insights concerning language structure with the same basic vocabulary.

The solution based on a limited symbol inventory expresses a commitment to a particular concrete solution to a problem. If more than one solution presents itself, it is up to the analyst, with his prior knowledge of the theory, to present his own chosen alternative in the most rigorous fashion possible within the limits of that theory. Of many solutions that are adequate to represent the structure in a given set of data, one solution will usually turn out to be simpler than the others.

Solutions that are rigorously formulated are easily understood by others familiar with the same notation. If, in practice, it becomes necessary to introduce new symbols by analogy with the old, each new symbol should be explained as it is introduced. The resulting description can then be interpreted without ambiguity.

Use of Meaning. In using a functional model for the description of language, no apology is given for the use of meaning. The recognition of the lexical meaning of forms, and the grammatical meanings which these forms have in syntax, is essential to the system. In general, the tagmemic system follows the principle enunciated by Fries (1952:8) that the use of meaning is unscientific only when "the fact of our knowing the meaning leads us to stop short of finding the precise formal signals that operate to convey that meaning."

A translation is given with the data, often supplemented by a word for word gloss of the forms. First the individual words and word parts must be isolated, together with their meanings, by comparing recurring partials in the language. When there is a change in meaning parallel to a change in form, the meaning change is attributed to the form change. The forms and meanings isolated are listed in a lexicon. In the second step, these forms are programmed into the patterns of the language. Formulas are constructed that describe how morphemes combine to form words, words to form phrases, phrases to form clauses, and clauses to form sentences. This set of formulas constitutes the grammar. The points in the pattern are named with functional labels, and the forms that occur at these points are labeled with form or category labels from the lexicon.

Verification of the Model. With the formulation of the tag-memic model in terms of grammar and lexicon, the problem has been solved, but it is useful to follow this work with verification procedures. One method of doing this is to calculate, for each finite problem, the exact number of sentences that can be generated by a given solution.

If the solution to a problem is a commitment, the analyst should be aware of the full implications of this commitment. He should be aware that the solution he proposes, whether he makes the calculation or not, does in fact generate an exact number of sentences. The attempt to determine this number leads to a fuller realization of the generative power of the grammar, and focuses attention upon restrictions which should be imposed on the grammar, and included in the solution.

With each grammar produced, there is an underlying structural description assigned to each sentence generated. The analyst should be aware, not only of the number of sentences generated by the model he has created, but of the number of underlying structural patterns, and the number of sentences that belong to each of the structural patterns. The number of structural patterns generated is a function of the number of optional elements occurring at any level from sentence to word; the number of sentences generated is a function of the number of morphemes that happen to belong to each morpheme class isolated.

Conclusion. The tagmemic model is only one of many models used in linguistic analysis. Because of its functional orientation, and its well-developed discovery procedures, it is useful in teaching language analysis to beginners, and ideally suited even for the more advanced in a field methods situation. With the new emphasis upon verification procedure, it can be demonstrated that the model has generative capacity, and that it generates a well-defined set of sentences that can be calculated exactly and generated by computer. The model also generates a set of phrase structure descriptions which represent the "deep structure" of the sentences generated. Finally, it assigns explicit function to all points of the branching patterns in that underlying structure.

The science of language analysis profits from the existence of conflicting theories; each can learn from the other. The tagmemic system has been applied to many languages of the world with considerable success, and many of the current language descriptions of unknown languages are done in some form of tagmemic description. Anyone interested in the science should be acquainted with this functional approach to language, simply in order to understand what others are doing. Those using this approach should also be familiar with other current grammatical models.

TABLE 1: THE SYSTEM OF GRAMMATICAL LEVELS

SENTENCE LEVEL
Base + Intonation

CLAUSE LEVEL
Subject + Predicate + Object + Adjuncts

PHRASE LEVEL
Relater + Axis, and Endocentric Word Groups

WORD LEVEL
Stems + Derivations + Inflections

MORPHEME LEVEL
The ultimate level of analysis

1 TAGMEMIC ANALYSIS

Tagmemic analysis is a set of procedures for the description of language, with a basic grammatical unit called the *tagmeme* mapped into string-type constructions located at specific levels in the grammar. The system and theory were developed by Kenneth L. Pike, and used by the Summer Institute of Linguistics for the training of language analysts. The system was designed to meet concrete field problems. Because of the large number of linguists who have come to use the system and the frequency of their publications, the system of tagmemic analysis is now one of the major systems of analysis in modern linguistic science.

Early Tagmemic Theory. The notion of the tagmeme as a basic unit of grammar, consisting of a functional slot and a list of the mutually substitutable items that fill the slot, first appeared in Kenneth L. Pike's *Language in Relation to a Unified Theory of the Structure of Human Behaviour*, Part I, 1954, and Part II, 1955. The term "tagmeme" was substituted for the original name, "grameme," in a later article by Pike, "On Tagmemes nee Gramemes" *(IJAL,* **24:**273–278, 1958). In this article, Pike describes how he arrived at the notion of the tagmeme by working with artificial languages with a constant lexical inventory but varying grammatical structures, and contrasts his use of the word "tagmeme" with that of Bloomfield. The tagmeme is a unit, parallel to the phoneme and the morpheme, in a triple grammatical hierarchy of phonology, lexicon, and grammar. All three basic units are shown to be trimodally structured in a later article: "Language as Particle, Wave and Field" *(The Texas Quarterly,* 1959, **2:**37–54). Finally, the last volume of Pike's original work was published as Part III (1960) to complete the theoretical

13

framework. All three volumes have recently been republished in a single volume (The Hague, Mouton and Co., 1967). Bibliographies have been updated, and footnotes added to reflect recent discoveries in linguistics.

Later Developments. With the tagmeme clearly defined as a unit, Robert E. Longacre, in his article, "String Constituent Analysis" (*Language*, 1960, **36**:63–88), shows how these units combine in a string type analysis which is radically different from the binary type constructions used in the older immediate constituent model. The cuts in tagmemics are simultaneous at each level of the grammar, with multiple branching in a single formula, whereas the immediate constituent type of analysis is based on a system of successive binary cuts. This system is reduced to practice in Longacre's *Grammar Discovery Procedures* (The Hague, Mouton and Co., 1964), which explains analytic procedures at the sentence, clause, phrase, and word levels. Finally, the main points of the theory are summarized by Longacre in a later article, "Some Fundamental Insights of Tagmemics" (*Language*, **41**:65–66, 1965).

With unit and constructions now clearly defined, Pike next turned his attention to the grammatical system, and developed the idea of the grammatical matrix as a field system in two articles: "Dimensions of Grammatical Structure" (*Language*, **38**:221–244, 1962), an exposition of matrix theory, and "A Syntactic Paradigm" (*Language*, **39**:216–230, 1963), a practical application of the matrix theory. In these articles, the grammatical matrix is described as an array, similar to the systematic arrangements found in word paradigms and phonemic charts. While recognizing the usefulness of matrices to show relations between constructions, Longacre, in *Grammar Discovery Procedures*, also recommends the use of grammatical transformations. The use of both methods in the same description is not contradictory; the two ways are "not immiscible" (1964:16).

Pedagogical Materials. The application of the tagmemic system has been greatly aided by the practical work of the teachers of the Summer Institute of Linguistics and the pedagogical textbooks prepared for this teaching program. Beginning with Velma Pickett, *An Introduction to the Study of Grammatical Structure*, and Benjamin Elson, *Beginning Morphology and Syntax*, a set of revised texts was published in 1962, including Benjamin Elson and Velma Pickett, *An Introduction to Morphology and Syntax*, and the *Laboratory Manual for Morphology and Syntax*, by William R. Merrifield, Constance M. Naish, Calvin R. Rensch, and Gillian Story. These works provide a clear and simple method of applying tagmemics in practice, together with problems needed to exercise these skills.

Although this brief survey has been confined to the principal texts available in tagmemic theory, many other analysts have contributed to the system by solving problems of particular languages using tagmemic methods. References to these tagmemic publications, with a critical appraisal of each, may be found in "A Guide to Publications in Tagmemic Theory," by Kenneth L. Pike, published in *Current Trends in Linguistics*, edited by Thomas A. Sebeok (The Hague, Mouton and Co., 1966, III, 365–394).

THE UNIT: THE TAGMEME

The unit in tagmemic analysis is the tagmeme, the correlation of a functional slot with the class of items that fill that slot. This unit is not merely a form unit, as in other grammatical models, but a composite of function and form. For a complete understanding of this basic unit, we will consider: (1) the definition of the tagmeme, (2) the kinds of tagmemes that may occur in construction, and (3) tagmemes as essential units of the grammar.

The Tagmeme Defined

The tagmeme is defined as "the correlation of a grammatical function, or slot, with the class of mutually substitutable items that fill that slot" (Elson and Pickett, 1962:57). It is a slot-class correlative in which both function and form are explicitly named. This concept of a grammatical function, correlated with a set of manifesting items, is the first of four fundamental insights of tagmemics (Longacre, 1965:65).

The Functional Slot. A slot is a position in a construction frame. Functional slots are positions in construction frames which define the role of linguistic forms in the construction, relative to other parts of the same construction. Functions are grammatical relationships. They answer the question of what the form does in the construction, and are labeled as subject, predicate, head, modifier, and the like. Functional slots may be identified by (1) position, (2) proportion, and (3) meaning, as described by Pike (1967:218–219).

The slot is defined by position in the construction frame. However, the function is structural rather than linear. Although normally functional slots will be found in a fixed position, the system provides for units that are movable and occur in more than one position. Further, cases of intonation and stress, which occur simultaneously with other elements, are by convention placed to the right of the accompanying elements. The linear order of the slot is not to be interpreted too rigidly.

The slot is also defined by structural meaning, that is, the meaning which is added to the lexical items filling the slot, over and above the lexical meaning as it appears in the dictionary. The structural meaning of the slot is indicated by the choice of slot label, for example, "Subject." Structural meaning, in turn, sets up a proportional relationship between items filling the different slots of a construction. One subject is to its predicate as any other subject is to any other predicate within the same construction. Items change, but the proportion remains constant.

The Filler Class. The filler class is the list of all the items that can fill the functional slot. These items are mutually substitutable within the slot. This filler class, by definition, is a distribution class, which in many cases is heterogeneous. Whatever fills the slot belongs to the distribution class, no matter what its form. These fillers must be sorted into form classes, and the symbol for each form class that occurs must be listed as part of the tagmeme. In the subject slot, for example, the fillers may include pronouns, proper nouns, noun phrases, clauses, infinitives, and participles.

Within the filler class, one class of forms may be the exclusive, or the typical filler. Particularly in case-marked systems, the slot may be identified by form class marked with a particular case. The subject fillers, for example, may be marked by the nominative case. When listing the filler classes, an effort must be made to find the typical filler of the slot, and identify it by formal markings where possible. Subject, in English, for example, is a slot filled by forms which can be replaced by the series *I, you, he, she, it, they* and is opposed to the object slot, which can be replaced by the series *me, her, him, them.*

Slot-Class Correlative. The tagmeme is neither a functional slot nor a filler class, but a correlation of both slot and class. If the forms of language are held constant, a new language structure can be created by changing the function of these forms. If the functions are held constant, a new language can be created by changing the forms. Both function and form are necessary in order to identify the units of grammar in any particular language.

Any linguistic sign is fully defined by its meaning, form, and distribution. The meaning of the tagmeme is carried by its functional slot. The form of the tagmeme consists of the form classes which are found to manifest this function in the sentences of the language. Finally, this form-meaning unit has a distribution in the constructions of the language.

The correlation of the functional slot with the filler class is a correlation of function and form. The tagmemic system is maximally explicit in the naming process. Function and form are both named in a notation, such as S:N, read as: "subject slot, filled by a noun phrase." We simultaneously name the form, by listing the forms that fill the slot to the right of the ratio mark, and name the function, by giving a label to the grammatical meaning carried by the forms to the left of the ratio sign. When this tagmemic unit is placed in a construction string, we can answer all these pertinent questions about the linguistic unit: What is it? What does it do? Where does it occur?

Kinds of Tagmemes in Constructions

Tagmemes are function-form correlatives which are distributed in the constructions of the language. Relative to the constructions in which they occur, tagmemes are of various kinds. They may be: (1) obligatory or optional to the construction; (2) nuclear or peripheral to the structure; and (3) distributed in fixed or movable positions.

Obligatory versus Optional Tagmemes. Tagmemes are either obligatory or optional to the construction in which they occur. An obligatory tagmeme is a tagmeme that occurs in every manifestation of the structure in the given data. It is marked with a plus (+) sign to indicate that it must occur whenever the construction occurs. An optional tagmeme is a tagmeme that occurs in some but not all of the manifestations of the construction. It is marked with a plus/minus (±) sign to indicate that it may occur, but need not necessarily occur, whenever the construction occurs. Every tagmeme in the construction string, including the very first tagmeme, must be marked as obligatory or optional.

Suprasegmentals may be marked with a minus (−) sign. This sign is interpreted as an obligatory tagmeme, but one which is not in linear order. It is used for the intonation patterns of sentences, and may be extended to include the suprasegmentals that affect the structure of the word, such as the features of pitch, tone, and stress.

The symbols that mark the tagmeme as obligatory or optional are also the concatenation symbols of the construction string. They may occur in the following combinations to express concatenation relations:

+A	+B	Tagmemes A and B are both obligatory
+A	±B	Tagmeme A is obligatory, B is optional
±A	∓B	Either A or B must occur, but not both.

By the use of parentheses, further relations of concatenation also can be expressed, with an obligatory or optional marker outside the parentheses.

$$+(+A \quad \pm B) \quad \text{for combinations A, AB (B requires A)}$$
$$\pm(+A \quad \pm B) \quad \text{for combinations A, AB, } \emptyset \text{ (B requires A)}$$
$$+(\pm A \quad \pm B) \quad \text{for combinations A, B, AB}$$
$$\pm(\pm A \quad \pm B) \quad \text{for combinations A, B, AB, } \emptyset$$

Particularly in cases where the affected tagmemes are separated in the linear string, the algebraic sign outside the parentheses may be placed upon a tie bar, connecting the tagmemes which show mutual dependence.

$$+(+A \quad \pm B) \quad \text{may be written} \quad \overset{+}{\overline{\begin{array}{cc} +A & \pm B \end{array}}}$$

Further combinations of obligatory and optional tagmemes, when more than two tagmemes are involved, are handled in similar fashion.

Nuclear versus Peripheral Tagmemes. Tagmemes are either nuclear or peripheral to the constructions in which they occur. This is not the same distinction as obligatory and optional. A nuclear tagmeme is a tagmeme that is diagnostic of the construction in which it occurs. It may be either obligatory or optional. A peripheral tagmeme is a tagmeme that is not diagnostic of the construction in which it occurs. It is always optional. Peripheral tagmemes are sometimes called satellite or marginal tagmemes.

All obligatory tagmemes are nuclear, but all nuclear tagmemes are not obligatory; all optional tagmemes are not peripheral, but all peripheral tagmemes are optional. The application of these two rules results in a three-way classification of tagmemes (Longacre, 1964:19): (1) nuclear and obligatory; (2) nuclear and optional; and (3) peripheral (and optional).

In clause structures, for example, the nuclear tagmemes are those tagmemes that help us to diagnose the clause structure, and generally include the subject, predicate, and object. Yet these tagmemes are, in different languages or in different situations in the same language, optional tagmemes. Thus, the subject is often optional at the clause level, the object is optional in transitive clauses, and even the predicate may be optional in predicate attribute constructions. Yet all of these tagmemes are nuclear, and are useful in separating clause types. A tagmeme may be both nuclear and optional.

Movable versus Fixed Order Tagmemes. Tagmemes are generally assumed to occur in the position in which they are represented in a fixed linear sequence. In the case of languages with movable word order, the statistically prominent order is represented in the string, but the movability of the tagmeme must be indicated.

If the tagmeme has two and only two fixed positions in the string, the alternate positions may be represented by writing the tagmeme in each position, in an either/or notation such as $\pm A \ldots \mp A$. If the tagmeme is freely movable within the string, one device which has been suggested is an arrow written above the movable tagmeme. If, in the same situation, the tagmemes are freely movable, but may not interrupt the nucleus, or SPO complex, then these nuclear elements may be enclosed in parentheses to limit the movability of tagmemes.

$$1.1 \quad tCl = (+S:N +P:tV +O:N) \overset{\longleftrightarrow}{\pm L:loc} \overset{\longleftrightarrow}{\pm T:tem}$$

The above formulation allows such constructions as (in regular order): SPO, SPOL, SPOLT, SPOT; but either L or T or both may occur before the SPO nucleus, and the order TL is permitted after the nucleus.

Etic and Emic Units of Grammar

Tagmemes are the essential units of grammar; but parallel to phonology and lexicon, the grammar has both essential units and nonessential units. The nonessential unit is called an etic unit, and is the first approximation of the analyst to the unit from the point of view of an outsider. The essential unit is called the emic unit, and is the unit of language from the point of view of a native speaker of the language. In grammar, the etic unit is called the tagma, and these tagmas are grouped as allotagmas of essential units, called tagmemes. Thus, in a parallelism suggested by Elson and Pickett (1962:131):

> Tagmas (and allotagmas) are to tagmemes, what
> Morphs (and allomorphs) are to morphemes, and what
> Phones (and allophones) are to phonemes.

The first approximation of the analyst is the tagma, a correlation of function and form. But after initial investigation, tagmas that are the same are grouped as allotagmas of one tagmeme. Tagmas that are different are set up as belonging to different tagmemes. Norms must be laid down to determine when tagmas are the same or different.

Tagmas as Etic Units. The isolation and classification of tagmas is called the science of tagmatics. It is essentially a cutting process, in which the slot-class correlatives discovered are isolated from each other in the linear string. The words and word sequences are grouped into units, and the string is cut simultaneously into its functional parts at a given level in the grammar.

In practice, every tagma is considered, in the first analysis, as if it were an invariant unit. One works as if every tagma were a tagmeme, that is, as if every tagmeme had one and only one allotagma. This is parallel to the science of morphetics, where the units isolated are morphs, but initially considered as if they were the only manifestations of the morpheme. Form and meaning are clearly isolated.

Once the slot-class correlatives have been initially formulated, it is possible to institute a grouping process and group together those tagmas which seem to have the same functional meaning, even though the fillers of the slots may be different. Thus, given such structures as S:N, a subject slot filled by a noun phrase, and S:pn, a subject slot filled by a pronoun, these may be combined as S:N/pn, a subject slot filled by either a noun phrase or a pronoun. Alternate filler classes are represented by the slash symbol (/) and repeated as often as needed. When variants of a tagmeme seem to have different grammatical meaning, the grouping process becomes more difficult.

Allotagmas of a Tagmeme. The tagmeme is the essential unit of grammar, but may be represented by one or more allotagmas. Since the unit is a function-form unit, the variants of a tagmeme may differ in function, or in form, or in both. Since the function-form unit has a distribution in the language, there may also be differences in distribution. The linguistic sign (LS) is fully described in terms of meaning, form, and distribution (MFD); the variants of the tagmeme will be variants: (1) of meaning, (2) of form, (3) of distribution, or some combination of these features.

If tagmas are totally different in form and meaning, and also in distribution, they belong to different tagmemes. If tagmas are partially different, that is, if they differ in one of these features, the following norms may be useful:

1. Tagmas differing in form alone are tagmas with the same functional meaning and the same position in the string. These are easily grouped as allotagmas of the same tagmeme, by listing the alternate fillers in the one tagmemic slot.
2. Tagmas differing in meaning alone may belong to the same tagmeme. Although the structural meaning of the tagmeme is the principal identifying feature, it is possible to carry over meanings from one's own native language into the target language. Therefore, unless the meaning difference is correlated with a parallel

difference in filler class or position in the string, group the elements as allotagmas of the same tagmeme.

3. Tagmas differing in position alone may belong to the same tagmeme, and would then be merely positional variants of the same unit. Unless change of position is correlated with change of meaning or with change of form, consider the units as variants of one tagmeme.

Tagmemes as Essential Units. The tagmeme is the essential unit of grammar which may be manifested by one or many tagmas. The unifying element in the tagmeme is the grammatical meaning attached to the slot, just as the unifying element in the morpheme is the meaning attached to the form, or set of forms. The tagmeme may have, as its variants: (1) form variants, made up of different filler classes; (2) positional variants, if the tagmeme is movable without change of meaning; and (3) variation in structural meaning, provided form and distribution are constant. The sum of these meaning variations would then be the meaning of the slot, as interpreted by native speakers in the target language. The area of meaning of the slot often does not coincide with the analyst's initial guesses in setting up the etic tagmas, prior to the tagmemic grouping process.

THE CONSTRUCTION: THE SYNTAGMEME

In tagmemic analysis, the unit is the tagmeme — a correlation of a functional slot with a filler class. These units are strung together in constructions. Once the unit of a grammatical description has been clearly defined, the next step is to consider how these units are put together in constructions. In tagmemic analysis, the construction is called the syntagmeme, reminiscent of DeSaussure's syntagm, "a combination supported by linearity, . . . always composed of two or more consecutive units" (1916:123). To understand the nature of the syntagmeme in tagmemic analysis, we consider, in order: (1) the definition of the construction, or syntagmeme; (2) the kinds of construction that occur; and (3) etic and emic constructions.

The Syntagmeme Defined

The construction, or syntagmeme, is defined as "a potential string of tagmemes, whose manifesting sequence of morphemes fills a grammatical slot" (Elson and Pickett, 1962:59). This definition includes the notions of (1) string constituency, (2) potential string, and (3) the internal and external unity of the construction. The concept of syntagmeme, as a "functionally contrastive string on a given level," is the second fundamental insight of tagmemics (Longacre, 1965:70).

String Constituents. There are two principal systems for the description of constructions, no matter what type of unit is used. The first is a string constituent type of analysis; the second is an immediate constituent (IC) type of analysis. In a string type analysis, the utterance is cut simultaneously into all of its functional parts. In making these cuts, the analyst is guided by his knowledge of function. In an immediate constituent analysis, the utterance is cut successively into binary constituents. In making these cuts, the analyst is partly guided by a knowledge of function as well as by the theory that all constructions, with rare exceptions, consist of two parts.

> *String Analysis* cuts this sentence into 5 parts at once: The slow, lumbering covered wagon / pulled / the pioneer's family / across the prairie / just yesterday.

> *IC Analysis* cuts this sentence in 4 successive cuts: The slow, lumbering covered wagon, /[1] pulled /[4] the pioneer's family /[3] across the prairie /[2] just yesterday.

Potential Strings. Given a string type of analysis, how many units are required for the string? Following DeSaussure, one would think that at least two consecutive units are required. However, in the tagmemic use of string analysis, there need not be two obligatory elements to make a construction. Constructions are also possible with one obligatory and one optional element. If the string is potentially expandable — and in any concrete set of data, if it is expanded in fact at least once — then the string is considered to be a construction.

Constructions in tagmemics are not obligatorily complex, but they must be at least potential strings. For example, in discussing the phrase, Pike says it is "either composed of a sequence of two or more words, or is one word which is optionally expandable in that same slot into a sequence of two or more words," (1967:439) and he formulates this as: a phrase is +(+word+word), +(+word ±word), but not +(+word).

The principle of the potential string allows for conciseness in the formulation of single words and phrases. The notation S:N, means that the subject slot is filled by a noun phrase. But the term "noun phrase" includes both single nouns and nouns taken together with modifiers. The notation S:N/n would be redundant, since N (noun phrase) includes n (noun). In practice, the symbol N (noun phrase) would be used only if the noun did, in fact, in the set of data, occur at least once with modifiers.

External Unity and Internal Unity. The external unity of the construction is determined by its occurrence in a higher level slot. To depend upon this occurrence for the unity of the construction is to start an infinite series. Somewhere there is a highest level construction, and this does not occur in a higher slot. In practice, in a grammar limited to the analysis of sentences, these sentences are bounded by their intonational patterns and are not considered as occurring in higher slots.

Although external unity is useful for lower level constructions, each construction has its own internal unity. This internal unity is based upon the correlativity of the tagmeme unit and the construction in which it occurs. The tagmemic functions are defined in terms of the construction in which they occur. For example, subject is meaningless without its relation to the other tagmemes of the string, such as predicate and object.

The tagmeme, then, is not only a unit, as Pike insists, but it also expresses grammatical relationships within the context of the construction. The construction cannot exist without the tagmemes as component parts, and the tagmemes cannot exist without reference to the syntagmeme, or construction. It is this built-in set of relations, of the whole to its parts, that gives the construction its internal unity, and this feature of internal unity is independent of whether or not the whole occurs in a higher slot.

Kinds of Syntagmemes

The syntagmeme, or construction, is a potential string of tagmemes. All of the strings are not of the same kind. Strings of various kinds occur at all levels of grammatical analysis. These construction types include: (1) exocentric and endocentric constructions, (2) closed and open-ended constructions, and (3) recursive and nonrecursive layering.

Exocentric versus Endocentric Constructions. Constructions may be of the exocentric or endocentric type. An endocentric construction is centered about one or more head tagmemes. An exocentric construction is not centered. In endocentric constructions, the whole construction may be replaced by a form similar in form class to the head of the construction; in exocentric constructions, where there is no head tagmeme, the whole construction does not fill the same slot as one of its parts.

In string-type analysis, endocentric constructions include multiple head constructions, such as coordinate phrase and appositive phrase, as well as single headed phrases, composed of nouns, verbs, adjectives, and adverbs with their modifiers; they are proper to phrase level. Exocentric constructions occur at phrase level only in the relater-axis phrase (prepositional phrase), but include most constructions at the clause and sentence levels, where the whole construction is not centered about any particular head tagmeme.

Closed and Open-Ended Constructions. Some constructions are closed, while others seem to have no limit to their expansion possibilities. When words are combined in a phrase, or phrases into clauses, these seemingly can be strung out in endless fashion, with no practical limit.

Coordinate constructions are open-ended at almost all levels except the word level, where morphemes are combined into words. At the phrase level, for example:

He went to the store and bought books, pencils, pens . . .

In this English example, the object slot, filled by a coordinate noun phrase, indicates a phrase level construction that can be extended without limit. The conjunction generally occurs before the last item recorded. The noun phrase in question might be formulated as follows:

1.2 $N_{co} = +H_1{:}n \pm H_2{:}n \pm H_3{:}n . . . +C{:}c +H_n{:}n$

The discontinuity of the construction is indicated by the three dots (. . .), and the final expression indicates how the construction has closure (see also formula 4.9).

Modification structures may be open-ended; and limitless numbers of modifiers can, in certain cases, be added at the will of the speaker. Placing these modifiers in predicate attribute position, as an expansion of the adjective coordinate phrase acting as attribute, we might have:

We want students who are bright, honest, diligent . . .

1.3 $Aj_{co} = +H_1{:}aj +H_2{:}aj +H_3{:}aj . . .$

Closure may be indicated in the same way as in the preceding noun phrase. In these examples, provision is made for constructions which may be infinitely long. With practical data, however, these potentially infinite constructions are, in fact, limited to a concrete length.

Recursive versus Nonrecursive Layering. As Chomsky has pointed out (1957:24), grammatical systems must have methods for handling recursive constructions. Tagmemics handles this recursiveness with layering formulas, but not all cases of layering are recursive.

Recursive layering demands a rule of the type $X \rightarrow X + Y$, where the same symbol occurs on both sides of the arrow, or "rewrite" sign. In tagmemics, this requirement is fulfilled, for example, by allowing whole clauses to fill clause level slots. In cases where the identical clause level symbol occurs on both sides of the equals sign, such a construction is infinitely recursive and may be repeated indefinitely.

The police said the assassin shouted he hoped he had killed him.

1.4 $tCl = +S:N +P:TV +O:tCl/pn$

The tagmemic formulation is a simple clause formula, in which the symbol tCl occurs on both sides of the equation, showing recursiveness. This formula, applied four times (as is evidenced by the repetition of four subjects, four verbs, and four objects), describes the sentence.

> The police said / the assassin shouted . . .
> The assassin shouted / he hoped . . .
> He hoped / he had killed him.
> He had killed / him.

Nonrecursive layering is an inclusion of phrase within phrase, or clause within clause, and need not be recursive. For example, an adjective phrase might be included within a noun phrase. Thus, in the phrase, *a very old man*, the word *very* modifies *old* in an adjective phrase. The whole phrase, *very old*, is then one of the modifiers of the word *man*.

Etic and Emic Constructions

Just as the tagmeme unit has etic variants, there are also both etic and emic constructions. The etic construction is the first guess of the analyst; the emic construction is the construction as used by a native speaker. Constructions are patterns; in order for patterns to be distinctive as patterns, they must differ in at least two points in the construction. In order to determine the emic constructions of a language, we must: (1) describe the etic constructions, (2) apply the rule of two differences, and (3) find the essential constructions of the language.

Etic Constructions. The first step in the discovery procedure is to write the strings representing constructions according to what is found in the data. In the beginning, it is better to list too many rather than too few construction types. Each element in the construction is marked as obligatory or optional. Even in preliminary analysis, some of these constructions will show similarities. At this point, one must consider whether two similar constructions are to be combined in one formula.

The presence or absence of an optional element is not sufficient reason for setting up a new construction type unless the optional element is also nuclear. Differences in obligatory elements should be carefully noted, as they probably indicate different construction patterns.

The tagmemic slot may have many different form classes as fillers. If these fillers are mutually exclusive, they are considered as filling the same slot in the structure, pending further investigation.

The most practical procedure, after identifying the morphs in the construction, is to set up a temporary formula for the longest utterances in the data, in order to get all of the slot-class units in the correct order. Many shorter sentences are included in the maximum formula.

Longacre's Rule of Two. In order for two constructions to be essentially, or emically, different, they must be different in two ways. Only with two differences can patterns differ as patterns in language. One of these two differences must affect the nuclear tagmemes, according to Longacre (1964:18):

> For two syntagmemes to be in contrast they must have more than one structural difference between them; at least one of these differences must involve the nuclei of the syntagmemes.

In applying the rule of two, it should be noted that nuclear is not the same as obligatory. The rule specifies that one difference must be nuclear, but this nuclear tagmeme may be either obligatory or optional.

Essential Constructions. After applying the rule of two, those constructions that are found in contrast—that is, those found to have two differences, one of which involves the nucleus—are called essential. If two differences are not found, the two constructions are listed as etic variants of the same construction and combined in one formula. Since the string is composed of tagmemes, the application of the rule depends upon knowing when tagmemes are different, and also depends upon the definition of nuclear tagmeme.

Tagmemes are listed as essential contrastive units if they differ in at least two of these features: (1) slot, (2) filler class, or (3) position. As already outlined in the section on the Unit, a difference in either slot meaning, or filler class, or position would only indicate that this is a variant of the essential unit, or tagmeme.

Tagmemes are nuclear if they are diagnostic of the construction in which they occur. The following are rules of thumb to determine if a tagmeme is nuclear, without reference to the construction as such:

1. If the tagmeme is obligatory, it is nuclear. Therefore a difference in obligatory tagmemes is always an essential difference.
2. If the tagmeme is a transform of a nuclear tagmeme, it is considered nuclear. Transform potential of a nuclear element thus specifies such elements as Agent (Ag:) as nuclear in the passive.
3. Tagmemes in concord with nuclear tagmemes are considered nuclear, at least at the clause level. The agreement in endocentric constructions is excluded from this rule. Thus, subjects tied to the predicate or objects governed by the predicate are nuclear.

The real difference in applying the rule of two revolves around the question of whether the external distribution of the construction as a whole should be considered as one of two differences. According to Longacre, external distribution is not a countable contrastive feature (1964:21). Constructions should be regarded as contrastive only when they show two differences in their internal structure.

Elson and Pickett (1962:134) suggest the use of external distribution as one of the two differences in their rule: "Assume that two similar constructions are different construction types if there is one internal difference . . . and a correlated difference of distribution of the construction as a whole." Pike (1962:232) agrees that a difference in external distribution, like a transform difference, may be counted, provided this distributional difference is paralleled by a difference in structural meaning. In practice, this difference in external distribution has been found to be useful in limiting the output of the grammar by setting up two different constructions which differ internally by only one feature but have a different external distribution.

THE SYSTEM: LEVELS OF GRAMMAR

A grammatical model should have clearly defined units, which enter into constructions, and these constructions should be organized into some kind of grammatical system. In tagmemics, the *unit* is the tagmeme, a correlation of function and form; the *construction* is a potential string of tagmeme units, the syntagmeme; and the *system* is the grammatical hierachy, arranged in a series of systematic levels. By geometric analogy, the tagmeme is a point, the construction a line made up of points, and the grammatical hierarchy lines arranged from higher to lower.

The model resembles an abacus, with beads as units, strung on horizontal wires to form constructions, with the wires arranged from higher to lower within a frame.

Grammatical Level Defined

A grammatical level is described as a relative position in space—where space is the grammatical hierarchy within which constructions may occur. Just as physical celestial objects cannot be located in space in any absolute way but only in reference to each other, so levels are relative positions in grammatical space defined in reference to each other. The concept of "structural levels, arranged in explicit systemic hierarchy," is the third fundamental insight of tagmemics (Longacre, 1965:72).

Hierarchical Level. According to Pike, language may be described in terms of a triple hierarchy of phonology, lexicon and grammar. Within the grammatical hierarchy, constructions are arranged at a series of well-defined levels. The development of the concept of levels within grammar is attributed to Longacre, who felt that there should be a close analogy with phonology, where a single phoneme may be a syllable. Similarly, in grammar, a single morpheme may be simultaneously a word, a potential phrase, and a clause, as in the English command *Go!* The most common levels in use are the sentence, clause, phrase, and word levels.

By grouping constructions at a series of natural levels, language structure is represented as an orderly mapping of lower level into higher level structures. Morphemes are mapped into words, words into phrases, phrases into clauses, and clauses into sentences, in an orderly manner. This regular mapping of smaller units into larger units is, by using levels, clearly distinguished from nesting and layering tendencies within the same grammatical level. Provision is also made in the system for atypical mapping of structures, for level-skipping, and for back-looping.

Tagmemic versus IC Levels. In tagmemic analysis, the analyst works with a series of levels within the grammatical hierarchy, normally the sentence, clause, phrase, word, and morpheme levels. Constructions are arranged in the grammar at one of the four construction levels. In IC analysis, the only levels represented are included under the terms immediate, mediate, and ultimate constituents. The immediate constituents are the results of the first cut, the ultimate constituents are morphemes, and mediate constituents are the results of any intervening binary cut.

In the analysis of a simple sentence, the first cut in both IC analysis and in tagmemics is to remove the intonation from the sentence base. In tagmemics, this is a sentence level construction; in IC the sentence base and its intonation are the immediate constituents. The final level of the tagmemic grammar is the level of ultimate constituents, the morphemes. The clause, phrase, and word level constructions of tagmemics correspond roughly to the mediate cuts of the IC grammar, except that the tagmemic levels are well defined whereas the mediate constituents of IC grammar are *ad hoc* constituents changing with each sentence analyzed.

IC analysis, according to Longacre, fails to reveal construction types of "maximum relevance and comparability" (1964:16), and fails to distinguish mapping of constructions from lower into higher levels, from layerings on the same level of analysis (1965:72). Tagmemics, on the other hand, places constructions within the grammar at well-defined levels, arranging the levels from higher to lower within the grammar.

Significance of Levels. The concept of levels places the strings or syntagmemes of the grammar in an ordered set of rules. Just as the idea of string allowed multiple branching in the grammar, so the idea of level orders the rules from higher to lower in some well-defined way. Within a level, however, considerable variety of construction is found, and ordering within the level is not so rigidly defined as to exclude different orderings with different sets of data.

The purpose of the level is to set up a hyperclass of constructions which are similar in some specified way. Once we have defined these contrastive characteristics, we may speak of sentence level, clause level, phrase level, and word level constructions. Each of these constructions is defined, again, in terms of its constituent tagmemes, which are then recognized as sentence level, clause level, phrase level, and word level tagmemes respectively. Consequently, the concept of level not only places the constructions in hierarchical order, it allows for a more positive identification of the tagmeme unit. The tagmeme is fixed at a definite level, or depth, in the grammar, and at the same time has a position in the linear construction string.

Kinds of Levels in Grammar

Grammatical levels form a telescopic system in which the constructions at lower levels are typically mapped into constructions at higher levels in the grammar. In tagmemics, levels above the sentence are of considerable importance; sentences occur in larger contexts. In this introduction, however, we consider only the sentence level and levels below the sentence. This includes: (1) the five typical levels of grammar, (2) atypical mapping of levels, and (3) the systematic organization of levels in a field structure of hierarchy.

Typical Levels of Grammar. The five typical levels of grammar are the sentence, clause, phrase, word, and morpheme levels. These correspond to the sentence, clause, group, word, and morpheme levels of M. A. K. Halliday's scale-and-category grammar. The first four levels are levels at which constructions occur. The final, or morpheme level, is not a level of construction, but an ultimate point of reference.

1. *The sentence level* is that level of the grammar at which the major and minor sentences of language are broken down into dependent and independent clauses, together with their intonation patterns.
2. *The clause level* is that level of the grammar at which the clauses are broken down into their subjects, predicates, objects, and various clause adjuncts such as time, place, manner, and circumstance.
3. *The phrase level* is that level of the grammar at which the structured word groups which are not clauses are broken down into words.
4. *The word level* is that level of the grammar at which the words of the language are broken down into their constituent morphemes, including the analysis of the processes of inflection, derivation, and compounding.
5. *The morpheme level* is that level of the grammar at which the morphemes are seen as the ultimate meaningful constituents of which the utterances of a language are composed. Each morpheme is listed in a lexicon accompanying the grammar, with its form, class, and gloss.

A tagmemic grammar will therefore consist of a set of formulas ranging from the sentence through the clause, phrase, and word levels, and this grammar will be accompanied by a lexicon of constituent morphemes. The five levels as listed are typical of most languages. It may be possible to establish more or fewer levels within a given language, but strong points of contrast between levels would have to be established in order to set up new levels in the grammar. A priori, the five-level system seems to correspond to natural units of language — found in most grammars — which native speakers feel intuitively are sentences, clauses, phrases, and words (see Pike, 1967:444).

Atypical Mapping. Although the normal processes of grammar call for a mapping of lower level constructions into higher levels, there are cases of atypical mapping, including level skips, layering, and loopbacks in the grammatical structure:

1. *Level skips* are omissions of a level in proceeding from higher to lower. When a level is skipped, a filler from a lower level construction is used in a higher level construction. The use of a phrase clitic, a bound form to fill a phrase level slot, is a typical example of skipping.

2. *Layering* is the inclusion of a construction within another construction at the same level (Elson and Pickett, 1962:59). Thus, clause within clause and phrase within phrase are examples of layering. This layering may be recursive or nonrecursive, as explained in the section on Tagmemes in Construction.

3. *Loopbacks* are inclusions of higher level constructions within the slots of a lower level construction. A relative clause filling the identifier slot in phrase structure is a typical example of a loopback. (See Practice 2, Clauses within Phrases, for examples.)

Field Structure of Hierarchy. Longacre has pictured the typical and atypical mappings of structures in a field (1965:75), as the fourth fundamental insight in tagmemic grammar. The following chart is adapted from Longacre's chart in *Language* (1965:76), eliminating levels above the sentence level. At clause level, for example, the chart may be read as follows:

1. If tagmemic fillers at clause level are words (W), this is level-skipping: the phrase level has been skipped and the clause slot is filled by a lower level form, the word.

2. If tagmemic fillers at clause level are phrases (P), this is normal mapping: clauses are normally filled by phrases in proper hierarchical structuring.

3. If tagmemic fillers at clause level are clauses (C), this is layering at a level: a clause is embedded within another clause. This layering need not be recursive.

4. If tagmemic fillers at clause level are sentences (S), this is back-looping: a higher level construction, the sentence, fills a slot in a lower level construction, the clause.

Tagmemic Fillers	Level Skipping	Normal Mapping	Layering at a Level	Back-looping
Above the Sentence	C	S		
At Sentence Level	P	C	S	
At Clause Level	W	P	C	S
At Phrase Level	M	W	P	C
At Word Level		M	W	P

Etic and Emic Levels of Grammar

The tagmemic system of analysis posits well-defined units called tagmemes, the correlation of functional slot with filler class. These units combine in syntagmemes, or constructions. The constructions in turn are grouped at the essential levels of grammar.

Just as there are etic and emic units, tagmas and tagmemes, and etic and emic constructions, so also there are etic and emic levels of grammar. Longacre (1964:16) suggests that these essential levels of grammar are "discoverable" for each language. Pike (1967:437) suggests criteria for setting up levels within a given language as follows:

1. Constructions at a level must specify the kind of constituents at that level, including their occurrence and relative order in construction.
2. Constructions at one level should be sharply in contrast with those at other levels, immediately above and below the given level.

If we accept the natural levels of grammar as the sentence, clause, phrase, and word, then within these levels we find there are three possible identifying characteristics of levels, three geological strata, with the functions of (1) relation, (2) coordination, and (3) subordination. These features may help to define the essential levels of grammar.

Relational Strata. Within a given level, provision should be made for taking a whole construction at that level, and relating it to higher level constructions. In tagmemic analysis, Longacre has pointed out the parallelism between relater-axis structures at the clause and phrase levels, with a proportion evident between relater and axis (1964:38):

Preposition: its object : : subordinator: its clause

Similar relational markers may be found at sentence level, where sequence markers are used to connect sentences in higher structures, distinguishing sentences in "absolute" and "included" position (Fries, 1952:240). At word level also, the process of inflection is relational and fits the word for syntactic use. So close is the parallelism between inflectional ending and preposition, that in some languages they are indistinguishable. These four natural levels show parallelism in the use of relaters:

At Sentence Level, S-Subordinator + Sentence
At Clause Level, C-Subordinator + Clause
At Phrase Level, Preposition + Phrase
At Word Level, Inflection + Word

In each of these structures, the relater is added to a whole sentence, clause, phrase, or word and fits it for use in higher level structures. If this parallelism is correct, it would seem that relational properties are one identifying-contrastive feature of an emic level.

Coordinate Strata. Within a given level, provision should also be made for the coordination of two whole constructions to form a single coordinate construction at that level. In an article on scale-and-category grammar, R. D. Huddleston suggests that coordination be included at the various levels of the grammar ("Rank and Depth," *Language*, 1965:41). The levels of this grammar are sentence, clause, group, and word.

In tagmemic analysis, some provision is made for coordination at phrase level, where noun phrase + noun phrase = coordinate noun phrase. This is paralleled at the word level by compound words, and at the clause level by the coordination of clauses to form compound sentences. This parallelism, if followed rigidly, would produce the following structures:

Coordinated Sentence = Sentence + Sentence
Coordinated Clause = Clause + Clause
Coordinated Phrase = Phrase + Phrase
Coordinated Word = Word + Word

The schema is accurate for compound words and coordinate phrases, but suggests some indeterminacy between clause and sentence levels, where the coordination of clauses results in a compound sentence, and raises the question whether clause and sentence are really distinct levels. The parallelism does suggest, however, that coordination might be a second identifying-contrastive feature of the emic level.

Subordinate Strata. The units at a level must be broken down into constituent parts. This is the last or subordinate layer of structure at a level and constitutes the notion of level in its narrowest sense. Whatever else happens at a level, whole constructions must be broken into parts.

1. Sentence is composed of bases, margins, and intonation.
2. Clause is composed of subjects, predicates, objects, and adjuncts.
3. Phrase is composed of head and modifiers.
4. Word is composed of roots and derivations.

If this process of subordination is considered as the third identifying-contrastive feature of an emic level and occurs in conjunction with the two features of relation and coordination, the subordination feature is limited. It does not overlap with the other two features.

Word level becomes a single level, with layers of inflections, compounding, and derivation. Phrase level is a single level, with relater-axis phrases, coordinate phrases, and modification structures. Clause level, as found in current use, is mainly subordinate structure, with the coordinate and relational features used to form compound and complex sentences at the sentence level. If levels are well defined as reference points, they may serve as a basis for future universal grammars, by forewarning us what to expect in the structures of different languages.

PRACTICE 1: TAGMEMIC FORMULATION

The tagmemic model consists of a series of syntactic statements at the sentence, clause, phrase, and word levels. In the analysis of a single sentence, those elements which can be omitted from the structure are marked as optional, and all other elements are marked as obligatory. Write the tagmemic formulas at each level for the following sentence from Longacre (1960:63):

> The slow, lumbering covered wagon pulled the pioneer's family across the prairie just yesterday.

At the sentence level, the sentence base is separated from its final intonation contour. The intonation slot is marked with a minus sign to indicate it is suprasegmental. The intonation, if unknown, is marked ICF.

Sentence Level Construction:

Sent = +Base:tCl −Into:ICF

Read: A sentence consists of a base slot filled by a transitive clause and an intonation slot filled by a final intonation contour.

At the clause level, the clause that constitutes the sentence base is analyzed as a string made up of subject, predicate, object, and the sentence adjuncts of time and place. Slot names are marked with capitals; fillers have capital letters for word groups and small letters for words.

Clause Level Construction:

tCl = +S:N +P:tv ±O:N ±L:RA ±T:Tem

Read: A transitive clause consists of a subject slot filled by a noun phrase, a predicate slot filled by a transitive verb, an optional object slot filled by a noun phrase, an optional location slot filled by a relater-axis phrase, and an optional temporal slot filled by a temporal phrase.

At the phrase level, the word groups that fill clause level slots are analyzed into constituent words. Slot names are marked with capitals; fillers have capital letters for word groups and small letters for words.

Phrase Level Construction:

$$RA = +R{:}rel +Ax{:}N \qquad \text{across} + \text{(the prairie)}$$

Read: A relater-axis phrase consists of a relater slot filled by a relater (preposition), and an axis slot filled by a noun phrase.

$$N = +Det{:}det \pm Pos{:}pos +H{:}n \qquad \text{the} + \text{pioneer's} + \text{family}$$

Read: A noun phrase consists of a determiner slot filled by a determiner, an optional possessive slot filled by a possessive, and a head slot filled by a noun.

$$Tem = \pm Int{:}int +H{:}tem \qquad \text{just} + \text{yesterday}$$

Read: A temporal phrase consists of an optional intensifier slot filled by an intensifier and a head slot filled by a temporal word.

At the word level, words that consist of more than one morpheme are analyzed into constituent morphemes. Slots have small letters; fillers have small letters if they are either morphemes or words. (For possessive noun phrase, see formula 4.13.)

Word Level Construction:

$$pos = +nnuc{:}ns \pm num{:}plm +pos{:}posm \qquad \text{pioneer} + \text{-'s}$$

Read: A possessive consists of a noun nuclear slot filled by a noun stem, an optional number slot filled by a plural marker, and a possessive slot filled by a possessive marker.

$$tv = +vnuc{:}tvs \pm t{:}tm \qquad \text{pull} + \text{-ed}$$

Read: A transitive verb consists of a verb nuclear slot filled by a transitive verb stem and an optional tense slot filled by a tense marker.

$$aj = +core{:}ivs/tvs +ajzr{:}\{\text{-ing}\}/\{\text{-ed}\} \qquad \text{cover} + \text{-ed}$$

Read: One type of adjective consists of a core slot filled by a verb stem (transitive or intransitive), and an adjectivizer slot filled by the (derivational) suffixes, {-ing} and {-ed}.

SUPPLEMENTARY READINGS 1

Cook, Walter A., S.J., *On Tagmemes and Transforms*, Washington, D.C., Georgetown University Press, 1964. A summary of the tagmemic system, including the use of transforms and generative potential.

Elson, Benjamin, and Pickett, Velma, *An Introduction to Morphology and Syntax*, Santa Ana, Summer Institute of Linguistics, 1964. Standard text for beginning morphology and syntax in tagmemics.

Longacre, Robert E., "String Constituent Analysis," *Language*, 36:63–88, (1960). Compares tagmemic string construction with IC analysis.

, *Grammar Discovery Procedures*, The Hague, Mouton & Co., 1964. For procedures of tagmemics, including the use of transforms and the generative potential in terms of a set of rewrite operations.

, "Some Fundamental Insights of Tagmemics," *Language*, 41: 65–76. For tagmeme, syntagmeme, hierarchy, and field structure.

Monograph Series on Languages and Linguistics, 18th Annual Round Table, No. 20 (1967), E. L. Blansitt, Jr, ed. Conference with panels on tagmemic theory, current research in tagmemic description, and grammatical analysis.

Pike, Kenneth L., *Language in Relation to a Unified Theory of the Structure of Human Behaviour*, Glendale, California, Summer Institute of Linguistics, Part I (1954), includes Chaps. 1–7, on behavior, morphemes, Part II (1955), includes Chaps. 8–10, phonemes, syllables, Part III (1960), includes Chaps. 11–17, tagmeme, syntagmeme. Reprinted in one volume with updated bibliographies and footnotes on current developments. The Hague, Mouton & Co., 1967.

, "On Tagmemes nee Gramemes," *IJAL*, 24:273–278, (1958). For the concept of tagmeme and its discovery.

, "Language as Particle, Wave and Field." *The Texas Quarterly*, 2:37–54, (1959). For the development of the trimodal nature of the unit.

, "Dimensions of Grammatical Structure." *Language*, 38:221–244, (1962). For the exposition of matrix theory as applied to grammar.

, "A Syntactic Paradigm." *Language*, 39:216–230, (1963). For matrix theory applied to a practical example.

, "A Guide to Publications Related to Tagmemic Theory." *Current Trends in Linguistics*, Thomas A. Sebeok, ed., The Hague, Mouton & Co., Vol. III (1966) 365–394. A survey and critical appraisal of literature on tagmemic theory and practice.

TABLE 2: SENTENCE LEVEL ANALYSIS

According to the Type of Intonation	According to the Type of Base	According to the Type of Clauses	According to the Type of Situation
Sentences with Final Intonation	Major Types with Complete Base	1. *Compound Sentence* two independent clauses with conjoining 2. *Complex Sentence* independent and dependent clause with embedding 3. *Simple Sentence* one independent clause, no dependent clause	1. *Statement (S)* formed to relay information 2. *Question (Q)* formed to elicit answer response 3. *Command (C)* formed to elicit action response
	Minor Types with Incomplete Base	1. *Sequential Sentence* from compound 2. *Marginal Sentence* from complex 3. *Elliptical Sentence* from simple	1. *Addition (A)* with statements 2. *Response (R)* with questions 3. *Exclamation (E)* in any context
		Nonelliptical Types no clause structure	Vocatives, greetings, calls, titles, mottoes

2 SENTENCE LEVEL

The sentence level of grammar is that level at which clauses are combined into larger units. All sentences occur in some linguistic or nonlinguistic context, but the structures above the level of sentence are so varied that it is more practical for the beginner to focus attention upon sentence structure and the structure of levels below the sentence. The sentence is a grammatical unit, a construction in which the constitute is any utterance with final intonation contour, and the constituents are the clauses, connecting particles, and intonation patterns.

Sentence Defined. The sentence has been defined by Bloomfield as "an independent linguistic form, not included by virtue of any grammatical construction in any larger form" (1933:170). This definition is paraphrased by Hockett as "a constitute which is not a constituent; a grammatical form which is not in construction with any other grammatical form" (1958:199). In tagmemic analysis, this grammatical independence is accepted as a relative independence, which must be structurally defined for each language. The possibility of higher level analysis is never excluded. In the definition of the sentence, the following features are essential:

1. *Sentences are relatively isolatable.* Sentences may be isolated, and any corpus may be reduced to sentences, with no residue (Longacre, 1964:17, fn. 14). The sentence is isolatable in its own right (Pike, 1967:442).
2. *Sentences have final intonation patterns.* In a practical approach to sentences, we accept them as we find them. Intonation patterns, with pause and other phonological features, help to isolate sentences.

3. *Sentences are composed of clauses.* The clauses combine in some kind of "patterned dependency" (Longacre, 1964:126) involving combinations of clauses which do not have the overall structure of a single clause. These clauses may be dependent or independent clauses.

Traditional Sentence. The sentence has traditionally been the focal point of attention in grammatical work, but its definition was based upon meaning. The sentence was defined as containing "a complete thought" and was composed of a subject "about which something is said" and a predicate, "what is said about the subject." This tradition dates back to Aristotle and the Greek logicians and is carried over via Priscian's Latin Grammar into the English grammars of today.

In the linguistic tradition dating from Bloomfield, an attempt was made to define the sentence, not according to its meaning but according to its form, as an independent linguistic form. Tagmemic analysis would add the further dimension of distribution and claim that the sentence is only one level of the grammatical hierarchy. Sentences are distributed in higher units and ultimately in the context of behavior. Discourse analysis, however, has been little developed. Elson and Pickett treat levels above the sentence only briefly (1962:127–128), and Longacre barely mentions them (1964:17, 125–126). Part of the difficulty is the fact that structures above the sentence occur in a wide variety of literary genres, including dialogue, poetry, and narration. Further references to levels above the sentence may be found in Pike (1966:372).

Sentence Types. The definition of sentence becomes more concrete once the decision is made as to what is acceptable as a sentence. The notion of sentence is realized in concrete sentence types. Classification of sentences may be based on any of the following features:

1. *According to the number and kind of clauses in the base,* sentences are classified as simple, complex, and compound. This feature is used by Pike (1967:442–443) and Longacre (1964:130) to separate sentences into multiple clause, simple clause, and nonclause types.
2. *According to the internal structure of the main clause,* sentences are complete or incomplete. These are also called major, or favorite, or full sentences, as opposed to minor sentences (see Bloomfield 1933:171, and Hockett, 1958:200). Minor types are completive or exclamatory.
3. *According to the type of response expected,* sentences are classed as statements, questions, and commands.

Although included in traditional grammars, these sentence types can be defined formally for a language.

4. *According to the nature of the actor-action relationship,* sentences are classed as active, middle, or passive. This classification is based on the voice feature and belongs more properly to clause level.

5. *According to the presence or absence of negatives in the main verb phrase,* sentences are classed as affirmative or negative sentences. This classification is best handled at the level of the verb phrase, at least in English.

SENTENCE LEVEL SORTING

In tagmemic analysis, it is possible to begin work at any of the well-defined levels of the grammar. The practical procedures followed here will be to begin at the sentence level and proceed to the morpheme level, omitting levels above the sentence. The sentence level is then practically viewed as the starting point in analysis. Accepting the corpus as a set of sentences, the first task of the analyst is to institute a *sort* of sentence types and reduce the continuous narrative or dialogue to sets of homogeneously grouped sentences of well-defined types. The task here is threefold: (1) to separate the kernel sentences from derived sentences; (2) to reduce multiple clause sentences to simple clause types; and (3) to separate sentence base from sentence intonation.

Kernel Sentences

Within a given language, certain sentences belong to a set of basic structures, and all other structures may be expressed as derived from these basic structures. The basic structures are called kernel sentences. We first identify the distinctive features of kernel sentences; then consider the derived sentences opposed to these basic structures; and finally show how the nonkernel sentences are derived from kernel sentences.

Distinctive Features of the Kernel. Traditionally, language analysis has focused upon the declarative sentence as of primary importance. With the introduction of transformational grammar, analysis has once more concentrated upon this basic type. In response to the question of which set of sentences belongs to the kernel, Chomsky answers, that for English at least, "the kernel consists of simple, declarative, active sentences" (1957:80). However, since both negative transformations and deletion transformations are included in the grammar, we assume that the kernel is also affirmative and nonelliptical.

A kernel sentence is defined as a sentence of the language

that is (1) simple, (2) complete, (3) statement, (4) active, and (5) affirmative. Any sentence that simultaneously has these five distinctive features is a kernel sentence; any sentence that lacks even one of these five features is a derived sentence. In our analysis, we first institute a *sort* of all sentences in the corpus to separate the kernel set from the nonkernel, or derived, set. Later on, we attempt to describe the derived sentences in terms of the kernel set, using either transformational rules or matrix displays, to show how nonkernel sentences are derived. In this way we concentrate attention on the basic sentence structures.

Derived Sentences. The notion of kernel sentences is more clearly understood when kernel and nonkernel sentences are compared. The derived sentences lack at least one of the five distinctive features of kernel sentences. Kernel and derived sentences may be contrasted as follows:

Kernel Sentences		Derived Sentences
Simple	versus	Complex, Compound
Complete	versus	Incomplete, Elliptical
Statement	versus	Question, Command
Active	versus	Middle, Passive
Affirmative	versus	Negative

In a sentence level sort, kernel sentences are separated from derived sentences, and primary attention is focused upon kernel sentences. The analysis of derived sentences is then related to the simple structures from which they are derived.

Transformation. The transformational rule is simply a rule of change. This rule has an input string, a rule of change, and an output string. With kernel sentences as input, it is possible to set up a series of optional rules that will produce the output, the derived sentences:

INPUT STRING   T-RULE   OUTPUT STRING
Kernel sentence + transformation = derived sentence

Tagmemic grammars formerly described all the sentences of a language by describing both kernel and derived sentences. The resulting description was a complete description, but often failed to show the relationships between similar sentences. With the introduction of transformational rules or matrix devices to show the relationships between sentences, it is still necessary to describe both kernel and derived sentences in order to discover the differences between structures. However, the final grammar may be considerably simplified by employing some type of transformational rule or matrix display, together with an analysis of only kernel sentences.

Early models of transformational grammar produced derived sentences by a series of optional transformational rules, deriving the nonkernel passive by an optional passive transformation, for example. In more recent transformational models, the kernel set of sentences is a "proper subset" of sentences generated; derived sentences are also generated by the grammar by including optional markers in the base. The changes in methodology in transformational grammars do not destroy the "important intuitive significance" (Chomsky, 1965:18) of the kernel.

Primary Sorting Procedures

The sorting process at sentence level is a preparation for the work of analysis at clause level. The first procedure is to reduce complex and compound sentences to simple clause structures. The results of this reduction should be the clauses of the corpus written one to a line, ready for analysis. The first procedure then is to (1) reduce the corpus to simple clause structures, (2) identify complex and compound sentence types, and (3) isolate intonational patterns.

Reduction. In the reduction process, the corpus is considered to be a body of sentences, made up of simple clauses. These clauses may be dependent or independent. An independent clause is a clause that may stand alone in a given language as a simple major sentence; a dependent clause is a clause which may not, in this language, stand alone as a simple major sentence type. If we consider independent clauses as type A, and dependent clauses as type B, with sentence boundary marked as #, we can define the following sentence types:

Simple Sentence	# A #	one A-clause only
Complex Sentence	# A + B #	one A, at least one B-clause
Compound Sentence	# A + A #	more than one A-clause

In the reduction of complex and compound sentences to simple sentences, we are performing an operation that is the reverse of the conjoining process for building compound sentences, and of the embedding process for building complex sentences. It is important that the formulas for complex and compound sentences be preserved as the corpus is prepared for clause level analysis. The formulas for these nonsimple type sentences will then be included in the sentence level. In this analysis, the following types of clauses may be found:

1. Independent clause types
   a. Simple independent type   A
   b. Sequential independent type   (c) + A
2. Dependent clause types
   a. Subordinated type   (r) + A = B
   b. Subordinate type   B = A type, with built in (r)

Whether clauses are dependent or independent in the sentence structure, the clauses may be analyzed together at the clause level neglecting the connecting particles (c) and relating particles (r) which pertain rather to sentence structure.

The results of the reduction process will be a series of simple clauses and a list of sentence formulas for complex and compound sentences complete with intonational patterns. Further sorting of simple clauses isolates the complete statements, active and affirmative.

Embedding Process. Dependent clauses are embedded within the structure of language at the sentence, clause, and phrase levels. The process of subordinating a clause to another structure is called the embedding process. Within the tagmemic system a decision concerning the level of embedding must be made for each dependent clause.

1. *At sentence level,* dependent clauses are embedded in sentence structures and fill marginal slots in that structure. The resulting structure is a complex sentence, formulated as margin + base. The structure of a complex sentence may be indicated by: (a) choice of clause type, (b) connectors, (c) sequence of tenses, (d) order of clauses (Longacre, 1964:128). Conditions, indirect discourse, and so on may be of this type.
2. *At clause level,* dependent clauses are embedded in the clause structure and fill the same slots as words and phrases. The resulting structure is a simple sentence with the overall structure of a single clause (Longacre, 1967:17). Time and place clauses are of this type.
3. *At phrase level,* dependent clauses are embedded into the phrase structure as modifiers. They fill identifier slots in the phrase formula and are an example of loopback in the hierarchy of clause within phrase. These are principally relative clauses, modifying single words in the phrase structure.

Conjoining Process. The conjoining process deals with the joining of similar constituents at any level. The elements conjoined may be clauses, phrases, or words. The conjoining process at the sentence level deals with the conjoining of clauses, that is, with the conjoining of strings of tagmemes which contain one and only one predicate in the string.

According to Alton L. Becker (1967:110), conjoining is (1) recursive in the linear sense, (2) context sensitive, in that constituents must be of the same type, and (3) generally optional. Conjoining at the clause and phrase levels deals with the joining of single tagmemes and need not be traced to complete underlying sentences. The constituents joined are the same in that they fill the same slot, but the fillers of the slot may be words or phrases.

In contrast, the conjoining of clauses to form sentences deals not with single tagmemes, but with strings of tagmemes. The strings which are conjoined are not necessarily complete structures, nor are they always dominated by the same node of the underlying phrase structure. Thus, in *She rode and I walked home*, S and P are conjoined; but the locational, L, while properly belonging to both clauses, occurs once. One method of handling the problem is to consider both clauses as complete structures and allow optional deletion of elements in one of the clause structures, thus deriving the compound from two simple underlying complete clauses.

Multiple Clause Formulation

In a tagmemic analysis restricted to the sentence and lower levels of analysis, the sentence level serves chiefly as a clearing stage to prepare the work of clause level analysis. Sentence level structures are recorded as simple or multiple clause structures, with their intonation patterns. The underlying structure of the sentence is then analyzed at the clause level.

Sentence Level Tagmemes. Sentence level constructions are those constructions in which the constitute is an isolated utterance, and the constituents are the clauses which constitute the sentence base, together with connecting particles and intonational or junctural features. The principal tagmemes useful in sentence level analysis are:

Base: *Base tagmeme*, filled by independent clauses (IndCl). Multiple base slots may be subscripted: $Base_1$ $Base_2$.

Marg: *Margin tagmeme*, filled by dependent clauses (DepCl). Margins occur only in complex and marginal sentences.

C: *Connector tagmeme*, filled by connecting conjunctions called connectors (c). These also occur at phrase level.

Into: *Intonation tagmeme*, filled by intonation contours marked as final (ICF), as nonfinal (ICN), or by pattern: 231 ↓.

The base and intonation tagmemes are always nuclear to the structure; the margin tagmeme is generally optional and peripheral; and the connector tagmemes may be nuclear if they are obligatory to the construction.

Sentence Level Constructions. Typical constructions at the sentence level are the formulations for simple, complex, and compound sentences. Each of these constructions will be accompanied by intonation patterns.

2.1 (Simple) Sent $= +$Base:Ind.Cl $-$Into:ICF

Read: A (simple) sentence consists of a base slot filled by an independent clause and an intonation slot filled by a final intonation contour.

In this simple sentence formula, the $+$ sign means that the sentence base is obligatory. The $-$ sign also indicates an obligatory tagmeme, but shows that the tagmeme is a suprasegmental, and not in linear sequence. The intonation pattern, if not known, is simply labeled ICF, for final intonation contour, or ICN for nonfinal intonation contour. If, however, the pattern is known, it may be marked, for example, as 231 ↓ .

In early stages of the analysis, the fillers of base and margin slots, respectively, are marked as independent clause (Ind.Cl) and dependent clause (Dep.Cl). Once the type of clause is known, however, these temporary symbols are replaced by concretely designated clause types.

Complex sentences consist of one independent and at least one dependent clause. Their sentence level formulas contain a margin tagmeme when the dependent clause is analyzed as part of sentence level structure.

2.2 (Complex) Sent $= +$Base:Ind.Cl
$\pm$Marg:Dep.Cl $-$Into:ICF

Read: A (complex) sentence consists of a base slot filled by an independent clause, an optional margin slot filled by a dependent clause, and an intonation slot filled by a final intonation contour.

Compound sentences consist of at least two independent clauses, and may or may not have dependent clauses as well. Such a structure will have at least two base tagmemes, and often connector tagmemes between clauses.

2.3 (Compound) Sent $= +$Base$_1$:Ind.Cl $\pm$C:c
$+$Base$_2$:Ind.Cl $-$Into:ICF

Read: A (compound) sentence consists of a base slot filled by an independent clause, an optional connector slot filled by a connector, a base slot filled by an independent clause, and an intonation slot filled by a final intonation contour.

Complex and compound sentences may show more than one intonation contour. If it is necessary to record more than one intonation pattern in the same sentence, a second intonation slot may be introduced for each clause in the pattern, usually filled by nonfinal intonations.

2.4 Sent = +Base:Ind.Cl −Into:ICN
 +Marg:Dep.Cl −Into:ICF,

2.5 Sent = +Base$_1$:Ind.Cl −Into:ICN ±C:c
 +Base$_2$:Ind. Cl −Into:ICF

Sentence as Initial String. In this introduction to tagmemic analysis, the symbol #Sent# is accepted as the initial string, or absolute starting point for analysis. Every analysis begins with this symbol, and proceeds as far as the ultimate constituents, or morphemes, in the utterance. In this limited analysis, every structure is dominated by a sentence symbol. This method is consistent and allows comparison with the structures of the transformational grammars. Secondly, a place is always provided for intonational patterns in the language, whether these are known or not known. The procedure is comparable to IC analysis, where the first cut separates the sentence base from its intonational pattern. In tagmemic analysis, the intonation pattern has a place only in sentence level construction, and contrasts of intonation must be handled at this particular level.

MAJOR SENTENCE TYPES

The kernel sentences of the language have been described as those which are: (1) simple, (2) complete, (3) statements, (4) active, and (5) affirmative. First, the simple sentences were opposed to complex and compound sentences. Now we investigate the feature of "completeness," and distinguish between major sentence types, which are complete sentences, and minor sentence types, which are noncomplete.

Major Type Defined

The major sentences of a language are sentences which have the feature of completeness; minor sentences lack this feature. The judgment as to whether or not a sentence is complete is determined by the type of clause base involved. If the base is an independent clause, the sentence is complete; if the base is only a dependent clause, or has no clause structure at all, then the sentence is incomplete. A major sentence is a sentence which has at least one independent clause.

Major sentences, as understood here, are the set of sentences described by Bloomfield (1933:170–172) as full sentences, favorite types, with the meaning "complete and novel utterance." The emphasis here is on the word "complete," which is opposed to "noncomplete" minor types.

Complete versus Incomplete. Whether or not a sentence is complete depends upon whether it contains an independent clause. Since an independent clause is a clause which can stand alone as a sentence, this definition is circular unless criteria are given for when a clause may stand alone as a sentence. This will depend upon the structure of the language in question.

English, for example, requires that an independent clause of the statement type contain both subject and predicate. In Latin, where the subject is already contained within the verb form, the subject is not obligatory. Sentences such as *veni*, 'I came,' are already complete.

Complete sentences may be simple, complex, or compound, since all of these structures contain at least one independent clause. But if the reduction process is completed first, then the single clause structures must be tested for completeness in the second step. In the early stages of analysis, the "standing alone" property may be tested with a native speaker; but as the analyst completes clause level analysis, he should become aware of the formal features of the particular language that determine when a clause may stand alone and when it may not. The intuitive analysis is then reduced to a formal analysis of the structure.

Major Kernel Sentences. A sentence that has the feature of completeness, and contains at least one independent clause, is a major sentence in the language. It may be simple, complex, or compound. Of these major sentences, only the simple major types belong to the kernel; the other major types, and minor sentences, are derived from the kernel. The features of simplicity and completeness may be used to set up a classification of kernel and derived sentence types as follows:

1. *Well-formed sentences (formata)* are both simple and complete. These sentences have one and only one independent clause—a clause which, by formal criteria, can stand alone in the language as a major sentence. This set of well-formed sentences contains the kernel as a proper subset.

2. *Transformed sentences (transformata)* are complete, not simple. These sentences are complex and compound. They are major sentences because they have at least

one independent clause, but are not part of the kernel because they are not simple. They may be derived from simple sentences by applying the processes of embedding and conjoining.

3. *Incomplete sentences (deformata)* are simple, not complete. These sentences include both dependent clause structures and nonclause structures which occur in the language as minor type sentences. When the clause structure is only partial, these sentences may be derived from simple, complete sentences by a process of deletion.

Simple Complete Sentences. The well-formed sentences that belong to the kernel next become the focus of attention for the analyst. The corpus is reduced to simple sentences, and the complex and compound major types are rejected as not belonging to the kernel. The simple sentences are sorted for completeness, and the minor type sentences with incomplete structure are rejected as derived. What remains is a set of simple complete sentences; these are then sorted according to the remaining three features of the kernel:

1. Statements, questions, and commands, which are identified according to the type of response expected. *Statements* (S) expect no particular response; *questions* (Q) expect an answer; and *commands* (C) expect an action response.
2. Active, middle, and passive sentences are identified according to the voice of the main verb form. *Active* sentences have subject-as-actor; *passive* sentences have subject-as-goal; and *middle* sentences have subject as both actor and goal. Some languages have a fourth voice, called *reciprocal*, in which the subject and object act in reciprocal action.
3. Affirmative and negative sentences are identified by the presence of a negating particle within the main verb phrase. The sentence may be said to be *negative* when a negative particle occurs with the main verb.

These last three features are used to form a kernel sentence matrix.

Sentence Level Matrix

Once the complex and compound sentences have been broken down by reduction and the complete sentences isolated from the incomplete, a sentence level matrix is set up that deals with simple, complete sentences. This matrix distinguishes the kinds of sentences described in the other three features of the kernel, namely: (1) statement, as opposed to question and command; (2) active, as opposed to middle and passive; and (3) affirmative, as opposed to negative.

Parameters of the Matrix. A matrix in mathematics is an array of rows and columns, in which the elements are the coefficients for a set of simultaneous equations. In linguistic analysis, a matrix is an array of rows and columns, an array in the sense in which this word is used in computer analysis. The elements of the array may be complete construction symbols or units which enter into construction.

The notion of matrix was introduced by Pike in a series of articles entitled "Dimensions of Grammatical Structure" (*Language*, 1962:221–244) and "A Syntactic Paradigm" (*Language*, 1963:216–230), in which grammatical structures are charted in much the same way as morphological paradigms. Longacre likewise makes use of matrices, as well as transformational rules, to show relationships between constructions. These two methods of showing structural relationships are "not immiscible" (Longacre, 1960:16). Both methods may be used in the same grammatical description.

A grammatical matrix charts constructions in different dimensions, or parameters. These parameters must be chosen before the matrix can be set up. For the sentence level matrix, two useful parameters are:

1. Sentence types, such as statement, question, and command.
2. Basic clause types, such as transitive, intransitive, and equational.

Together, these parameters give us a 3 × 3, or 9-element matrix of sentence types. These nine sentence types are useful for early analysis.

CLAUSE TYPE	STATEMENT	QUESTION	COMMAND
Intransitive	S-iCl John went.	Q-iCl Did John go?	C-iCl Go, John!
Transitive	S-tCl John ate it.	Q-tCl Did John eat it?	C-tCl Eat it, John!
Equational	S-eqCl John is good.	Q-eqCl Is John good?	C-eqCl Be good, John!

Matrix Operators. The analogy of a mathematical matrix may be carried one step further by the introduction of matrix operators. In matrix algebra, the matrix may be used as a unit in calculations. The whole matrix is multiplied by a single number, by multiplying each element in each cell of the matrix by the number, called an operator.

In tagmemic field theory, the derivation of construction types is represented as the multiplication of a matrix by a constant (Pike, 1962:226). Some of the constants which might occur in this use are the features of interrogation, emphasis, quotation, and negation. Each of the elements in the matrix is multiplied by the constant to derive new types (Pike, 1967:473, fn. 9). This operation is essentially the same as transformational rules which derive negatives, passives, and so on. In the sentence matrix given above, the first column is the basic kernel, and the Q and C columns are derived from the first column by use of Q and C operators respectively. The whole 9-element matrix may then be operated on by (operator #1) *negative*.

$$
\begin{vmatrix}
\text{S-iCl} & \text{Q-iCl} & \text{C-iCl} \\
\text{S-tCl} & \text{Q-tCl} & \text{C-tCl} \\
\text{S-eqCl} & \text{Q-eqCl} & \text{C-eqCl}
\end{vmatrix}
\qquad \text{X} \qquad \text{/Negative/}
$$

The product will be a 9-element negative matrix, with nine negative sentence types in addition to the nine affirmative sentence types in the original matrix. The transitive elements of the matrix may be operated on by (operator #2) *voice*.

$$
\begin{vmatrix}
\text{S-iCl} \\
\text{Q-tCl} \\
\text{C-tCl}
\end{vmatrix}
\quad \text{X} \quad \text{/Voice/} \quad =
\begin{vmatrix}
\text{S-tCl}_p & \text{S-tCl}_m & \text{S-tCl}_r \\
\text{Q-tCl}_p & \text{Q-tCl}_m & \text{Q-tCl}_r \\
\text{C-tCl}_p & \text{C-tCl}_m & \text{C-tCl}_r
\end{vmatrix}
$$

With the use of both operators, negative passive sentences are derived. Beginning with three clause types, a 9-element matrix is developed. With the use of both operators, 36 different sentence types may be derived. Of these 36, only three are kernel types and the other 33 are derived. If voice is only active/passive, as in English, there are three basic and 21 derived, or 24 types.

MAJOR SENTENCE TYPES				
At Sentence Level		At Clause Level		
Compound Complex Simple	Statement Question Command	Intransitive Transitive Equational	Active Passive	Affirmative Negative

Simple Clause Formulations

The sentence level is that level at which clauses combine to make sentences. In the case of simple clause structures, it is the level at which single clause bases combine with intonation patterns. In the formulation of these structures, only base and intonation tagmemes are required, with possible special tagmemes for sentence level particles. Simple major sentences are statements, questions, or commands; the clauses that fill the base slot are transitive, intransitive, or equational. In an initial sort of simple sentences, these features of the sentence matrix are considered first. The voice and negative operators are considered at the clause level of construction. Applying this type of sort to a problem in Sierra Popoluca (#165, *Laboratory Manual*, 1967), a corpus of 75 sentences was separated into five homogeneous sets, as follows:

S-tCl	S-iCl	S-eqCl	C-tCl	C-iCl
17	25	14	8	11

Working on the divide-and-conquer principle, the corpus was reduced to five manageable problems, which could be easily and clearly charted. No questions occurred in the corpus given.

Statements. Turning our attention first to the statements, which belong to the kernel, we formulate the sentence type for statement, assuming all statements have similar intonation and that this intonation is in contrast with the intonation patterns of the command sentences. In the formulas, sentences are assumed to be statements unless marked otherwise.

2.6   Sent = +Base:iCl/tCl/eqCl −Into:ICF

Read: A sentence consists of a base slot filled by an intransitive clause, a transitive clause, or an equational clause, and an intonation slot filled by a final intonation contour.

The individual fillers of the base slot, labeled as tCl, iCl, and eqCl, are then expanded at the clause level. The two points of contrast between this sentence level formula, and that for the command sentences given below, are found in the fillers of the base and intonation slots respectively.

2.7   C-Sent = +Base:C-iCl/C-tCl −Into:C-ICF

Read: A command sentence consists of a base slot filled by an intransitive or a transitive command clause, and an intonation slot filled by a final intonation contour for commands.

The fillers of the base slot, labeled as C-iCl and C-tCl, are then expanded at the clause level, and are demonstrably different from the corresponding fillers of the statement type sentence.

Commands. The commands of language, marked as C-iCl and C-tCl, usually differ from statements in their internal clause structure, and may differ as well in their intonation patterns.

Subjects in the second person are omitted or replaced by vocatives; verbs are in the imperative mood; and often the negative particles used with commands are distinctive. Other differences may occur, including restrictions on peripheral tagmemes. The differences at the sentence level may be listed as:

1. *Intonation Pattern.* May be special for commands; differences may be represented by a substitution transformation.
2. *Base Fillers.* May be different clause level strings as fillers; differences may be represented by a substitution transformation.
3. *Command Markers.* May be marked by special particles; differences may be represented by an addition transformation.

Questions. The questions of language may differ from statements by intonation pattern, by the use of special question markers, or by different internal clause structure in the fillers of the base slot. Question words are used in most languages, and change of order is a question-marking signal in English. Other changes may occur, such as limitation in the use of peripheral tagmemes in the clause structure. Differences at the sentence level may be listed as:

1. *Intonation Pattern.* Some patterns are used as question signals; differences may be represented by a substitution: 231 ↓ → 233 ↑.

   2.8 Q-Sent = +Base:iCl/tCl/eqCl −Into:233 ↑

   Read: A question sentence consists of a base slot filled by an intransitive, a transitive, or an equational clause, and an intonation slot, filled by the intonation pattern: 233 ↑.

2. *Base Fillers.* Question type clauses occur, as Q-iCl, Q-tCl, Q-eqCl in which the clause structure which forms the sentence base is different, while the intonation pattern may be the same as for statements.

   2.9 Q-Sent = +Base:Q-iCl/Q-tCl/Q-eqCl −Into:231 ↓

   Read: A question sentence consists of a base slot filled by an intransitive, a transitive, or an equational question clause, and an intonation slot filled by the intonation pattern: 231 ↓.

3. *Question Markers.* Questions may be signaled by special question markers, marked QM, used to transform any statement into a question; for example, Hindi uses unstressed {kyaa} as one method of marking questions.

2.10   Q-Sent = ±QM:{kyaa} +Base:iCl/tCl/eqCl
                    −Into:233 ↑

Read: A question sentence consists of an optional question
marker slot filled by {kyaa} and a base slot filled by an intransitive, transitive, or equational clause, and so on.

MINOR SENTENCE TYPES

An utterance either has final intonation or it does not have final
intonation. Those utterances found with final intonation contours are called sentences; those without final intonation contour
are fragments. It is to be expected that, with this definition of a
sentence, many types of sentences will be found that do not have
complete clause structures as a sentence base. These are the
minor sentences of language.

Minor Sentence Defined

A minor sentence is a sentence with an incomplete sentence
base and a final intonation contour. Since the contour is final,
the utterance is a sentence; since the base is incomplete, the sentence is a minor type of sentence. Some minor sentences have
clause structure, while others have no clause structure intended
or implied. Of the minor sentences with clause structure, some
are (1) sequential; some are (2) marginal; and some are (3) elliptical, with only partial clause structure.

Sequential Sentences. Minor sentences of the sequential
type are those sentences which, in fact, contain a complete independent clause, but also contain an obligatory sequence-marking
tagmeme. This type of sentence is not used to initiate discourse,
but is found in included position, with recognizable conjunctions
as sequence signals (Fries, 1952:250), for example: *also, besides,
consequently, however, likewise, thus, yet,* and so on. Elson and
Pickett (1962:121), following Waterhouse, "Dependent and Independent Sentences" (*IJAL*:29, 45–54, 1963) classify the sequential
sentence as a minor type. The sequence sentence has a connector
and an independent clause:

2.11   Seq-Sent = +C:c +Base:Ind.Cl −Into:ICF

Read: A sequence sentence consists of a connector slot filled
by a connector, a base slot filled by an independent clause,
and an intonation slot filled by a final intonation contour.

This minor sentence type is related to the compound sentence,
and the formula is identical with the second half of the compound
sentence formula (see formula 2.3). Without the final intonation

contour, this sentence could be joined to a preceding simple sentence to form a single compound sentence. Without the sequence marking tagmeme, since the base is filled by an independent clause, the structure could stand alone as a simple sentence in the language.

Marginal Sentences. The marginal sentence has a margin slot filled by a dependent clause and a final intonation contour. This type is derived from the complex sentence (see formula 2.2). and could be joined to a preceding simple sentence to form a complex sentence.

2.12   Marg-Sent = +Marg:depCl −Into:ICF

Read: A marginal sentence consists of a margin slot filled by a dependent clause, and an intonation slot filled by a final intonation contour.

The filler of the margin slot might be either a dependent clause of the relater-axis type, with the clause subordinated by a relater particle; or the filler might be an indefinite clause, in which the subordinating particle is also a constituent of the clause in which it stands, for example, indefinite pronoun.

Elliptical Sentences. The elliptical sentence is a sentence in which the clause structure is not complete, due to the deletion of some of its elements. This sentence type is directly derived from the simple sentence type (see formula 2.1). These sentences include, or are interpreted in terms of, elements understood in traditional grammar, or have a nonfinite verb filling the predicate slot in the structure.

These structures are similar to sequential or marginal structures, but differ from them in that they do not contain either a complete independent clause or a complete dependent clause; the clause structure here is a partial structure, or a nonfinite structure.

1. *Deletions.* After sequence marking tagmemes, subject deletion is common. The sequence marker connects the minor sentence with the preceding sentence, and the subject is understood to be the same.

> He finished his work at the office.
> And then went home. (subject omitted)

In marginal minor sentences, the subject and auxiliaries are often deleted, with a resulting participial form filling the predicate slot.

> What are you doing this evening?
> Watching television. (subject and auxiliary omitted)

2. *Nonfinite Verb Forms.* Partial clause structures also occur as minor sentences, which in normal use would be nominals in clause structure. The internal structure of these clauses is characterized by the form of the verb filling the predicate slot, which might be either (1) an infinitive form (marked $+P:V_{inf}$) or (2) a participle form (marked $+P:V_{part}$). These forms occur in combination with other clause level tagmemes, although the subject is generally omitted from the string.

Types of Minor Sentences

The minor sentences of language are not only characterized by their formal structure as sequential, marginal, or elliptical. They are also characterized, according to their function in the context of the situation, as (1) additions, (2) responses, and (3) exclamations. Although the tagmemic structure has been outlined according to form, the label of the construction should coincide with its use in the language.

Addition Sentences. Addition sentences (marked A-Sent) are minor sentences that occur in discourse as additions to statements already made. They occur with final intonation and are sentences. They do not have full clause structure and are minor sentences. In form, they may be sequential, marginal, or elliptical; or they may have only the structure of a word or a phrase. They are formulated:

2.13 A-Sent = +Base:depCl/phrase/word −Into:ICF

Read: An addition sentence consists of a base slot filled by a dependent clause, phrase, or word and an intonation slot filled by a final intonation contour.

These additions, qualifications, corrections, or afterthoughts need not be fully expressed in the language, as they are clearly understood in the given context as added to the previous sentence. The addition is part of a major sentence, a major sentence which can be reconstructed into a full sentence using elements from the preceding sentence. Thus:

He is leaving for summer vacation soon.   (Statement)
The day after tomorrow.   (Addition sentence)
He is leaving for summer vacation *the day after tomorrow.*

Response Sentences. The response sentences (marked R-Sent) are minor sentences which occur in response to questions. They are sentences with final intonation, but they often are minor sentences of the marginal or elliptical types, or have the structure of only a phrase or a word. Short responses are very frequent. They are formulated:

2.14 R-Sent = +Base:depCl/phrase/word −Into:ICF

Read: A response sentence consists of a base slot filled by a dependent clause, phrase, or word and an intonation slot filled by a final intonation contour.

The responses to questions need not be complete structures, as the response is fully intelligible in terms of the question asked. Where necessary, the full response can be reconstructed in terms of the original question into a full and complete major sentence-type.

Where are you going this afternoon? (Question)
To the supermarket. (Response sentence)
I am going *to the supermarket* this afternoon.

In reconstructing the full sentence, the question word *where*, which fills a location slot in clause structure, is replaced by the response phrase, *to the supermarket*, which fills the locational slot in clause structure. All other elements in the clause remain constant, except for the change of person, here, from speaker to nonspeaker.

Exclamatory Sentences. Addition and response sentences are minor sentences of the completive type; they complete a statement or a question that has gone before. These are opposed to the exclamatory type, which is syntactically independent (see Bloomfield, 1933:176). These exclamatory minor sentences might combine with any sentence as a peripheral exclamatory tagmeme, but when used in isolation with their own final intonation contour, they are minor sentences.

Completive minor sentences, including additions and responses, tend to have an underlying structure which ranges from simple word structures, such as a *yes* or *no* answer, through phrases, to elliptical, marginal, and sequential dependent clause structures.

Exclamatory minor sentences tend to be limited to simple word and phrase groups, with no underlying clause structure at all. Because of their syntactic independence, no underlying structure is implied. This lack of clause structure is evidenced by the lack of a predicate tagmeme. These structures are discussed in the following section, Nonclause Structures. The structure of minor sentences, with incomplete clause structure, may be charted as to sentence and clause level features. Each minor sentence type may then be characterized by picking one feature from each column in the diagram of the minor sentence types.

MINOR SENTENCE TYPES					
At Sentence Level		At Clause Level			
Sequential Marginal Elliptical	Addition Response Exclamatory	Intransitive Transitive Equational	Active Passive	Affirmative Negative	

Nonclause Structures

The minor sentences of language include single words or short phrases that do not have the underlying structure of a clause. These structures are characterized, in general, by the absence of a predicate or predicate-like tagmeme in the string, which defines a clause. Yet such forms do occur with final intonation and fall within the general class of minor sentences.

Calls, Greetings, Interjections. Minor sentences of this group have no clause structure and are generally limited to one or two words. They are functionally of the exclamatory type, syntactically independent.

1. *Calls, or vocatives*, are generally the names of persons or titles of address designating persons. Many case-marked language systems have a vocative case, used with or without exclamatory particles.

John!   Waiter!   Mr. Secretary!

2. *Greetings* in most languages are stereotyped expressions, used in a ritual for meeting people, initiating conversation, or leaving. Where the individual words had meaning, this original meaning is often lost.

Hello!   Goodbye!   Be seeing you!

3. *Interjections* are usually short and expressive, not expecting a particular response. They are used particularly to express strong emotion, such as pain, surprise, enthusiasm, but not limited to these uses.

Ouch!   Oh boy!   Doggone it!

Most of these types need no grammatical formulation. They are simply listed in the lexicon of the language for use in particular context situations; and they are listed as single lexical entries, without further analysis.

Titles, Mottoes, Inscriptions. This group of minor sentences is generally of greater length and indicates some of the phrase structures of the language. This type may overlap with favorite sentence types.

1. *Titles*, when they consist of more than one word, are generally a legitimate phrase structure, with the author included as an agentive. In reading, the structure is spoken with a single final intonation pattern.

Alice in Wonderland,   by Lewis Carroll

2. *Mottoes*, consisting of more than one word, show regular phrase structure. The type of phrase used may differ from language to language, as each culture has its own favorite phrase types in this use.

Latin: *In caritate et iustitia*   (An adverbial phrase)
French: *Liberté, égalité, fraternité*   (A nominal phrase)

3. *Inscriptions*, when limited to phrase structure, as well as spoken toasts, often begin, in English, with *To* meaning "dedicated to," followed by nominals, often with embedded modifying clauses.

Nontypical Structures. There are sentences in language use which do not conform to any of the major or minor sentence types. They are special uses of language which may be pitfalls for the unwary analyst.

Metalanguage is language about language. In this usage, some of the forms of language become the topic of conversation, and thereby become nominal in use, losing their original functional class, for example:

The is a definite article.   (*the* = a noun)

Using metalanguage, it is possible to string together lists of conjunctions, auxiliaries, and other parts of speech, in ways normally ungrammatical.

Between *hotdogs* and *and* and *and* and *hamburgers*
there is the same spacing given on the neon sign.

Once the forms in metalinguistic use are recognized, the grammatical structures appear to be quite regular.

Abbreviated language occurs in common use in headlines, in the writing of telegrams, and in some types of radio announcements. The structure is shortened by eliminating many of the function words, with the result that the message is cryptic, and often becomes ambiguous.

Army camps in the open   Is *camps* noun or verb?
Officers Flying Home   Is *officers* plural, possessive?

Anyone who has tried writing a ten-word telegram has experienced the difficulties of using this abbreviated form of language.

Certain types of written and spoken reports also have an abbreviated style, for example: the weather bulletins—a recitation of facts regarding clouds, wind, tides, and temperatures—or police descriptions of a suspect in a case, with name, height, weight, and identifying characteristics. These special uses of language must be interpreted in the light of their stylistic format.

There are other forms of language which are grammatical and neither abbreviated nor metalinguistic. These specialized uses of language are the aphorisms, or sayings, popular in a language, or the use of language in special fields such as sports, science, or business. The limited use of abstract inanimate nouns as subject, described as "less grammatical" by Chomsky, (1957:78), in such sentences as *Sincerity admires John*, is contradicted by the aphorisms:

Misery loves company.   Power corrupts.
Fortune favors the brave.   Love conquers all.

The use of simile and metaphor in both ancient and modern languages also allows for a wide range of subject-predicate combinations that would not be allowed by an overrestricted semantic component. The collocations of individual words, and consequent grammatical patterns, are used with considerable liberty in the sports field, where each sport has its own specialized vocabulary. These and other special forms of language must be interpreted in terms of its nonspecialized uses.

PRACTICE 2: SENTENCE LEVEL SORTING

The corpus is a set of sentences ready for analysis. The sentences, particularly in running text, must be isolated, sorted according to type, and then analyzed at the clause level. Procedures at the sentence level include reduction of the corpus to simple clause structures, and then recording of complex and compound structures with their intonations. Reduce the following paragraph and list the type of sentence patterns:

> As the sun set, he remembered, to give himself more confidence, the time in the tavern at Casablanca when he had played the hand game with the great negro from Cienfuegos who was the strongest man on the docks.
>
> Hemingway, *The Old Man and the Sea*

Reduction of the Corpus. Rewrite the paragraph, one clause to a line; isolate connectors, relaters, and simple clause patterns discovered.

+R	+S	+P	±O
1. as	the sun	set	
2.	he	remembered	the time in the tavern at Casablanca
3. to		give himself	more confidence
4. when	he	had played	the hand game with the great negro from Cienfuegos
5. X	who	was	the strongest man on the docks

Clauses within Sentences. After reduction of the corpus, complete formulas for complex and compound sentences can be recorded with intonation pattern. If clause (2) *main,* and clause (3) *purpose,* combine:

$$\text{(Complex) Sent} = \pm\text{Marg:F–tCl} +\text{Base:tCl} -\text{Into:ICF}$$

Read: A complex sentence consists of an optional margin slot, filled by a purpose clause (F), a base slot filled by a transitive clause, and an intonation slot filled by final intonation contour.

$$\text{F–tCl} = +\text{P:tv}_{\text{inf}} +\text{IO:refl.pn} +\text{DO:N} \qquad \text{(Purpose)}$$

Read: A purpose clause consists of a predicate slot filled by a transitive verb infinitive, an indirect object slot filled by a reflexive pronoun, and a direct object slot filled by a noun phrase.

Alternate Solution: If the complex sentence formula is not a useful pattern in the overall structure of the language, the purpose clause may be interpreted as filling a purpose slot within the main clause:

$$\text{tCl} = +\text{S:pn} +\text{P:tv} \pm\text{F:F–tCl} \pm\text{O:N}_{\text{id}} \qquad \text{(Main Clause)}$$

Read: The (main) transitive clause consists of a subject slot filled by a pronoun, a predicate slot filled by a transitive verb, an optional purpose slot filled by a purpose clause, and an optional object slot filled by an identified noun phrase.

Clauses within Clauses. Some dependent clauses will be found as fillers of clause level slots, with one clause layered within another clause. The temporal clause (1) fills a clause level temporal slot.

$$\text{tCl} = \pm\text{T:T–iCl} +\text{S:pn} +\text{P:tv} \pm\text{O:N}_{\text{id}} \qquad \text{(Main Clause)}$$

Read: The (main) transitive clause consists of an optional temporal slot filled by a temporal clause, and so on.

$$\text{T–iCl} = +\text{R:rel} +\text{Ax:iCl} \qquad \text{(Temporal)}$$

Read: A temporal clause consists of a relater slot filled by a relater and an axis slot filled by an intransitive clause.

Clauses within Phrases. Some dependent clauses will be found as fillers of modifier slots at the phrase level. These are generally relative clauses. Clauses (4) *when* and (5) *who* are of this type. The identifier (Id:) tagmeme is used for these loopback clauses.

$$N_{id} = +Det:det +H:n +Id:R-tCl \qquad \text{(Noun Phrase)}$$

Read: An identified noun phrase consists of a determiner slot filled by a determiner, a head slot filled by a noun, and an identifier slot filled by a relative transitive clause.

$$R-tCl = +T:rel.av. +S:pn +P:tV \pm O:N... \qquad \text{(Relative)}$$

Read: A relative clause consists of a temporal slot filled by a relative adverb, a subject slot filled by a pronoun, a predicate slot filled by a transitive verb phrase, and an optional object slot filled by a noun phrase, and so on.

SUPPLEMENTARY READINGS 2

Bloomfield, Leonard, *Language,* New York, Holt, Rinehart and Winston, Inc., 1933. See Chap. 11, "Sentence Types," 170–177, for the classical definition of sentence. Favorite (= major) types are distinguished from minor. The minor are completive or exclamatory.

Chomsky, Noam, *Syntactic Structures,* The Hague, Mouton & Co., 1957. Kernel sentences are the sentences which result when we apply only obligatory and no optional transformations (46). In English, the kernel sentences are simple declarative active (80) with no complex noun or verb phrases (107). All other sentences are derived.

Elson, Benjamin, and Pickett, Velma, *An Introduction to Morphology and Syntax,* Santa Ana, Summer Institute of Linguistics, 1962. Chap. 11, "Tagmemes and Constructions at the Sentence Level," 82–83, and Chap. 18, "Survey of Sentence Types," 121–128. The levels above the sentence are treated briefly in Chap. 19, 127–128.

Fries, Charles C., *The Structure of English,* New York, Harcourt, Brace and World, Inc., 1952. See Chap. 2, "What is a Sentence?" 9–28, for use of Bloomfield's definition versus traditional definitions. Chap. 3, "Kinds of Sentences," 29–53, based on situation and response.

Gleason, Henry A. Jr, *Linguistics and English Grammar,* New York, Holt, Rinehart and Winston, Inc., 1965. Chap. 14, "Joining Clauses," 329–350. Rejects division of sentences into simple, complex, and compound, in favor of IC coordination and subordination of clauses.

Liem, Nguyen Dang, *English Grammar, A Combined Tagmemic and Transformational Approach,* Linguistic Circle of Canberra, 1966. A Contrastive Analysis of Vietnamese and English, vol. I, Chap. 5, "English Sentence Types and Sentence Level Structures," 139–149. Lists major independent, major dependent, and minor types.

Longacre, Robert E., *Grammar Discovery Procedures*, The Hague, Mouton & Co., 1964. Chap. 4, "Sentence Level Procedures," 125–151. Treats sentence level after the levels of clause, phrase, and word.

, "The Notion of Sentence," *Monograph Series on Languages and Linguistics*, No. 20 (Washington, D.C., Georgetown University Press, 1967), 15–25. Defines sentence level as a level of clause combination, and classifies sentences by conjunction, alternation, implication, and negation.

TABLE 3: CLAUSE LEVEL ANALYSIS

According to the Type of Verb Form	According to the Distribution of Unit	According to Its Internal Structure	Characteristics of the Clause Type
Main Clause with Finite Verb Form	Independent Clause which can stand alone	1. *Transitive (tCl)* transitive verb, may take object 2. *Intransitive (iCl)* intransitive verb, takes no object 3. *Equational (eqCl)* equational verb, predicate attribute	Transitivity recognized if object occurs with the verb at least once. Intransitivity recognized if no object ever occurs with the verb Verb links subject with predicate attribute, noun, adjective, or adverb
	Dependent Clause which cannot stand alone	1. *Nominal Clause* acts like a noun 2. *Adjectival Clause* acts like adjective 3. *Adverbial Clause* acts like adverb	Recognized dependent by indefinite pronoun Recognized dependent by relative pronouns Recognized dependent by clause-type relaters
		Nonfinite Verb Forms with partial clause structure	Recognized as dependent by gerunds, participles, infinitives

3 CLAUSE LEVEL

The clause level of grammar is that level that is below the sentence level and above the phrase level. The clause is composed of words and phrases and, in turn, fills slots at the sentence level. The clause is a unit of grammar. It is a construction in which the constitute is a potential sentence base, and in which the constituents are the subjects, predicates, objects, and adjuncts that combine to form this base. Clause level analysis is central to the system.

Clause Defined. The clause is "a string of tagmemes that consists of or includes one and only one predicate, or predicate-like tagmeme, in the string, and whose manifesting morpheme sequence typically fills slots at the sentence level" (Elson and Pickett, 1962:64). In the wording of this definition, the following essential features should be noted:

1. *Clauses typically fill slots on the sentence level.* In typical mapping of lower constructions into higher levels, clauses combine to form sentences, or combine with intonation to form sentences. However, atypical mapping of clause within clause and clause within phrase occurs.
2. *Clauses consist of or include one and only one predicate.* Accordingly, there are as many clauses as there are predicate tagmemes. A single clause may, however, have a compound verb form in the predicate slot. Some languages have verb forms which, in themselves, constitute what Longacre calls a "clause-in-miniature," containing both subject and predicate; other languages require subject and predicate tagmemes.
3. *Clauses may have a predicate-like tagmeme.* Particularly

in the equational type structures, the predicate may be optional. In these cases there is another tagmeme, the predicate attribute tagmeme, which is obligatory. This predicate attribute occurs even when the linking verb does not occur and the clause unit has no predicate tagmeme.

Traditional Clause. The clause has traditionally been considered a unit of grammar and has been defined as "a group of words, containing a subject and a predicate, and used as part of a sentence." Clause units were subclassified as independent, or main clauses, and dependent, or subordinate clauses. An independent clause was defined as a clause that could stand alone as a sentence, and a dependent clause as a clause that could not stand alone as a sentence (see Warriner, 1965:53).

In tagmemic analysis, the clause is accepted as one of the fundamental units of grammar, but is defined as a word group containing one and only one predicate. This allows the inclusion not only of independent and dependent clauses, which have both subject and predicate, but also of partial clause structures under the label of clause. An infinitive or participle, expanded with objects or modifiers, is also classified as a dependent clause. The definition of independent clause is also amended. This clause must be able to stand alone as a major sentence in the language. The features that determine whether the clause can stand alone as a major sentence in the language will be unique for each language investigated.

Clause Types. The clause types traditionally investigated in the study of grammar must also be investigated in formal linguistic analysis. Whatever the system of analysis, provision must be made for describing known clause structures, and for stating the relations of dependency by which clauses are subordinated within sentence structure.

Independent clauses are classified by these features:

1. Transitivity: intransitive, transitive, or equational.
2. Voice: active, middle, passive, or reciprocal.
3. Negation: affirmative or negative.

Dependent clauses are classified by their structure:

1. Complete Clause Structures: Subordinated or subordinate.
2. Partial Clause Structures: Infinitives or participles.
3. Nonclause Structures: Base for minor sentences.

In the analysis of independent clause structures, primary

attention is given to kernel sentences. Simple, complete state-ments, whether transitive, intransitive, or equational, are analyzed first. Then these basic sentences are related to non-kernel sentences. Statements are opposed to commands and questions, active to nonactive, affirmative to negative.

In the analysis of dependent clause structures, clause struc-tures must be analyzed as filling slots at a particular level of analysis. The clause fills a marginal slot at sentence level, or the clause occurs filling a clause level slot in a *layering* structure, or the clause fills a phrase level slot in a *loopback* structure. Once the distribution of the clause is known, the clause may be further classified according to its function as nominal, adjectival, or ad-verbial, and according to its form as a complete, partial, or non-clause structure.

INDEPENDENT CLAUSES

The clause level in tagmemics is the heart of the analytic process. The sentence level provides a sorting ground for reducing sen-tences to homogeneous sets of clauses, apart from their intona-tion. After sorting, the underlying structure of the sentence is analyzed by taking apart its clause base, in terms of subject-predicate-object-adjunct tagmemes that form the underlying structure. The work done here is comparable to the upper level branching rules of a transformational grammar.

Independent Clause Defined

An independent clause is a clause that can stand alone as a major sentence in the language. This capacity to stand alone must be judged according to its acceptability by a native speaker of the language. Each language will have its own features of both external distribution and internal structure which formally categorize clause independence.

Nuclear Clause Level Tagmemes. Clauses are potential strings of tagmemes which include one and only one predicate in the string. Within that string, some tagmemes are nuclear, some peripheral. The nuclear tagmemes are diagnostic of the construction in which they occur and may be obligatory or op-tional; peripheral tagmemes are optional. In clause structure, subject-predicate-object are generally nuclear.

S: *Subject tagmeme* manifests the topic, or actor, or thing de-scribed. Subject may be obligatory or optional in the con-struction, and is often linked with the predicate by a cross-reference type of concord tie.

P: *Predicate tagmeme* manifests the type of action or serves as a link between the subject and its attribute. Predicate is obligatory in all clause constructions except the equational type construction.

PA: *Predicate attribute* manifests an attribute of the subject by a nominal, adjectival, or adverbial word group. It is linked to the subject by a linking verb and an agreement type of concord. It is always obligatory.

O: *Object tagmeme* completes the meaning of the predicate, and often is case-governed by the predicate in a government type concord tie. Objects may be specified as *DO:* direct object; *IO:* indirect object; or *OC:* object complement, in structures which take two objects.

Peripheral Clause Level Tagmemes. The peripheral tagmemes at clause level are not diagnostic of the construction, and are always optional. They fill in details of time, place, and manner, and are mainly adverbs and adverbial phrases or clauses. Typical peripherals are:

L: *Location tagmeme* answers the question *where* and places the verbal action in a place setting. The fillers of this slot are adverbs of place and their substitutes. Locative adverbs are labeled *loc.*

T: *Temporal tagmeme* answers the question *when* and places the verbal action in a time setting. The fillers of this slot are adverbs of time and their substitutes. Temporal adverbs are labeled *tem.*

M: *Manner tagmeme* answers the question *how* and fills in the details of the circumstances of the action. The fillers of this slot are adverbs of manner and their substitutes. Manner adverbs are labeled *av.* In initial analysis, this slot is used to differentiate manner from time and place, as a catchall for all adverbs except those of time and place.

I: *Introducer tagmeme* introduces a clause and occurs almost always in initial position. In later analysis, introducers may turn out to be temporals, or sequence signals proper to the sentence level. Introducers are labeled *i.*

The Drama Analogy. The grammatical relationships in the clause structure have been explained by Longacre, using the analogy of a drama. The dramatis personae, or roles, are the nominals, subjects, and objects. The plot is the verbal action. The scenery, or props, are provided by the adverbial elements of place, time, manner, and so on (1964:35; 1965:65). To this, we would add the costuming department, manifested by adjectival words and phrases, used as fillers in the predicate attribute slot. This four-fold classification parallels the−AL ('acts like') designation of Trager and Smith (1951:74), and the functional classes of Fries (1952:76). These terms are extended to include both single words and word groups.

Fries	Trager-Smith	Longacre
Class 1 Words	nominals	Roles, dramatis personae, S:, O:
Class 2 Words	verbals	Plot, verbal action, P:
Class 3 Words	adjectivals	Costuming features, PA:
Class 4 Words	adverbials	Props, scenery, L:, M:, T:, I:

The drama analogy is within the tagmemic tradition, and sets up classes of tagmemes which are similar in function. The role-plot distinction seems to be a fruitful line of investigation for discourse analysis (Pike, 1967:246, fn. 14; Gleason, Georgetown Monograph Series: No. 21, 1968:39–63). It is also the basis for the case grammar of Charles Fillmore (1968), who seeks to establish deep structures with *plot*, tense and mode, in one branch, and *role*, agent and goal, in another, marked by case.

Clause Level Matrix

At sentence level, a sentence level matrix was set up with the principal sentence types—statement, question, command—in one dimension and the principal clause types in the other. At clause level, a clause level matrix may be set up with the principal clause types in one dimension and the nuclear tagmemes in the other dimension. This type of matrix reveals the differences in structure between clause types.

Clause Type	Subject	Predicate	Object
1. Intransitive	$\pm$S:N	+P:iv	$\emptyset$
2. Transitive	$\pm$S:N	+P:tv	$\pm$O:N
3. Equational	$\pm$S:N	$\pm$P:eqv	+PA:N/Aj/Av

In preliminary sorting, it is assumed that these three types of clauses will be found in a language, but further investigation may require that these types be subclassified or that new types of clauses be added.

Intransitive Clause. An intransitive clause is defined as a clause which contains an intransitive verb. This verb, in turn, is a verb which can never take an object. According to the rule of two (see p. 26), this clause must differ from other clauses by two structural differences, one of which affects the nuclear tagmemes of the construction. The differences here are: (1) absence of object tagmeme, (2) filler of predicate slot, and (3) inability of intransitive verbs to transform into passive. All are nuclear. A typical clause level formula for an intransitive clause would be:

3.1   iCl = +S:pn +P:iv $\pm$L:loc   He went home.

Read: An intransitive clause consists of a subject slot filled by a pronoun, a predicate slot filled by an intransitive verb, and an optional location slot filled by a locative.

Transitivity could have been defined in a different way, so that verbs that occur sometimes with and sometimes without objects are classified as both transitive and intransitive. However, transitivity is often marked in the verb form, and verbs so marked for transitivity do occur without objects at times. Therefore the tagmemic system permits the use of optional objects and classifies intransitive verbs as verbs that never take an object, and transitive verbs as verbs that have the capacity to take an object.

Transitive Clause. A transitive clause is defined as a clause that contains a transitive verb. This verb, in turn, is a verb that has the capacity to take one or more objects. This capacity to take an object is demonstrated by the occurrence of the object with the verb at least once. According to the rule of two, the transitive clause differs from other clauses in: (1) the presence of an optional object, (2) filler of the predicate slot, and (3) the ability of the transitive clause to transform into the passive. A typical clause level formula for the transitive clause is as follows:

3.2 tCl = +S:pn +P:tv ±O:n   He ate dinner.

Read: A transitive clause consists of a subject slot filled by a pronoun, a predicate slot filled by a transitive verb, and an optional object slot filled by a noun.

Every verb is either transitive or intransitive; but transitive verbs can be further subclassified as: (1) semitransitive, with optional object; (2) transitive, with obligatory object; and (3) ditransitive, with two objects. In English, for example, verbs occur with one object, with both indirect and direct object, or with object and object complement.

Equational Clause. An equational clause is defined as a clause that contains an equational, or linking, verb. The verb connects the subject with the predicate attribute, which may be nominal, adjectival, or adverbial. In this structure, the PA: slot is obligatory and in agreement with the subject. In some languages the subject is omitted, in others, the predicate linking verb is omitted. In English both are obligatory. A typical clause level formula for the equational clause is as follows:

3.3 eqCl = +S:pn +P:eqv +PA:N   He is the chief.

Read: An equational clause consists of a subject slot filled by a pronoun, a predicate slot filled by an equational verb, and a predicate attribute slot filled by a noun phrase.

In investigating equational clauses, it is often useful to test the clause formula in different tenses. Many languages that allow a zero link in the present tense have an overt linking verb form in the past tense. This clause type is sometimes classified into: (1) equational, if the predicate attribute is a noun; and (2) stative, if the predicate attribute is an adjective (Elson and Pickett, 1962:113). In Liem's analysis of English, clauses beginning with *It* and *There* are set up as stative clauses (1966:160–161) distinct from the equational type clause.

Derived Clause Types

Independent clauses are used as the fillers of the base slot of both kernel and derived sentences. The basic list of nuclear and peripheral tagmemes is sufficient for most kernel sentences. For derived sentences new tagmemes must be established. The derivation of sentences from the kernel may be shown by indicating the contrastive patterns. The principal derived sentences are: (1) commands and questions, opposed to statements; and (2) passive and negative, opposed to active and affirmative; to these may be added (3) emphatic clauses.

Questions and Commands. The sentence types opposed to statements are questions and commands. These differ from statements by features at the sentence level, at the clause level, or both.

Questions differ from statements at the sentence level by intonation patterns, or by special question markers, or by the type of clause used (see p. 53, Questions). The differences in the structure of the clause are:

1. *Use of question words* as fillers for clause level slots. In English, for example, questions are recognized by the words *who, what, when, where, why, how*, generally with a shift of the slot to initial position.

   3.4 Q-eqCl = +S:Q-pn +P:eqv +PA:N

   Who is the chief?

2. *Change of order*, in English, is used as a question marking signal. The first verbal auxiliary, if there is one, is placed before the subject; where there is no auxiliary, some form of the verb *do* is used.

   3.5 Q-iCl = +Aux:aux +S:pn +P:iv ±L:loc

   Is he going home?

Commands differ from statements at the sentence level by intonation patterns, by command markers, or by a special type of clause base (see p. 52, Commands). The principal differences in clause structure are:

1. *Subject deletion* in imperatives of the second person. The subject is often supplied by a vocative form, which is syntactically independent.

2. *Verb forms* are often formally marked by an imperative mood, which is different from the regular finite verb forms of the language.

    3.6   C-tCl = +P:tv$_{imp}$ ±O:N (John!) Eat your dinner!

3. *In commands, the form of the negative* is often different from that of statements (see Sierra Popoluca, {d^{y}a}, 'not,' versus {odoy}, 'don't'). Other differences may be found, including limits on peripheral tagmemes.

Passive and Negative. The basic sentence types may change from active to passive, middle, or reciprocal voice; affirmative sentences may be changed into negative. These changes are proper to clause level.

Passive clauses differ from active clauses by changes in the subject of the active clause and changes in the voice of the verb.

1. *Subject* of the active clause becomes agent (Ag:) of the passive. Object of the active clause becomes subject of the passive clause.

2. *Verb forms* for active and passive differ in the marking of the voice feature. In the passive clause, the predicate slot is filled by a passive verb form.

    3.7 tCl = +S:N$_1$ +P:tv +O:N$_2$

                             Clyde robbed the bank.

    3.8 tClp = +S:N$_2$ +P:tvp +Ag:RA

                      The bank was robbed by Clyde.

Negative clauses differ from the active in the presence of a negative within the main verb phrase. The negative is best expressed at the level of the phrase as one optional element in the phrase level string. In larger problems, it is often convenient to use a negative T-Rule.

    3.9 *Topt Negative*   S + P + O ⇒ S + Neg + P + O

This rule, used in Sierra Popoluca (#165), indicates that the negative {d^{y}a} is inserted in the clause level string, immediately before the predicate.

Emphatic Clause. Changes of order, combined with change of meaning or the use of emphatic particles, may indicate that a special emphatic clause type is required in the language. Since tagmemes may be movable, simple change of position may place different elements in focus; but this does not indicate the need for a new clause type. The emphatic clause must differ from others by two structural differences. For example, in Cashinahua (#164), the object is moved and marked with a particle.

3.10 E-tCl = $+$O:N_m/pn$_m$ $\pm$M:RA $+$S:N/pn $+$P:tv/tV

The object slot normally occurs immediately before the predicate. In the emphatic type clause, the object slot is moved to first position, and the noun phrase or pronoun is marked with a special emphatic particle {-ra}. There is a corresponding change of meaning to strong emphasis. In the *Laboratory Manual* by Merrifield, emphatic stress is indicated by underlining the forms stressed. Palantla Chinantec (#125), Northern Tepehuan (#126), Kalagan (#168, #170), and Bukidnon Manobo (#169) are sample problems dealing with emphatic clause structures.

DEPENDENT CLAUSES

Dependent clauses are clauses that may not stand alone as major sentences, though they occur, with final intonation, as minor sentences. To understand the use of dependent clauses within major sentence structure, we consider the external distribution of the clause, the functional meaning of the clause, and its internal structure.

External Distribution of Clauses

Dependent clauses fill subordinate positions in major sentences. The process by which a clause is subordinated is called an *embedding* process. The structure in which the clause is embedded is called the matrix; the dependent clause that is embedded is called a constituent. In a tagmemic analysis, embedding may take place at the sentence level, the clause level, or the phrase level.

Sentence Level Embedding. A dependent clause embedded in a sentence structure is called *margin*, and the resulting sentence is a complex sentence, consisting of base, margin, and intonation. Clauses embedded at sentence level form the only true complex sentences and are formulated in a complex sentence formula (see p. 46). Nominal and adjectival dependent clauses are never embedded at the sentence level but fill noun and adjective slots at clause and phrase level. Embeddings at sentence level are called marginal.

The structure must be a true multiple clause structure, what Longacre calls a "patterned dependency," involving more than one clause but not having the overall structure of a single clause (1964:128). Within this structure, there may be restrictions governing the type of clause used, connecting particles, order of clauses, and sequence of tenses, which assist in deciding whether a structure is a complex sentence. Some of the types suggested by Longacre are direct and indirect quotation, conditions, effect-cause, circumstance-event, and antecedent-consequent (1964:130). A fuller description of sentence types is found in "The Notion of Sentence" (18th Annual Round Table, Georgetown University Monograph Series No. 20, 1967:15–25).

In English, certain sets of correlative particles seem to indicate that the structure is a multiple clause sentence structure, and that the sentences that use these particles are truly complex sentences. For example:

> *Conditional:* if . . . then
> *Concessive:* although . . . nevertheless/still/yet
> *Causal:* since/because . . . therefore

Clause Level Embedding. In clause level embedding, the structure has the overall structure of a single clause, even though embedded clauses occur in the structure. The dependent clauses fill clause level slots and are parallel to constructions where the same clause level slots are filled by single words or by phrases. In their external distribution, these clauses may be nominal, filling subject and object slots, or adverbial, filling adjunct slots such as time, place, or manner.

The embedding of clause within clause is a particular case of the recursiveness of a tagmemic grammar when the same symbol occurs to both right and left of the equals sign (see p. 24). Nonrecursive embedding of clause within clause also may occur when the clauses do not have the same symbol. Any occurrence of clause within clause is called a *layering* in the system.

In English, and other languages as well, introductory clause particles may signal the type of clause and the kind of slot it fills in the structure. For example:

> *Temporal:* before, while, after, when, until
> *Locational:* whence *(from)*, whither *(to)*, where
> *Manner:* as, like, as if

Phrase Level Embedding. In phrase level embedding, the structure has the overall structure of a single phrase. If the phrase is relater-axis, then the clause may be embedded as the object of a preposition, a nominal. If the phrase is a modification structure, then the clause is embedded as a single modifier related, as an adjectival, to the phrase head.

> *Nominal clause:* Here is a recording of *it.*
> Here is a recording of *what was said.*

Adjectival clause: The man was my uncle.
                       The man *who came to dinner* was my uncle.

In English, adjectival clauses embedded at phrase level are usually relative clauses, whose antecedent is the head noun of the phrase. The order in English is that single word modifiers precede, and phrases and clauses follow (see also p. 96):

Single modifiers + Head noun + Phrases + Clauses

The embedded clauses that fill nominal slots at phrase or clause level are indefinite clauses, in which the relative indefinite pronoun is nonanaphoric. It has no antecedent in the sentence structure. Relative pronouns are *who, whose, what, which, whom;* indefinites are *whoever, whatever, whichever,* and any nonanaphoric relative pronoun. Any occurrence of clause within phrase is called a *loopback* in the system.

Functional Meaning of Clauses

Dependent clauses are embedded into sentence structure. They are partially defined by their external distribution. The first fact that must be determined is the level at which the clause is embedded. The second fact that must be determined is the functional use of the clause. At the sentence level, clauses fill marginal slots in the sentence structure, as already treated under complex sentences. Clauses embedded at clause and phrase levels can be identified according to their functional meaning.

Nominal Dependent Clauses. Dependent clauses embedded at the clause and phrase level have nominal functions. Dependent clauses may serve as the subject or object of clauses, or they may function as the object of a preposition, at the phrase level, in relater-axis structure.

Nominals at clause level are subjects and objects; they fill the same slots in the structure as pronouns, nouns, or noun phrases. For example:

Subject: *He* practices language analysis.
             Whoever takes this course practices language analysis.

3.11   tCl = +S:indef.Cl +P:tv +O:N
3.12   indef.Cl = +S:indef.pn +P:tv +O:N

Nominal dependent clauses are generally introduced by indefinite relatives that have no antecedent, such as: *whoever, whatever, whichever,* and more rarely, simple relative pronouns used without an antecedent. The indefinite nominal dependent clause may also occur as object.

Object: John said *it.*
John said *that he wanted to go home.*

Nominals at phrase level are objects of prepositions; they fill the same slots in relater-axis phrases as pronouns, nouns, or noun phrases. The restrictions on internal structure are the same as at clause level. For example:

RA Object: Here is a recording of *it.*
Here is a recording of *what was said.*

3.13   RA = +R:rel +Ax:indef.Cl
3.14   indef.Cl = +S:indef.pn +P:tVp

The indefinite clause is discovered within the axis slot of the relater-axis construction, and then is analyzed according to its clause structure.

Adjectival Dependent Clauses. Dependent clauses embedded at the clause and phrase level are found with adjectival function, filling the same slots in clause or phrase structure as adjectives. They may act as predicate attribute in clause structure, or as modifiers in the phrase:

1. *Adjectivals at Clause Level.* The only occurrence of adjectives at the clause level is in the predicate attribute slot (marked PA:), which also takes nominal and adverbial clauses. In some languages, the use of an *auxiliary + participle* may be interpreted as a *linking verb + attribute* construction, with the attribute slot filled by an adjectival partial clause.
2. *Adjectivals at the Phrase Level.* The most common use of dependent clauses in adjectival function is the use of relative clauses as modifiers. These occur after the head noun, and fill identifier slots (marked Id:). The phrase is called an identified noun phrase. For example:
The *old* man was my uncle.
The man *who came to dinner* was my uncle.

3.15 N_{id} = +Det:det +H:n +Id:rel.Cl
3.16   rel.Cl = +S:rel.pn +P:iv +L:RA

The relative clause is said to manifest the identifier tagmeme, and the use of clause within phrase constitutes a loopback in the grammar.

Adverbial Dependent Clauses. Dependent clauses embedded at the clause level fill peripheral slots of time, place, and manner. They are often introduced by relative and indefinite prowords of the adverb class.

Locational: He went *there.*
He went *wherever he wished.*

3.17   iCl = +S:pn + P:iv ±L:L-iCl
3.18   L-iCl = +R:rel +Ax:iCl

Temporal: John will fix the porch *then.*
John will fix the porch *when he has time.*

3.19   tCl = +S:np +P:tV +O:N ±T:T-tCl
3.20   T-tCl = +R:rel +Ax:tCl

In both of these examples, the clauses are subordinated by the use of a temporal or locational relater. The clauses are dependent, and specified as to function by the use of the subordinating particles.

Internal Structure of Clauses

Dependent clauses are classified according to their external distribution as embedded at a particular level, and as fulfilling specific nominal, adjectival, or adverbial function at that level. Dependent clauses may also be classified according to their internal structure as clauses which are: (1) subordinated by a relater, (2) subordinate because of a built-in relater, or (3) partial clause structures and therefore dependent. The recognition of these types helps in setting up the analysis of the dependent clause, once it has been discovered in the structure.

Subordinated Clause Types. Dependent clauses of the subordinated type have an overt relater marking dependency. The test for this type of clause is to remove the relater. If the clause without the relater is an independent clause, then the clause with relater is a subordinated type. These clauses are analyzed as relater-axis structures, consisting of two tagmemes, a clause subordinator, and a clause as axis, in a way parallel to the analysis of prepositional phrases. This analogy is established by Longacre (1964:38) in the following set of relations (see also p. 32):

Preposition: its object : : subordinator: its clause

The class of clause subordinators is the class of subordinating connectors and includes relative and indefinite adverbials as well. The subordinated type of clause is typically found in adverbial use at the clause level.

Subordinate Clause Types. Dependent clauses of the subordinate type have no overt relater, but have an internal relative or indefinite pronoun which is a *portmanteau* representation of relater and pronoun. If the relative is removed, the resulting structure is not a clause; if the relative is replaced by the equivalent pronoun, the resulting clause is an independent clause. The relative acts both as a constituent of the clause and as a subordinator, making the clause dependent in the sentence. Thus in *the man who came to dinner*, the relative *who* = R + *he*. It acts simultaneously as subject of the sentence, and as clause subordinator.

Relatives are often omitted, as Koutsoudas has observed (1966:292), in object position, but are never omitted in the subject position. The relative which is object of the preposition is also often omitted. For example:

the girl *whom* he likes	becomes	the girl he likes
the girl *whom* he gave the ring to	becomes	the girl he gave the ring to
the girl *who* lives next door,	but not	*the girl, lives next door.

The relatives and indefinites that are adverbial in function are never omitted, because they serve as clause subordinators in a relater-axis type construction, and are obligatory to the construction.

Partial Clause Structure. Dependent clauses that show only partial clause structure are identified by the presence of a predicate tagmeme, together with other clause level elements obligatory or optional to the string. The principal dependent clauses of this type in English are the participles and infinitives, used with other clause level elements in an embedded string. Other languages show similar use of nonfinite verbs.

Participle Clauses. In English, the two participles, past and present, are used as part of an embedded string, which is described as a partial clause structure. Their use is nominal or adjectival, and they fill the same structural positions as other subordinated and subordinate clauses. For example:

Subject: *Watching baseball* is entertaining.
Object: He enjoyed *playing the horses*.
RA Phrase: He found a new method for *raising money*.

The participle clauses fill nominal slots in the clause or RA phrase structure. They may be labeled as dependent (depCl), with an internal structure consisting of a predicate slot filled by participle (tv$_{part}$), and other clause level slots in the string. In adjectival use, for example:

Past Participle: The ship, *lost in the storm*, was recovered.
Present Participle: The dog, *barking loudly*, ran away.

The participle clauses here fill adjectival slots in the phrase and are best characterized as identifiers (marked Id:) in the same way as the equivalent dependent clauses of the subordinated or subordinate type. They resemble deleted versions of the more complete dependent structure:

> The ship, (which was) lost in the storm, was recovered.
> The dog, (which was) barking loudly, ran away.

In external distribution, the participle clause types fill the same slots as other dependent clauses; they differ only in their internal structure. They are formally different fillers in functionally identical slots.

Infinitive Clauses. In English, the infinitive is recognized by the infinitive marker, *to*, together with the base form of the verb. Infinitives occur either without subjects or with subjects in the objective case. When a subject occurs with the infinitive, it is often simultaneously the object of the main verb, in a portmanteau manifestation (Longacre, 1967:326). For example:

Without Subject: *To err* is human.
With subject: I asked *him to go home.*

In the occurrence of infinitives without subject, the infinitive and the other clause level tagmemes which it dominates are interpreted as filling a single slot, as a clause embedded within the overall pattern. In the example given, the infinitive fills the subject slot, $+S:iv_{inf}$. In portmanteau representation, the analysis gives precedence to one element. The second example may be interpreted as the string, $+S +P +IO$ *(him)* $+DO$ *(to go home)*, or as an SPO string with *him* internal to the embedded clause, acting as subject of the infinitive.

CLAUSE LEVEL ANALYSIS

The clause level stands below the sentence level and above the phrase level. Sentences are composed of clauses, which, in turn, are composed of words and phrases. At the sentence level, complex and compound sentences are reduced to simple clause structures by the procedures outlined in the section on reduction. At the clause level, the simple clauses are separated into homogeneous groups, and these clauses are then analyzed into subject, predicate, objects, and adjuncts.

Clause Level Sorting

Once the corpus has been reduced to a set of simple clauses, these clauses must be homogeneously sorted. In problems prepared for analysis, the clauses are often presorted and give the appearance of being contrived. Each analyst should be able to presort clauses himself, so that every problem he does will, in fact, have clauses of the same type.

Kernel Sentences. The clause types that underlie kernel sentences should be sorted out and analyzed first. Derived, nonkernel structures can then be analyzed as variations upon the kernel type structures. Kernel sentences are simple, complete, statements, active, and affirmative.

At the sentence level, simple complete statements are isolated by reduction and sorting, as follows:

1. *Simple sentences* are isolated by reduction, listing one clause to a line. Complex and compound sentences are not discarded, but are broken down into simple sentences; relaters are removed and relative pronouns treated as if they were personal pronouns.
2. *Complete sentences* are subject to analysis; incomplete sentences are filed as "residue" until after complete sentences are analyzed. Then incomplete structures become intelligible in the light of the complete structure.
3. *Statements* are separated from questions and commands. Mark each simple complete statement as S, Q, or C, and begin the analysis with the study of statements only. Questions and commands are treated later.

At the clause level, the clause bases underlying the simple complete statements isolated at the sentence level are analyzed. These are first sorted into basic clause types, such as transitive, intransitive, and equational:

1. *Transitivity:* Mark each clause as iCl, tCl or eqCl, according to whether the verb seems to be a transitive, intransitive, or equational verb.
2. *Affirmative clauses* should be separated from negative. The negative type is generally characterized by a negative particle in the verb phrase.
3. *Active clauses* must be separated from middle and passive. The clause structure for nonactive clauses is generally distinctive.

Charting the Data. Once clause types have been sorted, each type is analyzed singly. Within that type, any group of clauses of the same type may be analyzed as a set of structures. Convenient quantities range from 12 to 24 clauses, although there is no theoretical limit to the number. A chart is a list of all the clauses in the given data, separated into string constituents. List clause level elements, such as S: subject, P: predicate, O: object, PA: predicate attribute, at the top of the page, and under each heading list the words or phrases that fill these particular slots. Peripheral elements may initially be labeled as T: temporal, L: Locational, I: introducer, and M: manner. Elements in the string should be listed, in the chart, roughly in the order in which they occur in the data. If the order is not fixed, use the statistically predominant order. If only one element is movable, it may be listed in both positions. A partial chart of the data in Sierra Popoluca (#165, *Laboratory Manual*, Merrifield, 1967) for transitive clauses, showing subject, predicate, object, and locational slots, is given below.

	±S	+P	±O	±L
1.	tu·m pʌ·šin	ipaʔtne	ikawah	
	'a man'	'has found'	'his horse'	
2.	heʔm šiwan	dʸa ikoʔcgakum	heʔm ikawah	
	'that John'	'did not hit again'	'his horse'	
9.	(heʔm pʌ·šin)	iwatpa	ikama (X)	yʌʔm
	'that man'	'will make'	'his cornfield'	'here'
12.	heʔm kawah	ikuʔtne	haʔyaŋmok	
	'that horse'	'has eaten'	'much corn'	

In clause 9, the subject occurs after the verb. In this case, the position occupied by the subject is marked (X), and the subject, in parentheses, is placed in the regular column marked subject. Even in a preliminary survey of the transitive clause type it should become obvious that the regular order is SPO, with an alternate order POS expressed in clause 9. In the data thus far, all three elements are obligatory. However, further analysis of transitive clauses shows both subject and object are missing in some clauses, and so these are marked as optional to the construction. Some clause fillers are words; some are phrases.

Tagmemic Grammar

A tagmemic solution is given in terms of a grammar and lexicon. The grammar is a list of formulas at the sentence, clause, phrase, and word levels, with whatever restrictions and assumptions are required. The lexicon is a list of the morphemes which occur in the data, together with their form, classification, and gloss. To this are appended whatever morphophonemic rules are required.

Tagmemic Formulas. Grammar is represented by formulas. We label this section of the solution "GRAMMAR," and state the level of construction to which the formula belongs. The formula consists of a construction symbol to the left, an equals sign, and a string of tagmemes to the right of the equals sign. Tagmemes are marked as obligatory (+) or as optional (±) depending upon whether they always occur, or only sometimes occur, within the construction.

Formulas use capital and small letters. Capital letters refer to slots or fillers greater than the word; small letters refer to slots or fillers representing words or morphemes. Thus, the slots at sentence, clause, and phrase levels are capital letters. If the fillers are phrases or clauses, they are marked with capital letters. Fillers which are words or morphemes are marked with small letters.

GRAMMAR

Sentence Level Construction:

Sent = +Base:tCl −Into:ICF

Read: A sentence consists of a base slot filled by a transitive clause, and an intonation slot filled by a final intonation contour.

Clause Level Construction:

tCl = ±S:N +P:tv ±O:N

Read: A transitive clause consists of an optional subject slot filled by a noun phrase, a predicate slot filled by a transitive verb, and an optional object slot filled by a noun phrase.

The labels and readouts of the formulas are not part of the solution, but are added for the sake of clarity. In submitting solutions, include the labels, but exclude the readout which only restates what the formula says.

Restrictions and Assumptions. When restrictions or assumptions are necessary to the solution, they are added immediately after the formulas of the grammar. Besides these essential formal statements, no comments should be necessary. The solution should be stated in such a way as to express a nonambiguous commitment.

Restrictions are strictly formal and should pertain to grammar, not to lexicon. They generally deal with the facts of co-occurrence and are of the form: Item A excludes Item B, or Item A requires Item B. Many restrictions can be built into the solution, using available devices. For example:

1. Mutually exclusive fillers in a single slot may be listed as alternates, using the (/) notation. Thus, N/pn, means "noun phrase *or* pronoun."

2. Mutually exclusive tagmemes can be listed in an "either . . . or" notation, as ±A ∓B, meaning either A or B, but not both (see p. 17).

Assumptions are strictly formal, and involve a conclusion by the analyst which is beyond the given evidence. Those assumptions should be stated which have caused a modification of the grammatical formula.

Maximum Generation Potential. The maximum generation potential (MGP) of a given solution is the total number of sentences that may be generated from a given grammar and lexicon. This number is finite and calculable, whenever the data is limited. To calculate the MGP:

1. Count the number of morphemes in a given class, and list this number below the symbol of that filler class in the lowest level formula.
2. If the slot is optional, add +1 (to account for the possibility of zero occurrence within that slot) to the number of real morphemes.
3. Multiply the resulting totals to obtain the number of combinations possible in each single construction. Place this total under the label of the construction in any higher level slot in which it occurs.
4. Continue the same procedure, working from lower to higher levels, until the MGP is determined for the construction marked "#Sent#." This is the total number of sentences generated by the solution.

Restricted Generation Potential. If there are restrictions in the solution, the number of sentences will be less. The total number of sentences, less the restricted sentences, gives the restricted potential: RGP = MGP − restricted sentences. No general rules can be given to cover all possible restrictions, but these suggestions may help:

1. Classes may be divided into subclasses and calculated one at a time. Thus, nouns as subject or object may be called n_1 and n_2.
2. Mutually exclusive items must be added together to form one set, to which zero is added only once, if the set is optional.
3. Where concord of items is expressed, the numbers, genders, and persons must be calculated separately, for example, singular versus plural constructions.

Tagmemic Lexicon

The lexicon is the "total stock of morphemes in a language" Bloomfield (1933:162). In a particular language problem, the lexicon is the total list of morphemes in the particular language, together with the morphophonemic rules which describe morpheme variants. The lexicon is the second half of a tagmemic solution.

Form, Class, Gloss. The lexicon accompanying a tagmemic grammar has entries listed in three columns, one for the morphemic form, one for the classification, and one for the gloss or translation:

1. *Form* is entered in the first column. Where the morpheme is invariant, the phonemic form is entered. If the morpheme has variant forms, either the morpheme is listed as a base symbol in braces { }, or all forms of the morpheme are listed, separated by alternation signs.
2. *Class* is entered in the second column. This is the form class label chosen to represent the morpheme class in the formulas of the grammar. The classification, in the lexicon, must be identical with the form class symbols used in the filler slots of the grammar, so that the forms can be automatically programmed into the formula.
3. *Gloss* is entered in the third column, always in single quotes. The gloss is the assumed meaning of the morpheme. It is not an exact translation. Forms with contrasting meanings must be clearly identified, and the gloss should show where their meaning is contrastive.

Zeros in the Lexicon. Both zero morphs and zero morphemes may occur in the lexicon. Zero morph is a zero representing one alternate of a morpheme, in cases where the morpheme has nonzero alternates. Zero morpheme is a zero representing the only alternate for a morpheme. To set up a zero morpheme, zero must be one of a structural series, a filler of a tagmeme which has overt elements as fillers. Thus, some languages have pronominal affixes for first and second persons, but the third person is recognized by the absence of any form. In these cases, a clear positive meaning is assigned to zero in this particular slot.

If zero is listed as meaningful in the lexicon, then the slot which it fills is marked as obligatory; it must occur, but one filler may be zero. If zero is not listed in the lexicon, then the slot remains optional wherever, in at least one case, the slot remains unfilled. Care should be taken that zeros do not proliferate in analysis. Zero morphs are in contrast with overt variants of the same morpheme; zero morphemes are in contrast with other fillers of the same tagmeme. Only in these contexts is the zero notation meaningful.

The Classified Lexicon. The entries of the lexicon should be in a fixed order. One possible order is alphabetical, but this is not always the most useful. An alternative method is to use a classified lexicon. The morphemes of the lexicon are classified according to a tripartite system, into: (1) nouns and noun modifiers; (2) verbs and verb modifiers; and (3) uninflected particles. Morphemes can be separated into these three groups, and then listed alphabetically, where required, within these classifications. This system allows ready reference to all verb forms, all noun forms, and so on, at a glance. For example:

		(form)	(class)	(gloss)
I.	The Noun System:			
	Nouns	p∧·šin	n.	'man'
	Adjectives	ha?yaŋ	aj.	'much'
II.	The Verb System:			
	Verbs	pa?t	tvs.	'find'
	Adverbs	y∧?m	loc.	'here'
III.	Particles	dʸa	neg.	'not'

Again, the classifying labels are not part of the solution, but are included as a descriptive convenience, enabling the analyst to locate immediately the set of nouns, verbs, and so on, which are included under each form class label.

Morphophonemics. If all morphemes are invariant, then no morphophonemic statement is required. If, however, some of the morphemes have variants, then this is indicated by the notation { } in the form column, and a statement is included within the lexicon giving the form and distribution of the morpheme variants. This may be done in several ways:

1. *Solution by Allomorphs.* Each variant is listed as an allomorph of the morpheme, and a distribution statement is added for each allomorph, telling where, under what conditions, the allomorph will occur.

2. *Solution by Morphophonemes.* One base form is given in morphophonemic notation, in which phonemes which are variable are marked in capital letters, and phonemes which are constant in the form are marked in small letters. The distribution statement then lists the changes that occur in the variable phonemes only. This is useful in partial changes.

3. *Solution by Process Rule.* The process rule is a general statement which explains the changes which occur, in terms of a process or change. These rules may be expressed in terms of transformational statements, involving either whole forms or parts of forms. Thus, the summary process rule

$$A \rightarrow B \ / \ X\_\_\_Y$$ may be read as:

A is rewritten as B in the environment X___Y, where either X or Y may be null.

The rule is adequate, in that it explains what change takes place (A becomes B) and explains in what particular environments this occurs. The environment may be phonemic, morphemic, or even tagmemic.

PRACTICE 3: CLAUSE LEVEL STRUCTURE

Write the sentence level formula for the following set of sentences, showing the type of clause present. Isolate subjects, predicates, objects, and adjuncts and write a clause level formula. Write the lexicon, and calculate the maximum generation potential of the solution. The material is taken from Thomas J. Egan, C.SS.R., *Tereno Grammar.*

TERENO (Mato Grosso, Brazil)

1. kaliwano kuriko yaye kohoyene
   'The children played here today.'
2. koituke neukacheke
   'He worked yesterday.'
3. chaane imoko horokocheno yotike
   'The people slept there during the night.'
4. ceeno koyoho
   'The woman spoke.'
5. imoko
   'He slept.'
6. ceeno koituke yaye
   'The women worked here.'
7. hoyeno kuriko horokocheno neukacheke
   'The men played there yesterday.'
8. kaliwano koyoho yaye yotike
   'The child spoke here during the night.'

Problem 3: TERENO (Brazil)

GRAMMAR   (240 Sent)

Sentence Level Construction:

Sent = +Base:iCl −Into:ICF

Read: A sentence consists of a base slot filled by an intransitive clause, and an intonation slot filled by a final intonation contour.

Clause Level Construction:

iCl = ±S:n +P:iv ±L:loc ±T:tem

Read: An intransitive clause consists of an optional subject slot filled by a noun, a predicate slot filled by an intransitive verb, an optional location slot filled by a locational adverb, and an optional temporal slot filled by a temporal adverb.

LEXICON   (13 morphs)

I. Noun System:
   Nouns (4)

chaane	n.	'people'
ceeno	n.	'woman/women'
hoyeno	n.	'man/men'
kaliwano	n.	'child/children'

II. Verb System:
    Verbs (4)

imoko	iv.	'slept'
koyoho	iv.	'spoke'
koituke	iv.	'worked'
kuriko	iv.	'played'

Adverbs (4)

horokocheno	loc.	'there'
yaye	loc.	'here'
kohoyene	tem.	'today'
neukacheke	tem.	'yesterday'
yotike	tem.	'during the night'

SUPPLEMENTARY READINGS 3

Elson, Benjamin, and Pickett, Velma, *An Introduction to Morphology and Syntax*, Santa Ana, Summer Institute of Linguistics, 1962. Chap. 7, "Tagmemes and Constructions at the Clause Level," 64–72; Chap. 17, "Survey of Clause Types," 108–121, active, reflexive, passive, indefinite, stative, imperative, optative, interrogative, emphatic, and various types of dependent clauses.

Fries, Charles C., *The Structure of English*, New York, Harcourt, Brace and World, Inc., 1952. Chap. 9, "Structural Meanings, Subjects and Objects," 173–201; Chap. 12, "Immediate Constituents, Layers of Structure," 256–273, with branching rules given 271–272. For word classes, Class 1, 76; Class 2, 80; Class 3, 82; Class 4, 83.

Gleason, Henry A., Jr., *Linguistics and English Grammar*, New York, Holt, Rinehart and Winston, Inc., 1965. Chap. 7, "Syntactic relations," 138–167, with traditional and IC diagrams; Chap. 13, "Clause Patterns," 299–328, with transformations, 304–306.

Greenberg, Joseph H., *Universals of Language*, Cambridge, Mass., The M.I.T. Press, 1963. Chap. 5, "Some Universals of Grammar with Particular Reference to the Order of Meaningful Elements," 73–113, treats SPO order in language and prepositional/postpositional contrast.

Koutsoudas, Andre, *Writing Transformational Grammars*, New York, McGraw-Hill, Inc., 1966. Chap. 7, "Conjoining," 231–232; Chap. 8, "Embedding," 269–270, in transformational grammars.

Liem, Nguyen Dang, *English Grammar, A Combined Tagmemic and Transformational Approach*, Linguistic Circle of Canberra, 1966.

Chap. 1, "Independent Declarative Clause Types," 1–20, with summary chart I.2, listing 10 independent declarative types. Minimum and expanded formulas are given, with examples.

Longacre, Robert E., *Grammar Discovery Procedures*, The Hague, Mouton & Co., 1964. Chap. 1, "Clause Level," 35–73, including drama analogy, 35; rule of two, 47; and clause matrix, 70.

———, and Williams, Ann F., "Popoluca Clause Types," *Acta Linguistica Hafniensia*, vol. X, no. 2, 161–186 (Copenhagen, 1962). Distinguishes 6 kernel (statement) clause types and 12 derived (interrogative) clause types, based on formal criteria.

TABLE 4: PHRASE LEVEL ANALYSIS

According to the Type of Grouping	According to the Type of Structure	According to the Internal Structure	Characteristics of Phrase Type
Phrase as a Structured Word Group	Exocentric Noncentered	*Relater-Axis (RA)* relater and phrase	Recognized by relater class
	Endocentric Multiple Head	1. *Coordinate Phrase* similar phrases, different referents 2. *Item-Appositive (IA)* similar phrases, same referent	Recognized as same type phrases with conjunction Recognized as same type phrases without conjunction
	Endocentric Modifier-Head	1. *Noun Phrase (N)* with noun head 2. *Verb Phrase (V)* with verb head 3. *Adjective Phrase (Aj)* with adjective head 4. *Adverb Phrase (Av)* with adverb head	With possessives, determiner, adjective With auxiliaries, negative, adverbs With intensifiers, degree markers With intensifiers for adverb class

4 PHRASE LEVEL

The phrase level of grammar is that level that is below the clause level and above the word level. The phrase is composed of words and typically fills slots at the clause level. It is a construction in which the constitute is a close-knit morpheme sequence which functions as a typical unit at the clause level, and whose constituents are words. Phrases are word groups that fill the same slots at clause level as are filled by single words. This level is comparable to the "group level" of Halliday's scale-and-category grammar.

Phrase Defined. The phrase is defined as "a unit composed of two or more words potentially, which does not have the characteristics of a clause, and typically, but not always, fills slots on the clause level" (Elson and Pickett, 1962:73). In this definition, the following features must be noted, in order to understand phrase level construction:

1. *Phrases typically fill slots on the clause level.* In typical mapping of lower level constructions into higher, words combine to form phrases, and phrases combine to fill clauses. The phrase is discovered at the clause level as a functioning unit, and is analyzed into constituent parts at the phrase level. The clause level slot is filled either by words or by word groups; if the group is not an embedded clause (see p. 74), then the word group is a phrase.

2. *Phrases do not have the characteristics of a clause.* Functioning word groups may be clauses or phrases. Clauses are recognized as having one and only one predicate tagmeme in the string (see p. 65). All other word groups are

phrases. Even the verb phrase, which fills the predicate slot, is distinguished from clause, and has its own internal unity, although the same word group may be phrase, clause, and, with intonation, sentence.

3. *Phrases consist potentially of two or more words.* The phrase is a potential word group. It is not obligatorily complex. The phrase symbol signifies both the head word in isolation and the head word with modifiers.

Traditional Phrase. The phrase has traditionally been considered a unit, but the various types of phrases have often lacked systematic treatments. The phrase has been defined as a word group not containing subject and predicate, which functions as a single part of speech. Some of the phrase types treated include: (1) prepositional phrases, (2) coordinate and appositive phrases, and (3) modification phrases. Verbal phrases are often extended to include infinitives and participles.

In tagmemic analysis, the definition of clause is extended to any word group containing one and only one predicate, so that word groups which contain a predicate are listed as clause structures. Infinitive or participle constructions that contain, potentially, other clause level tagmemes are listed as embedded clause structures. The phrase, on the other hand, is extended to include "potential phrases," that is, single words with optional modifiers are listed as phrases. Thus, according to Pike (1967:439), a phrase is +(+word +word), or +(+word ±word), but not +(+word). A phrase is a unit which is composed of either two or more words, or is one word which is optionally expandable.

Phrase Types. The phrase types of traditional grammar may be organized systematically according to formal features as exocentric and endocentric structures. The latter may have one head or many. An exocentric construction is a noncentered construction. Endocentric constructions are centered constructions, in which the whole construction fills the same clause level slots as the head of construction. Endocentric constructions may be multiple head or single head constructions. In multiple head construction, the two or more heads may be coordinated or, if they have the same external referent, may be in apposition. These basic construction types are listed by Hockett (1958:184–185).

Phrase types may be outlined as follows:

1. *Exocentric Phrase:* prepositional phrase.
2. *Endocentric Phrase:* fills same slots as head words:
   A. *Multiple Head Phrase:* more than one head word:
      (1.) *Coordinate:* heads have different referents.
      (2.) *Appositive:* heads have same referent.

B. *Modifier-Head Phrase:* only one head word.
     Noun, verb, adjective, adverb phrases.

From this outline of phrase types, it may be seen that the phrase level is essentially the level of endocentric construction. All phrases are centered about head words except the prepositional phrase, in which the relater, or preposition, is attached to the word or word group and fits this word or group for a particular syntactic use. Elsewhere, phrases are structured word groups filling the same slots as the head of construction.

RELATER-AXIS PHRASES

The phrase level of grammar deals with structured word groups which are not clauses. Since these word groups are of various kinds, we find within the phrase level, various geological strata or layers. One such layer is the layer of relation. Words or word groups, together with a phrase relater, act as functioning units. These are called relater-axis phrases.

Relater-Axis Phrase Defined

A relater-axis phrase is a structured word group with two immediate constituents, one of which is a phrase relater, and the other a word or word group governed by the relater and called the axis. This construction type is exocentric because neither the relater alone, nor the axis alone, may fill the same clause level slots as the relater-axis group.

Relational Structure. In our discussion of the features which might be found in emic levels of structure within a language (see p. 32), we suggested that levels may be characterized by three geological strata: the layer of relation, the layer of co-ordination, and the layer of subordination. At the phrase level, the layer of relation is exemplified by the relater-axis type construction, which is a phrase, but of a type different from other phrases.

The function of the relater, in this type of structure, is to relate the whole constitute of the axis, whether word or phrase, to the grammatical structure of which it is a part. The relater acts as a sky hook, which takes the word or word group that is its axis and ties it into the structure. The function of the relater here is analogous to the clause level relater, which subordinates clauses to sentence structure, and to inflectional endings at the word level, which relate the word form to syntactic use.

This structure should always be treated as an immediate constituent structure with two and only two constituents, the relater and its axis. The reason for this is that the axis, in turn, will often prove to be another phrase, of an endocentric type, similar in structure to the other endocentric phrases of the language. In an ordered analysis, the relater-axis phrase must always be analyzed before the phrases that might constitute the axis. First, remove the relater, then analyze the axis together with other endocentric structures. This will generally lead to economy of description, although it is possible, with multiple nesting structures, to have a relater-axis phrase within a simpler phrase, containing, in turn, a simpler phrase.

The axis is often "governed" by the relater. Government is one type of concord in which the case is determined by the other words in the structure. Government occurs in relater-axis phrases, and also in the relation between verbs and objects in many languages.

Phrase Relaters. The relater-axis construction may be recognized by the set of phrase relaters of the language. Phrase relaters are a group of function words, opposed to clause level relaters (subordinating conjunctions) on the one hand, and to inflectional endings on the other. In languages which have no written literature, it is often difficult to determine whether relaters are bound or free. If free, they are phrase relaters; if bound, they are inflectional endings. One clue to their identity is whether they occur in construction only with single words, or with word groups. Those relaters which govern word groups tend to be free relaters.

Relater is preferred to the term "preposition," because all relaters in all languages are not preposed. The relaters of English are called prepositions; the relaters of Hindi are called postpositions, and always occur after the word or words they govern. Greenberg (1963:77) has attempted to correlate the order of Subject-Predicate-Object, with the use of prepositions and postpositions in language structure. He concludes:

Type I:	PSO	always prepositional	(Univ. 3)
Type II:	SPO	mainly prepositional	
Type III:	SOP	mainly postpositional	(Univ. 4)

Relaters need not be single words, whether prepositional or postpositional. Most languages contain complex, as well as simple, relaters. The best procedure for these complex relaters is simply to include them within the closed list which contains single word relaters.

Relater Class. The most useful way to define classes of function words is either to list the set exhaustively or to give such a representative list of the function word class that other members may be recognized in similar positions. The function word class is then defined as this typical list plus all other words which fill similar slots in syntactic structure. For English, a typical list of prepositional relaters is as follows:

about	in
above	into
across	of
after	off
against	on
among	out
around	over
at	through
before	to
behind	under
between	until
by	up
down	upon
during	with
for	within
from	without

The prepositions of this list are included within the 1000 most frequently used words in English, according to the Thorndike count (1944). Similar lists may be found in Fries, (1952:95), and in Lado (1964:123).

Types of Relater-Axis Phrase

Relater-axis phrases are similar in their internal structure; they are all composed of two obligatory tagmemes, a relater and an axis. But they may be distinguished according to their external distribution. The relater-axis phrases fill different slots in clause and phrase level structures, and on this basis may be distinguished as nominal, adjectival, and adverbial types. This basis for contrast is used in many traditional English grammars and corresponds, at clause level, to the drama analogy (see p. 68).

Adverbial Relater-Axis Phrases. Those relater-axis phrases that fill the same clause level slots as single adverbs are adverbial relater-axis phrases. These occur at the clause level of analysis, filling peripheral slots of time, place, manner, as props or scenery for the central action.

Temporal relater axis phrases answer the question *when* and fill slots at the clause level normally filled by adverbs of time. Temporal relater-axis phrases may be recognized by their external distribution; they fill temporal slots in clause structure. They may also often be recognized by their internal structure. The temporal relaters may be listed as a separate class, for example, *before, until, during, since, after,* are typical temporal relaters. Other relaters in this class include: *in, at, on, about,* used with time phrases. Principal relaters in a set can often be systematically arranged in a chart, as suggested by Lado (1964:123):

before	during	after
until	at	since

Locational relater-axis phrases answer the question *where* and fill slots at the clause level normally filled by adverbs of place. Locational relater-axis phrases may be recognized by their external distribution; they fill locational slots in clause structure. They may also be recognized by internal structure. The locational relaters may be listed as a separate subclass of relaters, for example, *into, in, out of, through, around, over, under, to, from, up, down, on, off,* are typical locational relaters (see chart, Lado, 1964:123).

into	at	out of
to	in	from

Manner relater-axis phrases answer the question *how* and fill slots at the clause level normally filled by adverbs of manner. In early stages of the analysis, it is useful to group all adverbial phrases except time and place under the manner label, and then establish more particular classes as the analysis proceeds. The manner phrases show distinct subclasses, such as instrument, accompaniment, purpose, cause, benefactive, and so on. Typical relaters in this function are: *for, against, by, by means of, with, without, like.* Excluded from this grouping would be such nuclear slots as agent, marked with *by*, and indirect object, marked with *to* or *for*.

Adjectival Relater-Axis Phrases. Those relater-axis phrases that fill noun modification slots at phrase level, or the predicate attribute slot at the clause level, are adjectival relater-axis phrases. They fill the same slots as single adjectives in clause and phrase structure. Phrases which fill modifier slots at the phrase level are nested phrases and manifest a layering (see p. 31) of phrase within phrase. In English, nested relater-axis phrases occur immediately after the head noun and before clauses:

Single modifier + Head noun + Phrases + Clauses

The descriptive function of the nested relater-axis adjectival phrase may often be demonstrated by transforming the relater-axis phrase into a preposed modifier. For example:

the mayor *of* Boston	becomes	Boston's mayor
the girl *with* the red hair	becomes	the red-haired girl
the man *in* the gray flannel suit	becomes	the gray-flannel-suited man.

The transformed phrase illustrates another type of adjectival relater-axis phrase, in which a bound relater, or *phrase clitic*, governs the phrase. The use of bound relaters, such as $\{-Z_2\}$, 'possessive,' and {-ed}, 'having,' is an example of level skipping (see p. 31); a bound form, belonging to the word level, is used in a higher level construction (here a phrase construction).

Nominal Relater-Axis Phrases. When phrases occur in nominal nuclear slots at the clause level and are marked by specific particles rather than case endings, they resemble, in a superficial way, the relater-axis phrase. But relater-axis phrases more typically fill peripheral slots at the clause level, or modifier slots at the phrase level. Therefore it is often advisable not to use the relater-axis terminology for the nuclear slots in analysis. One alternative is to consider these phrases as "marked" nominal phrases, and the particles involved as "markers" for nominal slots.

1. *Indirect object*, in English, is often marked with *to* or *for*. But this case is also marked by position, and the marker here is optional. For example:
   I gave the money *to* him.   I gave him the money.

2. *Infinitive forms*, in English, are marked with *to*. But this marking belongs to the infinitive form, and does not mark the whole embedded clause. In the predicate slot of the embedded clause, the verb form can be listed as V_{inf}, which is then analyzed as marker + verb base.
   I allow him *to come*. $(iV_{inf} = to + iv)$

Marked nominal phrases are treated in the same way as the cases of a case inflected language. Latin has subjects in the nominative case, and objects in the accusative case; Japanese marks these same slots with particles {o} and {wa}. Latin has indirect objects in the dative case; English marks these cases with {to} and {for}, or by position. If these marked nominals, with markers that are free forms, are treated in the same way as case-marked nominals, in which the markers are bound forms, then the fillers of nuclear clause level slots need never be formulated as relater-axis phrases.

Formulating Relater-Axis Phrases

The relater-axis phrase is a phrase that always consists of two obligatory tagmemes, a relater and an axis (Elson and Pickett, 1962:75, 106). The relater is a preposition, a postposition, a noun in special use, or a bound particle. The axis may be a word, another phrase, or an embedded clause. The phrase is called RA, and the obligatory tagmemes are marked as +R: (relater) and +Ax: (Axis) and are placed in the order in which they occur in the given construction.

Typical Mapping. Relater-axis phrases that fill typical clause level slots of time, place, and manner are examples of typical mapping of phrase into clause. When relater-axis phrases are discovered at the clause level, they are analyzed before those phrases that constitute the axis alone. For example:

During the afternoon he worked at the university.

4.1 $iCl = \pm T{:}RA_1 + S{:}pn + P{:}iv \pm L{:}RA_2$

4.2 $RA_1 = +R{:}rel_1 + Ax{:}N$ during +(the afternoon)

Read: A (temporal) relater-axis phrase consists of a relater slot filled by a relater (class 1), and an axis slot filled by a noun phrase. (Class 1 = *before, during, after,* and so on.)

4.3 $RA_2 = +R{:}rel_2 + Ax{:}N$ at +(the university)

Read: A (locational) relater-axis phrase consists of a relater slot filled by a relater (class 2), and an axis slot filled by a noun phrase. (Class 2 = *into, in, out of, to, at, from,* and so on.)

The noun phrase which fills the axis slot is subsequently analyzed as a head-modifier type of phrase, and is generally similar to other noun phrases found at the clause level in subject and object slots.

Atypical Mapping. Relater-axis phrases that fill phrase level slots are examples of layering of phrase within phrase. Relater-axis phrases that have bound forms as relaters are examples of level-skipping. Both are cases of atypical mapping, for they are outside of the normal mapping of the lower level constructions directly into higher level constructions. Both are adjectival in function, and both are illustrated in normal adjective type constructions, as well as in special possessive constructions.

Layering of clause within phrase is handled by means of the identifier tagmeme (see p. 76). This tagmeme is always manifested by embedded clauses and never by embedded phrases. The phrase that contains the embedded clause is called an "identified" noun phrase (N_{id}).

Layering of phrase within phrase is handled by means of the modifier tagmeme, filled by an (adjectival) relater-axis phrase. In English, this modifier tagmeme follows the head noun when the relater is a free form. For example:

The girl with the red hair

4.4 $N = +Det:det +H:n \pm Mod:RA_3$

4.5 $RA_3 = +R:rel_3 +Ax:N$ with +(the red hair)

Read: An (adjectival) relater-axis phrase consists of a relater slot filled by a relater (class 3), and an axis slot filled by a noun phrase. (Class 3 = *of, in, with,* and so on.)

Level-skipping, in which a bound relater is used to govern a phrase, is best analyzed at the phrase level before the phrase that constitutes the axis. The alternate solution, of treating the phrase as a word stem and performing the analysis at the word level, fails to demonstrate the use of bound particles (generally restricted) as phrase clitics.

The red-haired girl

4.6 $N = +Det:det \pm Mod:RA_4 +H:n$

4.7 $RA_4 = +Ax:N +R:\{-ed\}$ (red hair) + -ed

Read: An (adjectival) relater-axis phrase consists of an axis slot filled by a noun phrase, and a relater slot filled by the bound relater {-ed}.

Government is a type of concord that may occur in relater-axis phrases. If the choice of case, for the axis, is determined by the choice of relater, then the axis is said to be "governed by the relater." To program into the grammar a subroutine for selecting the proper case with each relater, the R: and Ax: slots are connected by a concord tie: $+R: \overset{c}{\frown} +Ax:$ Such a device automatically selects the correct case. In Latin, for example, it would select *urbem,* after *ad,* in *ad urbem,* 'to the city,' and would select *urbe,* after *ab,* in the phrase, *ab urbe,* 'from the city.'

MULTIPLE HEAD PHRASES

With the exception of the relater-axis phrases, the phrase level of structure is endocentric. Endocentric phrases are coordinate or subordinate. The coordinate endocentric phrases are multiple head phrases, in which the multiple head phrase fills the same slot as either of its constituent heads. The layer of coordination, or conjoining, is the second layer of phrase level construction.

Multiple Head Phrase Defined

Multiple head phrases are defined as structured word groups which contain more than one head. The heads of constructions may be single words, or they may be subordinate phrases. If the two heads have the same referent, the construction is appositive; if the two heads have not the same referent, the construction is strictly coordinate.

Coordinate Structure. Every level of the grammar should admit the possibility of conjoining elements at that level, according to Huddleston (1965, 41), cited on page 33. The conjoining process has been defined by Noam Chomsky (1957:36) in the following rule:

> If S_1 and S_2 are grammatical sentences, and S_1 differs from S_2 only in that X appears in S_1 where Y appears in S_2, and X and Y are constituents of the same type in S_1 and S_2 respectively, then S_3 is a sentence, where S_3 is the result of replacing X by X+ and +Y in S_1.

In an article entitled "Conjoining in a Tagmemic Grammar of English" (18th Annual Round Table, Georgetown University, No. 20, 1967, 109–121), Alton L. Becker sets up rules for conjoining for tagmemics, with emphasis on the decision procedure involved in choosing constituents of the same type. The similarity must be based on function rather than on form. Restricting conjoining to the phrase level sets up the following rules:

1. *Conjoining is independent of form.* That is, phrases may be joined to words, or phrase to phrase, or word to word. However, constituents will be of the same functional type, such as nominal, adjectival, and so on.
2. *Conjoining is dependent on function.* Elements conjoined must fill the same functional slot, that is, they must belong to the same tagmeme. Elements joined are both subjects, predicates, temporals, locationals, and so on.
3. *Conjoining at phrase level tends to be open-ended*, providing the grammar with what Becker calls "linear recursiveness" (see p. 45), which is opposed to the recursiveness due to layering or embedding.

Phrase Connectors. Multiple head phrases that are coordinated may be recognized by a limited set of function words called connectors. The coordinate phrase may be joined by zero connectors, by single connectors, or by double connectors. The elements connected in the coordinate phrase have the same general function, but have different external referents:

Parataxis:	Read Ibsen, Tolstoy
One connector:	Read Ibsen and Tolstoy
Two connectors:	Read both Ibsen and Tolstoy

The functional meaning of the phrase may change according to the type of connectors used. These connectors are: (1) additive, such as: *and;* (2) disjunctive, *but not;* (3) alternative, *either/or;* (4) comparative, *rather/than.*

In contrast, the appositive multiple head phrase is characterized by zero connector, and the heads of construction have both the same grammatical function and the same referent in the extra-linguistic world:

> Apposition: Read Tolstoy, the author of *War and Peace*

If connectors are introduced, the phrase is interpreted as coordinate, and the referents of the two heads of construction are presumed different:

> here in Washington   *Apposition:* here = in Washington
> here *and* in Washington   *Coordinate:* here $\neq$ in Washington

Connector class. The connector class, used in conjoining at the phrase level, is also used at the sentence level in combining clauses to form compound sentences (see p. 45). The following list of connectors is common in English; it is listed by Fries (1952:94–95) as Group E:

and	both .... and
but, but not	not .... but
not	neither ... nor
or	either .... or
rather than	rather ... than

In the listing above, Fries notes that the connector, *but,* used with words and phrases, is more common with adjectivals, *poor but honest,* or with adverbials, *slowly but carefully.* With nominals, this connector is common only with indefinite pronouns, in such expressions as *everything but, nothing but.* It is not common elsewhere with nominals or verbals. In tagmemic formulations, the first list is the list of single connectors, and the second list is the list of double connectors, which fill the first (c_1) and second (c_2) connector slots respectively. The connector slot, as part of phrase level, is marked with a capital letter, as C:; the fillers, being words, are represented by small letters, as c, or as $c_1 \ldots c_2$.

Types of Multiple Head Phrases

Multiple head phrases are divided into subtypes according to both formal and semantic norms. The two main types are coordinate phrase and item-appositive phrase. The coordinate phrase may be further subdivided as coordinate (1) noun, (2) verb, (3) adjective, and (4) adverb phrases. The list is not exhaustive; other parts of speech, including the function words, may often be coordinated by connectors.

Coordinate Phrases. These are multiple head phrases, generally joined by a connector, in which the heads of construction have different external referents. Heads of construction belong to the same function class and individually fill the same slots as the whole construction.

1. *Coordinated Noun Phrase*(N$_{co}$) The conjoining of two or more phrases of the nominal type. These include nouns, noun substitutes, and phrases with nouns as head, which fill the same tagmemic slot. For example:

> He and I
> Jack and Jill
> The old man and the sea

2. *Coordinate Verb Phrase*(V$_{co}$). The conjoining of two or more verb forms, whether these be main verbs, participles, or auxiliaries. The forms that are conjoined belong to the same functioning subclass:

> They were *singing and dancing.*
> He *could and should* pay the bill.

3. *Coordinated Adjective Phrase*(Aj$_{co}$). The conjoining of two or more phrases or words of the adjectival type. These include single adjectives, as well as intensified adjective phrases, composed of intensifier + adjective. The adjectives joined must be functionally the same and fill one slot.

> She was *young and very pretty.*
> There were *three or four* red flowers.

4. *Coordinate Adverb Phrase*(Av$_{co}$). The conjoining of two or more phrases or words of the adverbial type. These include both single adverbs and intensified or other relater-axis adverbial phrases. The adverbials must fill the same function as temporal, locational, manner, instrumental, and so on.

> He drove the car *slowly and with caution.*
> The snow fell *softly and very silently.*

Besides the function classes based upon the four major form classes, the function words also may often be connected. In this case, the group of words so connected fills the same slot as a single word would fill. For example:

> The bats flew *in, out, over, around, and through* the belfry.
> Come *on up out from down in under* there.

In the second example, the relaters are not coordinated. This example is rather a recursive application of a relater-axis construction.

Item-Appositive Phrase (IA). These are multiple head phrases, in which the two heads have the same extralinguistic referent, and are not joined by members of the connector class. Like the relater-axis phrase, the item-appositive phrase is best analyzed as consisting of two immediate constituents, that is, of two and only two obligatory tagmemes, the item tagmeme and the appositive tagmeme. As with coordinate phrases, the two heads of construction must fill the same tagmemic slot in the structure.

Concord in item-appositive phrases is more generalized, since the heads have the same referent, and we expect concord of gender, number, and case. But the grammatical forms used in apposition in language do not always neatly conform to this pattern. Item-appositive phrases are most commonly nominals; but other types of apposition may occur with parenthetical phrases, such as *that is* and *for example*, introducing appositives. Typical examples of item-appositive phrases include:

Tony, the barber   We, the people
He, the man in the street   You, the defendent

Item-appositive phrases are analyzed as multiple fillers of a single tagmeme and not as repetitions of the same tagmeme. Thus:

I live *here in Washington*

is first analyzed as Subject-Predicate-Locational, at the clause level. The single locational slot is filled by an item-appositive phrase (L:IA), and the item-appositive phrase is then analyzed as consisting of an item slot filled by *here*, and an appositive slot filled by the phrase *in Washington*. This analysis belongs to phrase level.

Repetition of Tagmemes. If like tagmemes are either coordinated or in apposition, how is it possible to have a repetition of the same tagmeme in the string? Either the tagmemes are the same or different; if the same, they may be analyzed as coordinates; if different, they are not repetitions of the same tagmeme but belong to two different tagmemes.

Items and appositives are analyzed as single fillers in the slot, for example, as a locational slot filled by an item-appositive phrase. Elements in apposition are certainly not repetitions of the same tagmeme but are complex manifestations of a single tagmeme.

Coordinate phrases with overt connectors are analyzed as a single coordinate filler of a single slot. Because of the connector, such phrases cannot be analyzed as repetitions of the same tagmeme but are complex manifestations of a single tagmeme.

Coordinate phrases with no overt connector constitute the difficult case. If they are functionally the same, they may be considered a case of a coordinate phrase with zero connector. If not, they should belong to different tagmemes. Repetitions should be regarded with some suspicion, and tagmemes should be tested for formal differences.

Formulating Multiple Head Phrases

The multiple head phrase is a phrase which consists of more than one obligatory head slot, with or without intervening connector slots. The two types of phrases are coordinate and appositive (Elson and Pickett, 1962:106). The same types are listed by Longacre as double-centered, coordinate, linking constructions (1964:74-75), as opposed to relater-axis constructions on the one hand, and modification structures on the other.

Coordinate Phrases. The coordinate phrase consists of more than one head tagmeme, generally all obligatory, and one or more connector tagmemes, which may be optional. Slots are marked with capitals. Fillers, if they are phrases, are marked with capitals; if they are words, with small letters. A typical formula for a coordinate noun phrase is:

4.8 $N_{co} = +H_1:N +C:c +H_2:N$ the old man and the sea

Read: A coordinate noun phrase consists of a head slot filled by a noun phrase, a connector slot filled by a connector, and a head slot filled by a noun phrase.

Alternate fillers for the head slot include pronouns (pn), proper nouns or names (np), and possibly nested appositive or coordinate phrases. Since serial, or open-ended, coordination often occurs in language at this level, a discontinuous notation may be used to indicate these open-ended constructions, in which new items may always be added (see also formulas 1.2 and 1.3).

4.9 $N_{co} = +H_1:N \pm H_2:N \ldots +C:c +H_n:N$

Read: A coordinate noun phrase consists of a head slot filled by a noun phrase, an optional indefinite series of head slots filled by noun phrases, a connector slot filled by a connector, and a final head slot filled by a noun phrase.

Coordinate verb phrase (V_{co}), adjective phrase (Aj_{co}) and adverb phrase (Av_{co}) are formulated in much the same way. Problems arise not in the formulation of the coordinate phrase, but in recognizing coordination.

He drove the car slowly and with caution.

This transitive clause shows a manner slot filled by a coordinate adverb phrase (M:Av$_{co}$) in which the first head slot is filled by an adverb (+H$_1$:av) and the second by a relater-axis phrase (+H$_2$:RA). Coordination must be recognized, and formulated, where it is discovered.

Item-Appositive Phrase. The item-appositive phrase consists of two and only two obligatory slots, the item (marked It:) and the appositive (marked App:). As with relater-axis phrases, the double capital (IA) designation is used to stress the fact that this construction is composed of two obligatory parts. A typical formula for an item-appositive phrase is as follows:

4.10   IA = +It:np +App:N   Tony, the barber

Read: An item-appositive phrase consists of an item slot filled by a proper noun and an appositive slot filled by a noun phrase.

Item and appositive are functionally identical, so it does not make much difference which element is called item, which appositive; both have the same external referent, and either can substitute for the whole construction.

Pronouns and noun phrases are regular fillers for the item-appositive phrases; clauses occur more rarely. The test for clauses in apposition is whether the clause could stand alone in place of the item-appositive phrase. According to this test, relative clauses which modify nouns are not in apposition, but fill identifier slots, modifying the head noun in the construction. In true apposition, the item can be deleted, and the result is still a sentence.

Concord in Multiple Head Phrase. The concord problems raised by multiple head structure concern both internal structure and external distribution. The internal structure of phrases involves agreement; external distribution of these phrases involves problems of cross-reference.

Cross-reference is concord of subject and predicate. If the subject is a coordinate noun phrase, cross-reference concerns the combined subject in both head slots; if the subject is an item-appositive phrase, the cross-reference is that of one of the head slots only. For example:

Jack and Jill *are*   plural subject, plural cross-reference
Tony, the barber, *is*   singular subject and cross-reference

Agreement is concord between parts of the same construction. In coordinate endocentric phrases, this concord is between the heads of construction. Since coordinate heads are "constituents of the same type," there will be at least case concord. In item-appositive phrases, there is also agreement; but since the two heads have the same referent, there is agreement of gender, number, and case, but not of person. For example:

> We, the people, are . . .
> You, the president, are . . .

In an item-appositive phrase with pronouns, the pronoun tends to dominate the construction and is in cross-reference concord with the verb. The appositive elements here belong to a different person category, but agree with the item in gender, number, and case.

HEAD-MODIFIER PHRASES

The first layer at phrase level concerns the relater-axis phrase, the second layer the multiple head phrases. The third level deals with the single headed phrases and the structure of modification. This latter layer is also endocentric, but is endocentric and subordinate. All of the elements of the phrase are subordinate to the single head tagmeme.

Head-Modifier Phrase Defined

The head-modifier phrase is a phrase in which one of the tagmemes is an obligatory head tagmeme, and the other tagmemes are modifiers which are subordinate to that head tagmeme. Most modification slots are optional; but in a particular language, as for the determiner slot in English, one or more modifiers may be obligatory, at least for some subclasses of head words.

Modification Structure. The modification structure is a subordinate endocentric structure in which there is one head slot and a series of (optional) modifier slots. The whole construction fills the same slot as the fillers of the head slot, or the equivalent substitute form. This layer of structure deals with the costuming in Longacre's drama analogy and seems to be a universal feature of languages.

Head-modifier constructions are further subclassified according to the form class of the words filling the head slot in the construction. Constructions for all the major form classes occur:

1. A *noun phrase* (N) is a head-modifier phrase with a noun as the head. The modifiers are adjectivals and include determiners, quantifiers, possessives, and descriptive adjectives, which may modify the noun.

2. *A verb phrase* (V) is a head-modifier phrase with a verb as head. The modifiers are adverbials used in a close-knit sequence with the verb, verbal auxiliaries or modals, and negatives.
3. *An adjective phrase* (Aj) is a head-modifier phrase with an adjective as head. The modifiers include intensifiers used to modify adjectives and the markers for comparison when these markers are free forms.
4. *An adverb phrase* (Av) is a head-modifier phrase with an adverb as the head. The modifiers include intensifiers that modify adverbs and the markers for comparison when these are free forms.

The designations of the head-modifier construction are strictly formal and based on the form of the head word. These designations are not to be confused with functional designations, such as nominal and verbal phrases, which deal with the function of word groups in syntax.

Noun Modifiers. The internal structure of head-modifier noun phrases is predictable in terms of the noun modifiers expected within the structure. These modifiers, generally but not always optional, are combined with a single head slot (marked H:) filled by the head noun.

Det: *Determiner tagmeme,* filled by determiners (det) including the articles: *a/an, the;* and the demonstratives: *this/that, these/those.*

Pos: *Possessive tagmeme,* filled by possessive pronouns (pos) such as: *my/mine, your/yours, his, her/hers, its, our/ours, their/theirs.* Nouns or noun phrases marked for possession also occur.

Qn: *Quantifier tagmeme,* filled by numerals (num) such as: *one, two, first, second;* or quantitative adjectives (qn): *all, many, more,* and so on.

Mod: *Modifier tagmeme,* filled by descriptive adjectives (aj) which may be broken into subclasses of color, size, quality, such as: *red/white, big/little, thick/thin, old/new, dry/wet.*

Verb Modifiers. The internal structure of verb phrases is also predictable; and elements in the string include modals and auxiliaries, together with negatives. More rarely, adverbs may be used in modifier or intensifier slots, when they form a close-knit verb sequence. This is particularly true of adverbs of manner, rarely of time and place. Adverbs generally fill peripheral clause level slots (Elson and Pickett, 1962:104).

Aux: *Auxiliary tagmeme,* filled by modals or auxiliaries distinct from the main verb form. Modals (mo) include: *can, may, must, shall, will.* Auxiliaries (aux) include forms such as: *have, be, do.*

Neg: *Negative tagmeme,* filled by negatives (neg) such as: *not, don't.* Negatives may be different for statements and commands, for example: Hindi statements use *nahīī* 'not'; Hindi commands use *mat,* 'don't.' Sierra Popoluca has a contrast between *dʸa* 'not' and *odoy,* 'don't.'

Adjective and Adverb Modifiers. The internal structure of adverb and adjective phrases is generally limited to a closed set of intensifiers, together with markers for comparative and superlative degree.

Int: *Intensifier tagmeme,* filled by intensifiers (int) and markers for comparison, in English: *more* and *most,* where these are free forms. Intensifiers include: *pretty, rather, very, really, truly,* and so on.

In English, there is growing use of a wide range of adverbs in intensifier function. Thus, such phrases as *remarkably intelligent* and *intensely interesting* manifest the intensifier + adjective construction.

Types of Head-Modifier Phrases

Head-modifier phrases are divided into subtypes according to the word which fills the head slot of the construction. The principal types parallel the major form classes, and are: (1) noun phrase (N), (2) verb phrase (V), (3) adjective phrase (Aj), and (4) adverb phrase (Av). Other word groups may occur in language, but they generally represent patterns that are not widely productive in the language.

Noun Phrase Subtypes. The noun phrase is a phrase in which the head word is a noun. This phrase type may be divided into different subtypes, according to the ways in which nouns are classified in the language. Nouns are classified according to distinctive features, as:

Common	Count	Animate	Singular
Proper	Mass	Inanimate	Plural

These features must be grammatically defined for the language, and may be inflective or selective categories (Hockett, 1958: 230). Inflective categories are grammatical meanings carried by inflectional endings; selective categories are grammatical features recognized by the choice of items in constructions. Some categories may show considerable overlap:

1. *Proper nouns* are "names," which can be preceded by neither a definite nor an indefinite article in English; *common nouns* may take articles. *Note*: Since names are unique, a definite article is often part of the name. For example: the whole phrase *the Amazon* is a name; *Amazon* does not occur.
2. *Count nouns* are items which are countable. *Mass nouns* refer to items which cannot be counted; they never occur with the indefinite article. For example: *a course, two courses;* but not **a music, *two musics.*
3. *Animate nouns*, in English, are those nouns which may be replaced by *he/she/they; inanimate nouns* may be replaced by the pronoun, *it*. These gender classes may overlap; for example: babies, household pets, which may be used functionally now as animate, now as inanimate nouns.
4. *Singular/plural*, in English, is in most cases an inflective category, which is marked for plural by the inflection $\{=Z_1\}$, 'plural.' However, in a limited number of cases, plural is selective, for example: *cattle* (plural).

Tagmemics formulates inflective categories at the word level by separating inflection from stem. Selective categories, such as gender (in English) and the count and common features, may require separate formulas. All categories are covered at the phrase level by concord ties, (1) of agreement within the endocentric phrase, (2) of cross-reference between subject and predicate, and (3) of government by verbs or relaters.

Concord Marking. Agreement is concord between head and modifiers in a modifier-head phrase. In tagmemics, concord is marked with a tie bar connecting fillers of the slots, and marked with a "c" for grammatical concord. This concord must be specified as to features, such as gender, number, and case.

$$\overset{\displaystyle c}{\overline{\qquad\qquad\qquad}}$$

4.11   N = +Det:det +H:n ±Mod:aj   la casa blanca

Read: A noun phrase consists of a determiner slot filled by a determiner, a head slot filled by a noun, and an optional modifier slot filled by an adjective (in Spanish).

Read "c": Concord of gender and number.

The concord tie is a feature of selectivity, and calls for a subroutine that selects the proper fillers for each slot. This subroutine is analogous to the square brackets of transformational grammar, as in Koutsoudas (1968:13). In writing a tagmatic manifestation of any one construction, items on the same line within the brackets are chosen. These are "etic variants of the emic construction" (Pike, 1962:236). The formulation in 4.11 may be made explicit in the following formulation:

$$\textbf{4.12} \quad N = +\text{Det:}\begin{bmatrix} \text{el} \\ \text{la} \\ \text{los} \\ \text{las} \end{bmatrix} +\text{H:n}\begin{bmatrix} \text{m.sg.} \\ \text{f.sg.} \\ \text{m.pl.} \\ \text{f.pl.} \end{bmatrix} \pm\text{Mod:aj}\begin{bmatrix} -\text{o} \\ -\text{a} \\ -\text{os} \\ -\text{as} \end{bmatrix}$$

The mechanics of concord are outlined by Elson and Pickett (1962:87–91), developed by Pike as "tagmas in reciprocally-conditioned variation," (1962:236), and specified by Dan M. Matson in "Tagmemic Description of Agreement" (18th Annual Round Table, Georgetown, 1967:103–108).

In a generative tagmemic model, we view the concord marking as calling up a subroutine that will select the proper modifiers according to the head word selected. The rule, as Matson has pointed out, is context-restrictive, and exponentiation (catesian multiplication) is not uniformly possible. The output must be broken down into four types of output as in the above example, with no cross-multiplication. Thus the output may be calculated separately for the noun phrases:

$$N_{msg} \qquad N_{fsg} \qquad N_{mpl} \qquad N_{fpl}$$

The subroutine would identify the head noun, with the selective feature, for example, *casa, n.f.;* (note that it can be marked for plural) and generate the phrases, *la casa blanca* and *las casas blancas*, while excluding the masculine articles and the adjectives with masculine endings. The output generated contains all grammatical and no ungrammatical sequences.

Formulating Head-Modifier Phrases

The head-modifier phrase consists of an obligatory head slot, with one or more modifier slots which may be obligatory or optional. Except for nested constructions, the subordinate endocentric type of phrase is generally analyzed as the last stage of phrase construction.

Noun Phrases. The noun phrase is a construction with a noun filling the head slot and with various noun modifiers in the string, for example: determiners, quantifiers, adjectives. Possessives are also noun type modifiers; but it is tactically often more useful to consider the item + possessor phrase as consisting of two and only two constituents.

In *item-possessor phrases* (IP), both item and possessor are obligatory and nuclear (Longacre, 1964:84). Either item, or possessor, or both may be marked. The string consists of +Item +Possessor. Attributes in the string belong to either item or possessor:

4.13 $IP = +Pos:RA + It:n$ (the pioneer's) + family

Read: An item-possessor phrase consists of a possessor slot filled by a relater-axis phrase, and an item slot filled by a noun.

4.14 $RA = +Ax:N +R:\{Z_2\}$ (the pioneer) + -'s

In cases where the possessive is a single word, such as a possessive pronoun that alternates with the determiner slot, it is more useful to analyze the possessive as part of the string modifying the head noun.

4.15 $N = +Det:det/pos \pm Qn:num \pm Mod:aj +H:n$
the/his three young children

Read: A noun phrase consists of a determiner slot filled by a determiner or possessive, an optional quantifier slot filled by a numeral, an optional modifier slot filled by an adjective, and a head slot filled by a noun.

Nonpossessed noun phrases, aside from the problems of possession and the marking of concord, tend to fall into a fixed pattern with the elements in fixed order, and only the head nuclear and obligatory. In internal structure, the one formula has many readings, depending upon whether the optional elements occur or do not occur in a given structure. In external distribution, it is often convenient to label noun phrases as N_1, N_2, and so on to limit their distribution in higher level structures.

Verb Phrases. The verb phrase is a construction with a verb as the head word and with various auxiliaries, negatives, and adverbs in the string. The problem of formulating verb phrases is often concentrated upon the special problem of the English verb phrase. In other languages, the verb phrase is often simpler and can follow a strict word level analysis. For example, in Hindi, verbs are either words, or participle plus auxiliary:

māĩ Jamshedpur *nahĩĩ jaataa huũ.*
'I am not going to Jamshedpur.'

4.16 $iV = \pm Neg:neg +H:iv_{part} +Aux:aux$

Read: An intransitive verb phrase consists of an optional negative slot filled by a negative, a head slot filled by a participle, intransitive verb, and an auxiliary slot filled by an auxiliary verb.

English verb phrases consist of discontinuous elements for the aspect perfective *have + en*, and progressive *be + ing*, as in the formula:

$$Aux = Tense\ (Modal)\ (Perfect)\ (Progressive)$$

formulated by Chomsky in *Aspects of the Theory of Syntax* (1965: 43), where modal is defined as the set: *can, may, must, shall, will*. To produce a tagmemic formula which is the equivalent of this analysis would require the mixing of phrase and word level constructions, for example:

4.17 iV/tV = +T:tm ±Mo:mo ±Asp$_1$:asp$_1$ ±Asp$_2$:asp$_2$
+H:iv/tv

Further rules would be required for permuting elements, and for the combination of morphemes into words to form the verb phrase. The solution of Elson and Pickett (1962:106) seems to mix levels of analysis.

One possible solution is to place the auxiliaries in three position classes, with Aux$_3$ = modals, Aux$_2$ = *have*, and Aux$_1$ = *be*, and correlate the occurrence of these with forms of the verb in *-ing*, *-en*. Thus,

1. Verb Phrase = +Aux$_3$ ±Neg +Aux$_2$			+Aux$_1$	+Head verb
(modal)	Modal	have	been	V-ing
	Modal	Ø	be	V-ing
	Modal	have	Ø	V-en
2. Verb Phrase = +Aux$_2$ ±Neg +Aux$_1$				+Head Verb
(have)	have	been		V-ing
	have	Ø		V-en
3. Verb Phrase = +Aux$_1$ ±Neg				+Head Verb
(be)	be			V-ing

The above forms are limited to the active voice. The negative is optional; forms that precede the negative are tense-marked in the construction.

PRACTICE 4: PHRASE LEVEL GROUPING

Write the sentence and clause level formulas for each of the sentences below. For every word group that functions as a unit at clause level, write a phrase level formula. Write the lexicon and calculate the maximum generation potential of the solution. The material was supplied by Teodore A. Llamzon, S.J., Philippines.

TAGALOG (Philippines)

1. kumain aŋ isda
      'The fish ate.'

2. nagluto aŋ tao naŋ matabaŋ baboy
   'The man cooked a fat pig.'
3. kumain aŋ malakiŋ tao naŋ manok
   'The big man ate a chicken.'
4. nagluto aŋ babae
   'The woman cooked.'
5. kumain aŋ baboy naŋ malakiŋ isda
   'The pig ate a big fish.'
6. kumain aŋ manok naŋ isda
   'The chicken ate a fish.'
7. kumain aŋ matabaŋ babae naŋ maliit na baboy
   'The fat woman ate a little pig.'
8. nagluto aŋ maliit na babae naŋ malakiŋ manok
   'The little woman cooked a big chicken.'

Problem 4: TAGALOG (Philippines)
GRAMMAR   (520 Sent)

Sentence Level Construction:

$\quad$ Sent = +Base:tCl −Into:ICF

Clause Level Construction:

$\quad$ tCl = +P:tv +S:N_1 ±O:N_2

Phrase Level Construction:

$\quad$ N_1 = +Det:det_1 ±Mod:aj +H:n_1
$\quad$ N_2 = +Det:det_2 ±Mod:aj +H:n_2

LEXICON   (12 morphs)

I. Noun System:

Nouns (5)	babae	n.1.	'woman'
	tao	n.1.	'man'
	baboy	n.1/2	'pig'
	isda	n.1/2	'fish'
	manok	n.1/2	'chicken'
Determiners (2)	aŋ	det.1	'the (subj)'
	naŋ	det.2	'a/an (obj)'
Adjectives (3)	malakiŋ	aj.	'big'
	matabaŋ	aj.	'fat'
	maliit na	aj.	'little'

II. Verb System:

Verbs (2)	kumain	tv.	'ate'
	nagluto	tv.	'cooked'

SUPPLEMENTARY READINGS 4

Becker, Alton L., "Conjoining in a Tagmemic Grammar of English," *Monograph Series on Languages and Linguistics*, No. 20, 109–121. Washington, D.C., Georgetown University Press, 1967.

Elson, Benjamin, and Pickett, Velma, *An Introduction to Morphology and Syntax*, Santa Ana, Summer Institute of Linguistics, 1962. Chap. 8, "Tagmemes and Constructions at the Phrase Level," 73–75; Chap. 16, "Survey of Phrase Types," 103–108, with head-modifier, coordinate, appositional, relater-axis, and close-knit verb phrase.

Fries, Charles C., *The Structure of English*, New York, Harcourt, Brace and World, Inc., 1952. Chap. 10, "Structural Meanings, Modifiers," 202–239, and Chap. 6, "Function Words," 87–109.

Gleason, Henry A., Jr., *Linguistics and English Grammar*, New York, Holt, Rinehart and Winston, Inc., 1965. Chap. 8, "Structure Signals," see "Parts of Speech and Function Words," 186–194, use of meaning.

Hockett, Charles F., *A Course in Modern Linguistics*, New York, Macmillan Company, 1958. Chap. 21, "Endocentric Constructions," 183–190 and Chap. 22, "Exocentric Constructions," 191–198.

Huddleston, R. D., "Rank and Depth," *Language*, 41: 574–586 (1965). Proposes a coordinate layer for all levels of the grammar, in a scale-and-category grammar of five (natural) levels.

Law, Howard W., "The Use of Function-Set in English Adverbial Classification, *Monograph Series on Languages and Linguistics*, No. 20, 93–102. Washington, D.C., Georgetown University Press, 1967. Sorting adverbials by form, function, and position.

Matson, Dan M., "Tagmemic Description of Agreement," *Monograph Series on Languages and Linguistics*, 18th Annual Round Table, No. 20, 103–108. Washington, D.C., Georgetown University Press, 1967. Tagmemic agreement reduced to subroutine using square bracket notation.

Warriner, John E., *English Grammar and Composition*, New York, Harcourt, Brace and World, Inc., 1951, revised 1965. Chap. 2, "The Phrase," 35–51, including traditional definition of phrase (36) and explanation of prepositional, verbal, and appositive phrases.

TABLE 5: WORD LEVEL ANALYSIS

According to Its Freedom in Use	According to the Formation Process	According to Its Internal Structure	Characteristics of the Word Type
Word as a Minimum Free Form	Inflection Outer Formation	1. *Nouns (n)*, with noun inflections 2. *Verbs (v)*, with verb inflections 3. *Adjectives (aj)* adjective inflections	Gender, number, case, possessive Tense, aspect, mood, voice Agreement with nouns, comparison
	Derivation Inner Formation	1. *Restrictive type* form class unchanged 2. *Governing type* form class changed	Nominalizer (nom) Verbalizer (vbzr) Adjectivizer (ajzr) Adverbializer (avzr)
	Compounds Core Formation	1. *Endocentric* compound same as one of the roots 2. *Exocentric* compound not same as one of the roots	Roots related as multiple heads, or head and modifier Roots unrelated, or one subordinated to the other

5 WORD LEVEL

The word level of grammar is that level which is below the phrase level and above the morpheme level. The word is composed of morphemes and typically fills slots at the phrase level. It is a construction in which the constitute is a minimally free form in the language and whose constituents are morphemes. Words are composed of one or more morphemes; the morphemes are the ultimate grammatical constituents, the minimum meaningful forms in the language.

Word Defined. The word has been defined by Bloomfield (1933:178) as "a minimum free form; a free form which does not consist entirely of two or more lesser free forms." The phrase "minimum free form" is to be understood as a minimally free form, that is, a free form which does not consist entirely of other free forms. The word "entirely" must be emphasized. If free forms are compounded, then something else enters into the composition of the compound to form the word.

In tagmemic analysis, word level construction is defined as a construction which consists, potentially, of two or more word level tagmemes, filled by morphemes. Word level includes the layers of (1) inflection, (2) derivation, and (3) compounding, and parallels the phrase level in which there are layers of relation, coordination, and subordination.

Elson and Pickett distinguish between word level constructions, which consists of a stem (or root) and an (inflectional) affix (1962:76), and stem level constructions, composed of two or more tagmemes which form the stem and fill the nuclear slot in words (1962:79). The disadvantage of separating a word and stem level is that the parallelism with the phrase level is destroyed, and

117

the stem is given preeminence among the linguistic forms of language, as if it had the emic status of such levels as the sentence, clause, phrase, and word in a language.

Linguistic Form. Forms that carry meaning are called linguistic forms. These forms may be simple, monomorphic forms, or they may be complex, polymorphic forms. Forms may also be classified as free or bound, and as stems or affixes.

Free forms are forms that can occur alone; *bound forms* are forms which cannot occur alone. If a form is found in one occurrence as free, it is listed as free. A form, once free, is always free.

Stems are forms that carry the basic meaning of the word; *affixes* add meanings to the stem. If a stem consists of a single morpheme, it is also called a *root*. Stems and roots may be bound or free, but affixes are always bound. The affixes are further classified as *prefix*, *infix*, *suffix*, or *suprafix*, depending upon whether they occur before, within, after, or simultaneously with the stem.

These are the forms that enter into the composition of words at the word level. If (A) is a free stem, (a) a bound stem, and (b) an affix, then the basic formulas for classifying word types are as follows (see Sapir, 1921:29):

1. *Simple Word* consists of a single morpheme and is free.   A
2.a. *Derived Word* consists of bound stem and affix.   a + b
   b. *Derived Word* consists of free stem and affix.   A + b
3. *Compound Word* consists of two free stems.   A + A

Bloomfield classified the first two types as primary words, simple or derived, and the last two types as secondary words, which contain a free form plus some other element in their composition (see Bloomfield, 1933:209).

Word Level Analysis. At the word level in tagmemics, as understood here, words are broken down into constituent morphemes. Thus:

1. *Simple words*, consisting of one morpheme, are not constructions and need not be represented at the word level. They are simply entered into the lexicon as free morphs. Words that show composition, and that contain more than one morpheme, are analyzed at this level.
2. *Complex words* are polymorphic; they may be broken down into stem and affix. The affixes may be inflectional or derivational. Inflectional affixes are removed first, then derivational affixes.

3. *Compound words* are polymorphic and consist of more than one stem or root. If the combining stems are free forms, then some other device is used in the language to combine these forms into a single word.

Exceptional cases at the word level include compound-compound words, such as *wind+shield+wiper*, complex-compound words, such as *gentle-man-ly*. These are analyzed as nested constructions at word level. The problem of phrase derivatives, such as *old maid-ish*, are best handled as loopbacks in the grammatical hierarchy (see p. 31). The phrase fills a word level slot, and the derivative is an adjective.

INFLECTIONS: OUTER FORMATIONS

Word level constructions are those constructions in which the constitute is the word; the constituents are the inflectional, derivational, and root tagmemes that enter into word structure. The outer layer of formation of the word is the layer of inflection. Inflectional affixes are first stripped from the word, then the stems of the words are analyzed into roots and derivational affixes.

Inflection Defined

Most languages of the world are characterized by some type of inflectional system. There is a contrast between inflected and noninflected forms. Where this contrast exists, inflections are recognized by the following set of distinctive features:

1. They are outer formations.
2. They are used as defining norms for major form classes.
3. They are relational in function, fitting words for use in syntax.

Outer Formations. Inflectional affixes, according to their form, are outer formations. The word has an onion-like structure, with inflections as the outer layer, derivations as inner layer, and roots at the core. When words are inflected, the inflectional affixes are found in the outer positions, furthest from the root. This does not mean that inflections may only occur at the outermost position. There may be series of inflections, but they are outer formations with respect to derivational affixes.

1. The word may be uninflected. If so, derivational affixes may occur in word final position. Therefore it is not true to say that any affix which is found in final position in a word is an inflectional affix.

2. The word may have more than one inflection. If so, one inflectional affix will appear in final position, and another inflectional affix in nonfinal position. Therefore it is *not* true to say that inflectional affixes occur only in word final position.
3. Considering word formation as a whole, the set of inflectional affixes tends to be outer and the set of derivational affixes tends to be inner. In one analysis of Latin (O'Brien, 1965:29), the Latin word is characterized by a stem, followed by three derivational affixes and three inflectional affixes, in that order. The three inflectional affixes are outer, and the three derivational affixes are inside the inflections.

It is generally true for English that no derivational affix ever occurs outside of an inflectional affix. Forms like *spoonfuls*, noun+derivation+inflection, are preferred over *spoonsful*, noun+inflection+derivation. Forms like *betterment* are regular verb+derivation formations, not adjective+inflection+derivation.

Wide Distribution. Inflectional affixes are general throughout a form class, and therefore are both limited in number and have a very high frequency of occurrence. Derivational affixes tend to be more numerous, but each derivation has very limited use in the language.

1. Inflections are general throughout a word class; they are used as the defining norms for the major form classes, such as noun, adjective, verb, and adverb. These word types are defined by their word paradigms. A noun is a word which takes the inflectional affixes of a noun.
2. Inflections are limited in number. In English, the noun has only two inflections, the verb has four, and the adjective two, for a total of eight. All other affixes in the language are classed as derivational. Even in highly inflected languages, such as Latin or Sanskrit, the inflectional systems are well defined and general throughout the word class.
3. Inflections have a high frequency of occurrence. Compared with the derivational affixes, which are limited to a few members of a class, inflections generally occur throughout the class and appear more often.

Relational Function. Inflections are relational markers, which fit the members of the major form class for use in syntax, rather than change the form class of words. This does not mean that uninflected forms do not occur in syntax; it means that once the inflection, or relational marker, is added to a form, that form is limited by that marker to certain positions in the syntactic construction. This relational marking takes place without changing the form class of the word. The changes made in the form of the word are syntactically relevant.

English, for example, has only two inflections for the noun stem, a plural and a possessive. The addition of a possessive suffix fits the noun for use in syntax as an adjectival; the noun, with the possessive marking, can only be used in slots normally filled by adjectives, and never in slots normally filled by (un-marked) nouns. Thus, John + {-Z_2} 'possessive,' forms *John's*, in such constructions as *John's hat*. Yet the form class of the word has not changed. To say that the form *John's* is now an adjective, is to imply that this form can undergo comparison in the same way as the simplest members of the adjective class. This form is not an adjective, because it cannot take the affixes {-er}, 'comparative,' and {-est}, 'superlative,' proper to that class.

The relational function of inflectional affixes may also be shown in the case-marked forms of a language. In Latin, nouns marked as nominative, genitive, dative, accusative, and ablative all have their own specific syntactic positions in constructions. They remain nouns, but are marked for special use in syntax as subjects, possessors, indirect objects, direct objects, or objects in construction with particular prepositions.

Types of Inflectional Systems

In inflected languages, inflected forms are opposed to non-inflected forms. Within the inflected forms, nouns and their modifiers can usually be distinguished from verbs and their modi-fiers. Noun systems, with nouns and adjectives, are generally characterized by gender, number, and case; verbal systems, including verbs and auxiliaries, by tense, mood, and voice. Un-inflected forms are defined by their syntactic use.

Inflectional Systems. In inflected languages, it is useful to establish a morphological sieve, which will sort out the form classes of the language according to their inflectional paradigms. The uninflected forms are first sorted according to their syntactic use, and then defined by listing. A typical sieve of this type may be set up for English as follows:

Inflected words, defined by inflection
1. Words not inflected for tense,
   but inflected for number and case   = NOUNS
      {Z_1}, plural
      {Z_2}, possessive

      but inflected for comparison   = ADJECTIVES
        {-er}, comparative
        {-est}, superlative

2. Words inflected for tense   = VERBS
    $\{Z_3\}$, 3d singular present
    $\{D_1\}$, simple past
    $\{D_2\}$, past participle
    {-iŋ}, present participle

Uninflected words, defined by syntactic use

Similar morphological sieves have been set up, for Latin, by Hockett (1958:221) and by O'Brien (1965:41). The purpose of the sieve is to sort the word forms of language and group them into major form classes which are clearly defined by the inflectional system of that particular language.

Noun systems are characterized by gender, number, and case. English has only plural and possessive inflections, but most Indo-European languages inflect nouns for number and case, and adjectives for gender, number, and case. Other useful categories include person, in pronouns. Verbal systems are characterized by tense, mood, and voice. Other useful categories are transitivity, aspect, person, and number of subject. The categories marked will vary from one language to another.

Inflectional Paradigms. The paradigm of a major form class consists of a single stem of that class, with the inflectional affixes which the stem may take. The paradigm serves as a definition of the form class; the forms need not take every inflectional affix, but to belong to the class the form must take some affixes of the set, as opposed to affixes of other paradigms.

1. *Noun* (n) is defined as a word that takes noun inflections. For example, in English, nouns show the following inflectional contrasts:

Base Form	Stem + Z_1	Stem + Z_2	Stem + Z_1 + Z_2
man	men	man's	men's

2. *Adjective* (aj) is defined as a word that takes adjective inflections. For example, in English, adjectives show the following inflectional contrasts:

Base Form	Stem + {-er}	Stem + {-est}
cold	colder	coldest

3. *Verb* (v) is defined as a word that takes verb inflections. For example, in English, verbs (except the verb *be*) show the following inflectional contrasts:

Base Form	Stem+Z_3	Stem+D_1	Stem+D_2	Stem+{-iŋ}
sing	sings	sang	sung	singing

Once the inflectional paradigms of a language have been established and the major form classes of the language defined, it is often possible to establish subclasses and classes of substitutes by the same paradigm.

4. *Pronoun* (pn), in its form, is a subclass of the noun. It does not add affixes which are inflections, but its forms fit the noun inflectional paradigm:

man	men	man's	men's
I, me	we, us	my, mine	our, ours
you	you	your, yours	your, yours
he, him	they, them	his	their, theirs
she, her		her, hers	

The alternates listed in each cell of the paradigm are positional variants, and the forms may be considered as allomorphs of the same morpheme. Thus, the morpheme {I}, has two forms, /ay/, 'I,' and /miy/, 'me.' The first occurs before verbs, the latter after verbs and as object of a preposition.

5. *Auxiliary* (aux) in its form, is a subclass of the verb, which fills part of the verbal paradigm, but not the whole paradigm. In English, the verb *be* has eight forms, most verbs have five or four, and the modals only two.

sing	sings	sang	sung	singing
be/am/are	is	was/were	been	being
can		could		

In some verbs, the five part paradigm only has four parts, because the D_1 and D_2 morphemes are identical in form. However, they may be recognized as different morphemes which happen to have identical shape. Likewise, the auxiliary *must* has one form, whether it is used in the past or the present tense, but it is still classed as a modal.

Word Level Formulas: Inflections

In combining the word and stem levels into a single word level in tagmemics, there is no basic change in writing tagmemic formulas. The word level formulas of earlier tagmemic grammars are simply the first layer of analysis; the stem level of these tagmemic grammars constitutes the two subsequent layers. The three layers, taken together, form a single word level.

Inflectional Constructions. An inflectional construction (formerly word level construction) consists potentially of two or more tagmemes, one of which is manifested by a stem or root, and the other by an (inflectional) affix (see Elson and Pickett, 1962:76). There are two kinds of tagmemes in this construction: (1) nuclear tagmemes filled by stems and (2) a series of affix tagmemes filled by inflectional affixes. Word level inflection formulas may be symbolized in the formula:

$$Word = Stem + Inflections$$

When dealing with inflectional constructions, it is immaterial whether the stem is simple (a root), or complex (affix derived), or compound (formed of more than one root). At this layer of construction, the stem is separated from all of its inflectional affixes. If the stem is not simple, it is analyzed later as a complex or a compound stem.

Word Level Tagmemes. The tagmemes in the first layer of word level construction are (1) nuclear slots filled by stems and (2) inflectional slots filled by inflections. The whole constitute is called a word. Some typical slot-class correlations at this stage of analysis are as follows:

	Word = Stem	+	Inflections	
n (noun)	nnuc:ns		pos:posm	num:numm
v (verb)	vnuc:vs		t:tm	md:mdm
aj (adjective)	ajnuc:ajs		comp:{-er}	supl:{-est}
av (adverb)	avnuc:avs			

At the word level, all slots and fillers are represented by small letters. Nuclear slots are filled by the corresponding stems, for example, nnuc: noun nuclear slot; ns, noun stem. For the inflections, the slot name is the name of the inflectional function, and the filler is called a *marker*. Thus *t:tm* is read as "tense slot filled by a tense marker"; *asp:aspm* is read as "aspect slot filled by an aspect marker." Nuclear slots are obligatory; inflectional slots may be obligatory or optional.

Typical Inflectional Formulas. The tagmemes which represent the inflectional layer of the word level are combined in formulas, which may either represent the full inflectional paradigm in the language, or may be written, *ad hoc*, for particular language problems.

　　1.　*Noun Formulas:* A typical formula for nouns, in English, would be as follows, assuming that number is a category which must be expressed:

　　　　5.1　n = +nnuc:ns +num:numm ±pos:posm

Read: A noun consists of a noun nuclear slot filled by a noun stem, a number slot filled by a number marker, and an optional possessive slot filled by a possessive marker.

An alternate formulation would list number as optional (±) but this obscures the fact that every noun in English expresses number, either singular or plural. Possession, on the contrary, is an optional category and constitutes the only case marking outside of the pronoun system.

2. *Verb Formulas:* A typical formula for verbs, in English, would be as follows, with either tense or aspect obligatory to the construction:

5.2 iv/tv = +vnuc:ivs/tvs ±t:tm ∓asp:aspm

Read: An intransitive or transitive verb consists of a verb nuclear slot filled by an intransitive or a transitive verb stem, and either a tense slot filled by a tense marker, or an aspect slot filled by an aspect marker (but not both).

This formula requires one inflection, and allows only one, with a verb stem. If tense occurs, it is present, marked by $-\phi$ or $\{Z_3\}$, or past, marked by $\{D_1\}$; if aspect occurs, the verb form is marked as a present participle, with $\{-i\eta\}$, or as a past participle, with $\{D_2\}$.

3. *Adjective Formulas:* A typical formula for adjectives, in English, would be as follows, with comparison markers optional:

5.3 aj = +ajnuc:ajs ±comp:{−er}/{-est}

Read: An adjective consists of an adjective nucleus filled by an adjective stem, and an optional comparison slot filled by {-er}/{-est}.

In this formulation, the adjective may show no comparison (positive degree) or it may take the optional comparative {-er} or superlative {-est} marker.

DERIVATIONS: INNER FORMATIONS

The top layer of word level construction deals with inflectional affixes; once these are stripped away, what remains is a word stem. This stem, which takes affixes, and other uninflected words of the language are then grouped together. Any stem or word which is not simple, that is, which consists of more than one morpheme, must be analyzed into its constituent parts. The next layer of construction deals with roots and derivational affixes.

Derivation Defined

Derivational affixes are affixes which are not inflections. If the inflections of language are defined as affixes which do not change the form class of the word, but fit the word for use in syntax in the sense explained above, then derivational affixes are affixes which can change the form class and merely establish words as members of the various form classes.

Inner Formations. According to their form, derivational affixes are inner formations. They are inner with respect to inflections, so that if derivations and inflections both occur, derivations are inner, closer to the stem, and inflections are outer, furthest from the stem.

Derivational affixes may occur in word final position, when the word is not inflected or the inflection has a zero manifestation. More than one derivational affix may appear in the same word. The position classes of the derivations must then be determined. The set of derivational affixes tends to be inner, while the set of inflectional affixes tends to be outer.

Restricted Distribution. Derivational affixes have a distribution that is very restricted; they are not general through a word class. They tend to be statistically more numerous than inflections, but each single derivation has a very limited work load.

Derivations establish a form in a particular class; by the derivational ending, one can recognize the word as belonging to a certain class. Derivations are practically unlimited in number; there is no theoretical limit to the number of derivations. English has over 60 common ones. Derivations have a low functional load. Each single derivation occurs rarely and is limited to a few set combinations with particular stems.

The range of productivity of a derivational pattern may vary from one or two isolated forms to a fairly general use with a particular form class, but rarely does a derivational affix combine with all the forms of a class.

Subordinating Function. Derivational affixes are markers which establish a form within a particular form class. They are of two kinds (Hockett, 1958:243):

1. *Governing derivational affixes* change the form class of the word to which they are added. Thus, *constitute*, a verb, + {-tion} = *constitution*, a noun.
2. *Restrictive derivational affixes* do not change the form class of the word, but change the meaning of the derivative. Thus, *state*, a noun, + {-hood} = *statehood*, a noun.

Whether or not the derivational affix changes the form class of noun, the constitute, once the derivation is added, is recognizable as a member of a particular class. *Constitution* is recognized as a noun and *statehood* is recognized as a noun. Once formed, the constitute is treated as the simplest member of the same form class, both in syntax and in the addition of inflectional affixes. The principal differences between inflection and derivation may then be summarized as follows (see Nida, 1949:99):

Inflections	Derivations
1. Tend to be outer formations, occur further from the stem than any derivational affix.	1. Tend to be inner formations, occur closer to the stem than any inflectional affix.
2. Tend to be less numerous, but with wide distribution. Each affix is used through the class.	2. Tend to be more numerous, but with limited distribution. Each affix limited to small subclass.
3. Used to fit words for use in syntax, but never change the form class of the word.	3. Used to establish words in a class, and generally change the form class of the word.
4. Inflected words do not belong to the same distribution class as uninflected members of the same class. The inflection is syntactically relevant.	4. Derived words do belong to the same distribution class as the underived members of the class. The change affected by derivation is morphologically relevant.
5. Inflectional paradigms tend to be well defined, homogeneous, and define major form classes.	5. Derivational paradigms tend to be ill defined, heterogeneous, and only define single words.

Because of the difficulties involved in characterizing inflection and derivation across languages, no clear-cut differences can be established. In each language, a judgment must be made, using the above general norms, as to what constitutes inflection; other affixes are derivational.

Types of Derivational Systems

Derivations are affixes which are not inflections; they are bound forms and may be prefixes, suffixes, infixes, or suprafixes. These affixes may be combined in derivational systems, based on the following differences: (1) derivations are governing or restrictive; (2) derivations establish a word in a form class; and (3) derivations differ in form, as one of the four types of affixes.

Governing Derivations. Derivations which change the form class of the stem are called governing derivations. They govern or determine the form class of the derivative. The newly formed derivative is marked by the formative, as a noun, verb, adjective, or adverb.

Noun formatives are derivational affixes that, when added to a given stem, form a noun. These derivations are called nominalizers (nom). Each language has its favorite patterns of nominalization. In English, nouns are generally formed from verbs, sometimes from adjectives.

1. *Favorite Pattern:* Verb + D.2-1 → Noun

break-AGE	resign-ATION	decis-ION	deliver-Y
arriv-AL	employ-EE	pay-MENT	CONvert (stress)
admitt-ANCE	catch-ER₁	defen-SE	bragg-ART
assist-ANT	freez-ER₂	depart-URE	associate /ey → ʌ/

2. *Secondary Pattern:* Adjective + D.3-1 → Noun

accur-ACY	social-ISM	good-NESS	activ-ITY
free-DOM	social-IST	social-ITE	tru-TH

Verb formatives are derivational affixes that, when added to a given stem, form a verb. These derivations are called verbalizers(vbzr). In English, verb formatives are comparatively rare. Verbs are the most basic form, in the sense they are used to derive other forms. The verbalizers that occur are causatives, a frequent verb formative in language.

1. *Favorite Pattern:* Noun + D.1-2 → Verb
   fright-EN   glory-FY   idol-IZE   (EN-joy, BE-friend)

2. *Secondary Pattern:* Adjective + D.3-2 → Verb
   cheap-EN   equal-IZE (EN-able)

Adjective formatives are derivational affixes which, when added to a given stem, form an adjective. They are called adjectivizers (ajzr). In English, adjectives are generally formed from nouns, rarely from verbs.

1. *Favorite Pattern:* Noun + D.1-3 → Adjective

season-AL	fortun-ATE	cub-IC	beast-LY
suburb-AN	ragg-ED	book-ISH	fam-OUS
circul-AR	wood-EN	child-LESS	cream-Y
vision-ARY	peace-FUL	life-LIKE	

2. *Secondary Pattern:* Verb + D.2-3 → Adjective

pay-ABLE	watch-FUL	creat-IVE	tire-SOME
confid-ENT		sens-ORY	

Adverb formatives are derivational affixes which, when added to a given stem, form an adverb. They are called adverbializers (avzr). Adverbs, in English, are generally formed from adjectives. Once it is formed, the adverb is a closed construction and is not used to form words of other classes, such as nouns, verbs, or adjectives.

1. *Favorite Pattern:* Adjective + D.3-4 → Adverb
   glad-LY   (the most productive of the derivatives)

2. *Secondary Pattern:* Noun + D.1-4 → Adverb
dai-LY   home-WARDS   rule-WISE   (A-shore)

Governing derivations always change the form class; in English they are mainly suffixes. Prefixes are included in parentheses.

Restrictive Derivations. Derivations which do not change the form class of the stem to which they are added, but merely change the meaning, are called restrictive. In English, they are mainly prefixes. Suffixes are included in parentheses.

1. *Noun Patterns:* Noun + D.1-1 → Noun
ANTI-body   UN-truth   (king-DOM)   (lord-SHIP)
EX-wife   (child-HOOD)   (duch-Y)
2. *Verb Patterns:* Verb + D.2-2 → Verb
AD-join   DE-brief   PRE-form   RE-dress
COL-locate   DIS-agree   PRO-rate   UN-do
3. *Adjective Patterns:* Adjective + D.3-3 → Adjective
ANTI-social   UN-real   (kind-LY)   (hard-LY)
IM-possible   (green-ISH)

There are no restrictive adverbializers. Adverbs do not form the base either for other form classes, or for further formation of adverbs.

Chart of English Derivational Affixes. The derivational affixes are marked as input-output; D.1-2, means noun becomes a verb. The restrictive derivations are found along the diagonal.

Stem Class	→ Noun	→ Verb	→ Adj	→ Adv
1. Noun	D.1-1	D.1-2	D.1-3	D.1-4
	kingdom	glorify	lifeless	rulewise
2. Verb	D.2-1	D.2-2	D.2-3	D.2-4
	payment	disagree	payable	No case
3. Adjective	D.3-1	D.3-2	D.3-3	D.3-4
	goodness	equalize	kindly	gladly

Word Level Formulas: Derivations

After words have been separated from the outer layer of inflection, the stems of words must be analyzed at that layer of grammar within the word level, sometimes called stem level, which includes the processes of derivation and compounding. Derivation deals with the addition of bound forms which are not inflections to roots. This is the second, or subordinate layer, of the word level.

Derivational Constructions. A derivational construction (formerly stem level construction) consists potentially of two or more tagmemes, one of which is manifested by a stem or root, and the other by some derivational affix. The stem or root is said to manifest a core tagmeme, and the derivation manifests a derivational tagmeme. The formula is:

$$\text{Complex Stem} = \text{Core} + \text{Derivations}$$

The term *complex* stem is sometimes replaced by *affix-derived* stem, or simply *derived* stem. The first tagmeme is a core slot filled by a root; and complex stems must be reduced to the ultimate roots of the word. However, in practice, it is more often the case that the formula must be written in terms of stems, not roots, to show the productivity of the formula. Hence, the functional term "core" is used in the formula.

Derivational Layer Tagmemes. The tagmemes in the second layer of word formation are: (1) core slots filled by stems, including roots, and (2) derivational slots filled by derivational affixes. With governing derivations, both slots are obligatory, and the derivations are called nominalizers (nom), verbalizers (vbzr), adjectivizers (ajzr), and adverbializers (avzr). Typical slot-class correlations at this layer of analysis are as follows:

Complex Stem	=	Core	+	Derivations
ns (noun stem)		core:vs/ajs		nom:D.2–1/D.3–1
vs (verb stem)		core:ns/ajs		vbzr:D.1–2/D.3–2
ajs (adjective stem)		core:ns/vs		ajzr:D.1–3/D.2–3
avs (adverb stem)		core:ajs/ns		avzr:D.3–4/D.1–4

For restrictive derivations, where the form class is not changed, the slot with the affix is optional. This slot may be labeled according to function, such as *nom:* in formula 5.7. All formulas apply not only to the stems of inflected words, but apply to uninflected words as well. The process of derivation is independent of the process of inflection.

Typical Derivational Formulas. Although the formulas given for inflections are best analyzed as strings of inflections with a single stem, the formulas for derivations, for full productivity, are best represented in terms of two and only two constituents, especially in English. The general order of word derivation in English may be represented as:

Verb	→	Noun	→	Adjective	→	Adverb
constitute		+ -tion		+ -al		+ -ly

This one formula represents the three favorite patterns, in English, for deriving nouns, adjectives, and adverbs. Verbs are generally basic forms. These favorite patterns may be represented, in tagmemics, as follows:

5.4   ns = +core:tvs +nom:{-tion}   constitute + -tion

Read: One type of noun stem consists of a core slot filled by a transitive verb stem and a nominalizer slot filled by {-tion}.

5.5   ajs = +core:ns +ajzr:{-al}   constitution + -al

Read: One type of adjective stem consists of a core slot filled by a noun stem and an adjectivizer slot filled by {-al}.

5.6   avs = +core:ajs +avzr:{-ly}   constitutional + -ly

Read: One type of adverb stem consists of a core slot filled by an adjective stem, and an adverbializer slot filled by {-ly}.

In the readouts of these formulas, we specify one type of noun stem, not the whole class of noun stems, as composed of verb stem and derivation.

Restrictive Derivations. For those derivations which do not change the form class, the derivational slot is marked as optional, and may be labeled according to function or meaning.

5.7   ns = +core:ns ±nom:{-hood}   child + hood

Read: One type of noun stem consists of a core slot filled by a noun stem, and an optional nominalizer filled by {-hood}.

5.8   ajs = ±neg:{im-} +core:ajs   im- + possible

Read: One type of adjective stem consists of an optional negative slot filled by {im-}, and a core slot filled by an adjective stem.

Where the derived noun forms a separate subclass in the language which is syntactically relevant, the derived stem may be marked as stem class 2, and the core stem as stem class 1, with the derivational affix as obligatory.

COMPOUNDS: CORE FORMATIONS

Inflectional constructions consist of stem and affix. The stem, bound or free, carries the basic meaning of the word. Affixes are bound forms, which add to the meaning of the stem, and are either inflectional or derivational. The stems which remain after the inflections are stripped away are: (1) simple, of one root;

(2) complex, with root and derivation; or (3) compound, consisting of root plus root. Roots form the innermost core of the word, and constitute the final layer of construction.

Compounding Defined

Compound stems are stems consisting of more than one root. Roots are monomorphic forms, which carry the basic meaning of words. Monomorphic stems are roots; polymorphic stems may consist of more than one root. Stems of more than one root are reduced to single roots at the compounding or coordinate layer of word formation.

Compound Recognition. When compounds are discovered composed of two roots, it is not difficult to analyze them as having two parts, or two roots. What is difficult is to recognize the distinctive features of compounds so that compounds are distinguished from phrases. Some features are:

1. *Phonological Features.* This includes such features as the patterns for consonants and vowels in the phonology of the language, and suprasegmental features, like stress. In English, words are characterized by a single primary stress, so that compounds are often recognized by stress pattern, and lack of juncture. For example: *bláck bírd* has primary stress on each word, and a juncture. *Bláckbird*, the compound, has one primary stress, and no juncture.

2. *Syntactic Features.* Compounds are distinguished from phrases, in that they have asyntactic features, which are contrary to phrase patterns:

   a. *Word Order.* In compounds, unusual orders may be found, and usual orders are not regular even for a particular compounded pattern. For example: *sea-sick*, noun followed by adjective, is not a usual phrase pattern. Verb + particle, as in *splash-down*, is regular for verbs, not for nouns.

   b. *Interruptibility.* The parts of a compound are not interrupted, but form a rigid noninterruptible pattern; the form is inseparable. For example: *dare-devil* cannot be used as *dare-the-devil*, which is a phrase.

   c. *Modification.* Elements of the compound cannot be separately expanded with modifiers, although the whole compound may be modified. For example: *sea-sick* may not occur as *deep sea-sick*, with *deep* modifying *sea*.

d. *Inflectibility.* Elements of the compound may not be separately inflected, although the whole compound may be inflected in its class. For example: *ash-tray*, may not occur as *ashes-tray*, with *ash* inflected for plural.

3. *Semantic Features.* Compounds tend to take on specialized meanings, and so attain idiomatic status. The meaning of the compound may be quite specialized, so that the meaning of its members is obscured. For example: a *blackboard* may be green, and may be made of slate, not wood. The features that set compounds apart may differ from language to language, but some initial investigation for each should be made on the basis of phonological, syntactic, and semantic features. The compound needs some binding force, so that it is not composed entirely of free forms, and can be differentiated from phrase structures.

Parts of a Compound. The simplest level of compounding is the joining of two simple roots; and this type of compound predominates in many languages. In English, the range of root-root compounds may be illustrated by listing some of the initial roots and verifying, from any dictionary, the vast number of compounds formed.

1. *Nouns as Initial Element*
   arm, eye, ear, foot, hair, hand, heart, lip, mouth, wrist, bird, bull, cat, cow, duck, ash, rail, rose, suit, steam, air, beach, rain, snow, time, light, moon, sun, star, wind, book, car, door, farm, house, lamp, shoe, tea, table, wall.

2. *Verbs as Initial Element*
   blast, break, cast, crack, drive, drop, count, carry, feed, line, lean, loop, kick, pull, push, pick, play, print, stick, shoot, splash, show, throw, take, turn, swim, wash, write, read, set, come, fall, go, run, sit, stand.

3. *Adjectives as Initial Element*
   black, blue, gold, green, grey, red, white, yellow, north, east, south, west, right, left, straight, big, small, hot, cold, high, low, long, short, far, near, brief, fair, top, sweet, tight, quick, slow.

4. *Adverbs as Initial Element*
   about, after, back, by, cross, down, fore, front, hind, in, off, on, out, over, in, under, up.

The second element of the compound is occasionally complex, and care must be taken to make the proper immediate constituent cuts, in order to determine the pattern for the compound and its underlying forms.

1. *Forms in -ER*, used as second root, fill the same function in the compound as simple forms. The construction is Noun + Noun (-ER). For example: *house-keeper* and *line-backer* are simple noun + noun compounds. The second noun is a derived form, with verb root + derivation.

2. *Forms in -ED*, used as second root, are generally phrase derivatives, with the -ED governing the whole phrase. (Noun + Noun) + -ED. Thus, for example, *red-haired*, in which *red* modifies *hair*, and the whole phrase fills the core slot in a derivational formula, governed by -ED.

Types of Compounding Systems

Compounds are stems or uninflected words consisting of more than one root. They may be bound or free, and the elements entering into compounds may be other stems. Compounds may be classified according to form class, according to the syntactic relationship between the two roots, or according to both.

Form Class of Compounds. Compound forms belong to some form class and function syntactically like simple or derived members of the same form class. Compounds may be classified by specifying (1) the form class of the constitute and (2) the form class and order of occurrence of the two roots entering into the compound. Classification by form is independent of syntactic relations between the two roots and resembles an algebraic equation.

Noun Compounds. Any major form + noun = noun compound. The second root is a noun and the first root may be a noun, a verb, an adjective, or an adverb. Examples of noun compounds are as follows:

Noun + Noun	(modifier-head)	ash-tray, arm-chair
Verb + Noun	(verb-object)	dare-devil, pick-pocket
Adjective + Noun	(modifier-head)	black-bird, red-coat
Adverb + Noun	(a-syntactic)	after-thought, back-talk

Verb Compounds. Any major form + verb = verb compound. The second root is a verb and the first root may be a noun, a verb, an adjective, or an adverb.

Noun + Verb	(object-verb)	house-keep, baby-sit
Verb + Verb	(coordinate)	dive-bomb, drop-kick
Adjective + Verb	(a-syntactic)	white-wash, sweet-talk
Adverb + Verb	(modifier-head)	down-grade, over-do

Adjective Compounds. Any major form (except verb) + adjective = adjective compound. The second root is an adjective and the first root may be a noun, an adjective, or an adverb. Verbs do not combine with adjectives.

Noun + Adjective   (a-syntactic)   sea-sick, ox-eyed
Adjective + Adj.   (coordinate)   blue-green, south-west
Adverb + Adj.   (modifier-head)   off-white, near-sighted

Adverb Compound. Adverb + adverb = adverb compound.

Adverb + Adverb (coordinate)   through-out, in-to

Special Noun Compound. Verb + adverb = noun compound. The first root is a verb, and the second root is an adverb. The compound differs from the verb + particle = verb construction, by a change of stress.

Verb + Adverb   (derived)   drive-in, blast-off

This last type of compound, in English, is the only compound composed of two roots in which the compound is not the same class as the second root.

Syntactic Relationships. The relationship between the two roots of a compound is generally the same as between those form classes elsewhere in the grammar, but is in highly condensed form. Where the grammatical relations are obscure, the compound is called asyntactic; the syntactic relations can be further described as endocentric and exocentric.

1. *Asyntactic Compounds*
   Noun + Adjective, sea-sick, = sick because of the sea.
   Adverb + Noun, back-talk, = derived from talk back

2. *Syntactic Compounds*
   a. Endocentric: at least one head root
       (1) Coordinate: two head roots
                   girl-friend = girl who is a friend
       (2) Subordinate: only one head root
                   black-bird = a modification structure
   b. Exocentric: neither root is the head
                   pick-pocket = one who picks pockets
                   splash-down = used as a noun or verb

The functional meaning of compounds may be further clarified by tracing them to their underlying sentence patterns (Lees, 1960:48). In noun compounds the type of phrase indicated by noun + noun, in terms of relaters, for example: *ash-tray = tray* for *ashes; arm-chair = chair* with *arms; sea-shore = shore* of *the sea; sun-light = light* from *the sun.*

Chart of English Compounds. The following chart is based on the form class of the roots and derived stem. The derived stem is always the same as the second root, except for the verb + adverb construction, which is listed here as a compound noun with single primary stress. The chart is based on form alone, in a manner analogous to the charting of consonant clusters in phonology. Once form classes have been sorted, they may be further differentiated according to functional norms.

Compound	+ Noun	+ Verb	+ Adj.	+ Adv.
1. Noun	N + N text-book	N + V baby-sit	N + Aj home-sick	N + Av No case
2. Verb	V + N turn-key	V + V dive-bomb	V + Aj No case	V + Av = Noun
3. Adjective	Aj + N blue-bird	Aj + V white-wash	Aj + Aj blue-green	Aj + Av No case
4. Adverb	Av + N back-talk	Av + V out-shine	Av + Aj off-white	Av + Av through-out

Word Level Formulas: Compounds

After inflectional and derivational affixes have been removed from words and stems, what remains are either single roots or compounds of more than one root. The analysis of compound stems into component roots is the third, or coordinate, layer of the word level.

Compound Stem Constructions. A compound construction (formerly part of stem level) consists potentially of two or more core tagmemes, manifested by roots. Both core slots may be obligatory, or one of the core slots may be optional. The general formula for compounds is:

$$\text{Compound Stem} = \text{Core}_1 + \text{Core}_2$$

The functional term *core* is used in the general formula because the full productivity of the formula often requires that the core slots be filled by stems. However, any analysis proceeds to the ultimate roots of the words. In English, the most common compounds are root + root.

Compound Layer Tagmemes. The tagmemes in the third layer of word formation are core slots filled by roots (or stems). In asyntactic constructions, exocentric and coordinate constructions, both core slots are obligatory. In endocentric subordinate construction, of the head-modifier type, the head core slot is obligatory, and the modifier optional.

Compound Stem	=	Core_1	+	Core_2
ns (noun stem)		$+\text{core}_1:\text{tvr/avr/nr}$		$+\text{core}_2:\text{nr}$
vs (verb stem)		$+\text{core}_1:\text{nr/vr}$		$+\text{core}_2:\text{vr}$

ajs	(adjective stem)	+core$_1$:nr/ajr	+core$_2$:ajr
avs	(adverb stem)	+core$_1$:avr	+core$_2$:avr
ns	(noun stem)	+core$_1$:vr	+core$_2$:avr

Compound Stem	=	Core$_1$ (mod)	+	Core$_2$ (head)
ns	(noun stem)	±core$_1$:nr/ajr		+core$_2$:nr
vs	(verb stem)	±core$_1$:avr		+core$_2$:vr
ajs	(adjective stem)	±core$_1$:avr		+core$_2$:ajr

In the above formulation, all of the core slots are unqualified as to their specific function. In more detailed analyses, the core slots are labeled according to function, obc: (object core) for the verb + object compound, and qc: (qualifying core) for modifier-head compounds. In an analysis that concentrates primarily on form, what is significant is the type of roots that enter the combination, not the specific function.

Typical Compound Formulas. The formulas for derivation and for compounding are best expressed in terms of two constituents. Where the stress pattern or other suprasegmentals are essential to the compound, these may be expressed using the (-) concatenation symbol, as was suggested for the intonation slot at the sentence level.

1. *In asyntactic or exocentric structures*, both roots are obligatory, and the construction is recognized by the form class of the roots.

   5.9   ns = +core$_1$:tvr +core$_2$:nr   pick + pocket

   Read: One type of noun stem consists of a core slot filled by a transitive verb root, and a second core slot filled by a noun root.

2. *In endocentric coordinate structures*, both roots are obligatory, and the two roots are in a coordinate relationship with each other.

   5.10   ajs = +core$_1$:ajr +core$_2$:ajr   blue + green

   Read: One type of adjective stem consists of a core slot filled by an adjective root, and a second core slot filled by an adjective root.

3. *In endocentric subordinate structures*, the first root, in English, is a modifier, and the second root is the head of the construction.

   5.11   ns = ±core$_1$:nr +core$_2$:nr   gate + house

   Read: One type of noun stem consists of an optional (qualifying) core slot filled by a noun root, and a second core slot filled by a noun root.

In any of the formulas where the stress pattern is significant, the stress pattern may be included in a slot, marked with a (-) concatenation symbol.

5.12 $ns = \pm core_1:ajr + core_2:nr\ \text{-stress:}$ $/\ \_\ \backslash$

black + bird

Read: One type of noun stem consists of an optional core slot filled by an adjective root, a second core slot filled by a noun root, and a stress pattern consisting of primary-secondary stresses, with no intervening (+) juncture.

PRACTICE 5: WORD LEVEL COMPOSITION

Write the sentence, clause, and phrase level formulas for the following sentences. For every word which shows composition, write a word level formula. List all the morphs in a lexicon and calculate the maximum generation potential of the given solution. The material was supplied by Cesar A. Hidalgo.

IVATAN (Philippines)

1. maymuhasa u mahahakay
   'The men are planting.'
2. mañivakami su paray
   'We are harvesting the rice.'
3. naymuhakami su uvi kakuyab
   'We planted yams yesterday.'
4. nañivasa u mavavakɨs sičaraw
   'The women harvested today.'
5. naymuhasa
   'They planted.'
6. mañivasia sičaraw
   'He is harvesting today.'
7. nañiva u mahakay su uvi kakuyab
   'The man harvested the yams yesterday.'
8. maymuha u mavakɨs su paray sičaraw
   'The woman is planting rice today.'

IVATAN (Philippines)
GRAMMAR   (540 Sent)

Sentence Level Construction:

   Sent = +Base:tCl −Into:ICF

Clause Level Construction:

   $tCl = +P:tv \pm S:N_1 \pm O:N_2 \pm T:tem$

Phrase Level Construction:

$N_1 = +Det:det.1. +H:n_1/N_2 = +Det:det.2. +H:n_2$

Word Level Construction:

tv = +t:tm +vnuc:tvs +subj:pn
n_1 = +nnuc:ns ±num:{-R-}

LEXICON   (16 morphs)

mahakay	ns.	'man'	may- ~ ma-	tm.	'present'
mavakɨs	ns.	'woman'	nay- ~ na-	tm.	'past'
{-R-}	num.m.	'plural'	-muha-	tvs.	'plant'
paray	n.2.	'rice'	-n̂iva-	tvs.	'harvest'
uvi	n.2.	'yams'	-kami	pn.	'we'
u	det.1.	'the(subj)'	-sa	pn.	'they'
su	det.2.	'the(obj)'	-sia ~ -Ø	pn.	'he'
sičaraw	tem.	'today'	kakuyab	tem.	'yesterday'

Morphophonemics:

1. {may}, 'present' = /ma-/before/ñ/, and /may-/elsewhere
2. {nay}, 'past' = /na-/before/ñ/, and /nay-/elsewhere
3. {-sia}, 'he,' = /-sia/ if no other subject, and /-Ø/ elsewhere.
4. {-R-}, 'plural' = a reduplication of the second -CV-syllable.

SUPPLEMENTARY READINGS 5

Bloomfield, Leonard, *Language*, New York, Holt, Rinehart and Winston, Inc., 1933. Definition of lexicon, 162, and word, 178. Chap. 13, "Morphology," 207–226; Chap. 14, "Morphologic Types," 227–246.

Elson, Benjamin, and Pickett, Velma, *An Introduction to Morphology and Syntax*, Santa Ana, Summer Institute of Linguistics, 1962. Chaps. 9 and 10, "Tagmemes and Constructions at Word (and Stem) Level," 75–81; Chaps. 14 and 15, "Survey of Stem Formation, and Word Types," 95–102. Word level includes inflection, stem level, derivation, and so on.

Fries, Charles C., *The Structure of English*, New York, Harcourt, Brace and World, Inc., 1952. Chap. 7, "Parts of Speech, Formal Characteristics," 110–141, including lists of derivational affixes.

Hockett, Charles F., *A Course in Modern Linguistics*, New York, Macmillan Company, 1958. Chap. 24, "Inflection," 209–213, and Chap. 28, "Derivations," 240–245, restrictive and governing types.

Lees, Robert B., *The Grammar of English Nominalizations*, The Hague, Mouton & Co., reprinted 1960. For the deep structure underlying nominal constructions in English.

Marchand, Hans, *The Categories and Types of Present Day English Word Formation*, Wiesbaden, Otto Harrasowitz, 1960. The most extensive work on English word formation to date.

Nida, Eugene A., *Morphology: A Descriptive Analysis of Words*, Ann Arbor, Mich., University of Michigan Press, 1949. Chap. 1, "Principles of Morphemic Analysis." In Chap. 4, the processes of inflection and derivation are contrasted, 99.

Sapir, Edward, *Language*, New York, Harcourt, Brace and World, Inc., 1921. Chap. 2, "The Elements of Speech," 24–41, word defined, 34; Chap. 4, "Form in Language, Grammatical Processes," 57–81; and Chap. 5, "Form in Language, Grammatical Concepts," 82–119.

Thorndike, Edward L., and Lorge, Irving, *The Teacher's Word Book of 30,000 Words*, New York, Columbia University Press, 1944; fifth printing, 1968. Frequency lists of English word forms; for use in establishing a basic vocabulary list on the basis of actual occurrence.

TABLE 6: STRUCTURAL DESCRIPTIONS

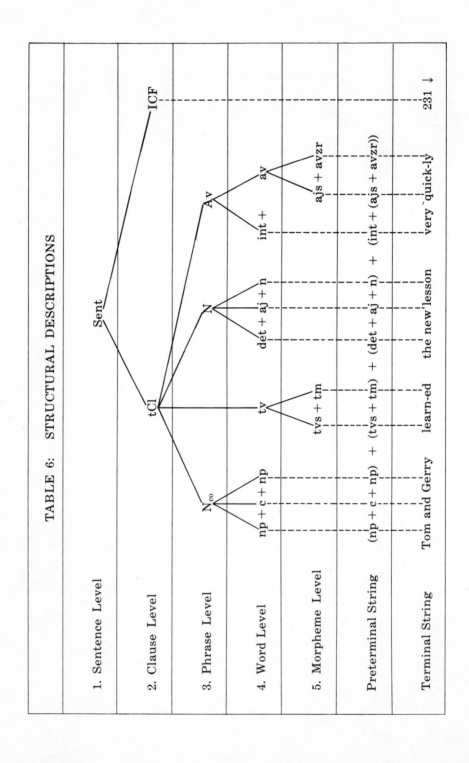

1. Sentence Level

2. Clause Level

3. Phrase Level

4. Word Level

5. Morpheme Level

Preterminal String $(np + c + np) + (tvs + tm) + (det + aj + n) + (int + (ajs + avzr))$

Terminal String   Tom and Gerry   learn-ed   the new lesson   very quick-ly

231 →

6 MORPHEME LEVEL

The morpheme level is the ultimate level of the grammar, but it is not a level of analysis. Beginning with the symbol for sentence, formulas are established at the levels of sentence, clause, phrase, and word. The morphemes are entered in the lexicon and programmed into the given formulas at the four levels of the grammar. The resulting morpheme sequences, with their underlying structural relationships, constitute what we call the morpheme level of the grammar.

Grammar has been defined by Koutsoudas as "a finite set of rules which generates an infinite number of grammatical sentences and no ungrammatical ones, and assigns to each sentence generated its proper structural description" (1966:4). At the morpheme level, it is useful to understand the relationships generated between the morphemes in the strings that are generated by the grammar.

1. *Grammatical patterns are generated,* and the morphemes are arranged in strings according to these grammatical patterns. These patterns may be expressed as generative rewrite rules. In tagmemic type grammars, these relationships are expressed in terms of the following:

    a. The functional slots of the tagmemes in construction
    b. The filler classes that are found in these functional slots
    c. The occurrence of morphemes as members of these filler classes

2. *Structural descriptions are generated* and each morpheme sequence generated has a well-defined underly-

ing structure applied to the string. Structures implicit in tagmemic formulas can be made explicit:

a. Underlying phrase markers can be constructed from the formulas.
b. These phrase markers can be reduced to preterminal strings.
c. Morphemes are programmed into strings to produce sentences.

In this final step, concrete morphemes can be programmed into arrays to produce a generative machine with an explicit generative capacity.

3. *Generative possibilities of the model.* Not only does the grammar generate patterns, complete with underlying phrase markers and preterminal strings, but the generative potential of the grammar can be calculated exactly for every finite language problem. The generative power of the model is demonstrated by calculating the number of:

a. *Combinations:* the number of elements in fixed order. The law of combinations enables us to reduce every conflated formula to an exact number of elements in a fixed formula. By an extension of this law, not only the number of formulas, but the number of elements in each of the formulas generated can be calculated.

b. *Permutations:* the number of elements in freely movable order. After the number of formulas and the number of elements in each formula are known, the number of permutations—that is, the number of formulas that can be formed if the elements are freely movable—can be calculated. This number will be a maximum and represent the greatest number of formulas possible with a given number of elements.

c. *Manifestations:* after the number of formulas and the number of morpheme class symbols in the formulas are known, concrete morphemes can be introduced from the lexicon, to produce sentences in the language. Manifestation is, in the first instance, the number of different filler classes in a given slot, but ultimately is the number of morphemes that can occur within a given slot. The generative power of the resulting formulas is calculated as a simple product of the numbers involved.

The generative possibilities of the tagmemic model were

first suggested by Longacre, in *Grammar Discovery Procedures* (1964:24), and were called: (R) readings; (P) permutations; and (E) exponents. We have chosen the terms *combination* and *permutation*, as these are the formulas used in the process taken from any college algebra text. Of the two terms *manifestations* and *exponents*, both suggested by Longacre, we preferred the tagmemic term *manifestation* rather than the mathematical term *exponent*, as the process does not deal with exponents in the sense in which this term is used in mathematics. The manifestation process can be further subdivided into manifestation of classes, which generates preterminal abstract strings of morpheme classes, and substitution, whereby concrete morphemes are introduced in place of class symbols to form the terminal strings which are the actual sentences of the language. Further references to the generative power of the model may be found in Longacre "Some Fundamental Insights of Tagmemics," *Language*, 41:65–70, 1965; in *On Tagmemes and Transforms*, Georgetown University Press, 1964; "The Generative Power of a Tagmemic Grammar," Georgetown University Press, 1967, 18th Annual Round Table, No. 20, 27–41; and Longacre, "Reply to Postal's Review," *IJAL*, 33:323–328, 1967.

GRAMMATICAL PATTERNS

Tagmemic analysis begins with the sentence and analyzes all of the utterances of the data as far as the ultimate morpheme level. The formal statement of the resultant grammar establishes a set of well-defined relationships between grammatical functions, between filler classes, and between the morphemes themselves.

Functional Slots Related

Tagmemic grammars consist of a set of formulas at the five levels of the grammar: sentence, clause, phrase, word, and morpheme. The units of this system are tagmeme units, correlations of functional slot and filler class. These units are strung into construction patterns, and the patterns occur at definite levels in a grammatical system.

Functional Slot. Traditional grammar has always dealt with grammatical functions. From the earliest grammars, we find terms such as *subject, predicate, modifier*, and *object*. Chomsky (*Aspects*, 1965:60) recognizes these functional terms and calls them grammatical relationships. In Chomsky's view, these "grammatical relationships" need not be explicitly stated in the formulas of the grammar, as long as they are well defined in the context of the theory. For example, a formula, such as S → NP + VP, purely in terms of form, implies that the NP is subject of the VP and likewise implies that the VP is predicate of the NP. Therefore a notation which specifies S:NP and P:VP is redundant.

Chomsky's argument is probably valid for immediate constituent type phrase structure components. If there are two and only two elements in the phrase, then there exists a binary relationship that can be predefined in the theory. Note, however, that these relationships are important to grammar, and prior to 1965 were not explicitly part of the theory. Chomsky's further observation (1965:69) that only "higher-level" relationships received explicit names is also a valid observation.

In a tagmemic grammar, however, the analysis is fundamentally different. The branching is not binary only, but follows a multiple type branching, string analysis technique. In this string, there may be many noun phrases, which have to be distinguished according to function. The labeling of function in such a grammar is no longer redundant; it is necessary. Such a labeling does not lead to a confusion of function and form. Nothing could be less confusing than explicit function-form symbols.

Functions in Construction. The functional slots of a tagmemic grammar are related to each other in the construction string. These relationships are indicated by:

1. *Position in the String.* Tagmemes mark definite positions within the construction frame — points in the pattern that can be recognized. For example, the subject in English normally precedes the predicate.
2. *Concatenation Symbols.* Tagmemes, even the first in the string, are marked with concatenation symbols, which indicate whether they are (+) obligatory or (±) optional to the construction in which they occur.
3. *Function Label.* The tagmeme is written in the form, slot: filler. The symbol to the left of the ratio sign (:) symbolizes the function. This function is opposed to all other functional labels within the same string.

Consequently, any particular grammatical unit can be described, from the formal statement, in terms of position (where it occurs), relative importance (obligatory or optional, peripheral or nuclear), and also in terms of its grammatical meaning (subject as opposed to predicate). For example, the subject in English may be described as that unit which, in a simple complete statement, occurs before the predicate, is obligatory and nuclear to the construction, is opposed to the other noun phrases of the construction, and carries the meaning "topic-of-sentence."

Functions in Grammar. The functional slots, related in constructions and specified at the various levels of the grammar, set up a grid of relationships into which the morphemes of language and sequences of morphemes are programmed. At the lowest levels, morphemes enter into word constructions, then words into phrases, phrases into clauses, and clauses into sentences. At each stage of the process, every form class entering into construction is named, and every grammatical function which unites these forms into constructions is also explicitly named. These names, or labels, are partially redundant at the lower levels of the grammar in such notations as tense: tense marker (t:tm), but are necessary at the phrase, clause, and sentence levels to adequately distinguish forms which enter into different kinds of constructions in a multiple branching system.

In summary, grammatical patterns are functional patterns; they are the blueprints of language. Into these patterns, the morphemes, or meaningful units of language, are programmed. As they enter construction, these forms take on the added grammatical meanings attached to the functional slots, so that the resulting meaningful utterance can be understood only if the structural meanings of the patterns are understood.

Filler Classes Related

Tagmemic grammars are functional grammars, with the underlying pattern manifest in the relationships established between the functional slots. These slots are filled by concrete forms. Because of the slot, these forms, or filler classes, are related to each other throughout the construction patterns in which they occur.

Filler Classes. Traditional grammars dealt not only with functional names, such as subject, predicate, and so on. They also named the various words and word groups, with such terms as noun, verb, noun phrase, and verb phrase. These form symbols, Chomsky identifies as "grammatical categories" (1965:64); and the transformational grammar he postulates is formulated in terms of form class symbols only, with function implicit in the theory. Rather than specify S:NP and P:VP, Chomsky leaves the functional definitions to the theory and states his generative grammar in terms of form class only, in such formulas as S → NP + VP.

However, as a generative grammar develops, more and more

functional terms are introduced into the form class symboliza-
tion, so that the distinction between function and form becomes obscure. Thus, in giving an illustration of a fragment of
a base component, Chomsky (1965:106), uses formulas no longer
binary and no longer formal. For example:

1. Sentence $\rightarrow$ NP + Predicate Phrase
2. Predicate Phrase $\rightarrow$ Aux + VP (Place) (Time)
3. VP $\rightarrow$ V (NP) (Prep-Phrase) (Manner)
4. Prep Phrase $\rightarrow$ Direction, Place, and so on

In a tagmemic grammar, terms such as predicate(phrase), place,
time, manner, and direction are considered functional; terms
such as NP, VP, Aux, Prep-Phrase (relater-axis-phrase) are considered formal. These are carefully distinguished in a notation
that specifies both form and function for every unit in the construction. The functional slots form a grid of grammatical relationships, and this grid is filled by words or word-groups from the
various formal grammatical categories. Thus:

$$\text{Function:} \quad \text{tCl} = +S +P \pm O \pm L \pm T \pm M$$

The transitive clause type of construction has a subject and
predicate, with optional object, place, time, and manner slots in
the string.

$$\text{Form:} \quad \text{tCl} = +\text{NP} + \text{VP} \pm \text{NP} \pm \text{Av/RA-phrase}$$

This same clause is manifested in a set of forms consisting of a
noun phrase, followed by a verb phrase, followed by an optional
noun phrase, and a series of optional adverbial or prepositional
phrases.

Filler Classes in Constructions. Filler classes are not tagmemes, but they manifest the tagmemes which are specified as
to both function and form. The functions set up the grammatical
relationships, which are then realized, in each single construction, by the occurrence of form-filling-the-function.

1. *Case Marking.* Single fillers are often marked for case,
   a case mark which coincides with the functional slot.
   Subjects are generally nominative; objects are either
   accusative, if there is such a case, or in a form of the
   direct case, as opposed to oblique genitive and adverbial
   cases.
2. *Relater Words.* Multiple, or word-group, fillers are often
   marked for the constructional slot in which they occur.
   Thus prepositions determine and mark the place, time,
   and manner slots in many different languages.
3. *Subcategorization Rules.* The fillers of slots may often be

categorized according to the slots in which they occur. Thus one set of pronouns (pn₁) may occur as subjects, while another set (pn₂) occurs as objects. The functional slot, and the grammatical relationships it implies, help us to subdivide classes into grammatically significant groups.

Filler Classes and Agreement. Agreement, or concord, is between forms in different slots. Using concord as a general term, the following types of concord may occur:

1. *Agreement* occurs in endocentric phrases, or between the subject and predicate adjective in an equational clause. Concord is marked by a tie bar between the slots concerned and must be specified in the grammar, as gender-number-case concord or any combination of these.
2. *Cross-reference* occurs between subjects and predicates in topic-comment constructions (Hockett, 1958:217). This is marked by a tie bar between the subject and predicate slots and must be specified. English has this concord only in the third person singular present.
3. *Government* occurs between verb and object, or preposition and object, and need not be marked. This type of syntactic linkage is already adequately marked by the case markings (for example: accusative) of the filler, in accordance with the paragraph on case marking above. For example, in Latin, one set of prepositions takes the ablative, one the accusative.

In summary, the filler classes which manifest functional slots are tied together by the functional grid. In addition, they often reflect these functional ties in a formal signaling device consisting of case markings, relater words, and subclasses within a class; or they are tied together by various types of concord or syntactic linkage, such as agreement, cross-reference, or government, with appropriate tie-markings.

Morphemes Related in the String

The tagmemic grammar is stated in terms of function and form; each tagmeme is a functional slot, a point in the grammatical pattern filled by a form class symbol. The correlation of function and form class constitutes the tagmeme, which enters into constructions at all levels of the grammar.

But the actual occurrences of tagmemes are the occurrences of forms-filling-a-function. In speech, it is the morphemes of the language which occur in morpheme sequences and manifest tagmemic function. These individual morphemes are programmed into the grammar from the lexicon, into those slots which admit morphemes of a given class.

Morpheme Fillers. The complete tagmemic solution includes grammar and lexicon. The lexicon lists all the morphs of the language or sublanguage, with their classification and gloss. The grammar consists of tagmemic formulas, in terms of function and form class. The morphemes can then be programmed into the grammar in that position in which the form class is specified, and in no other position. The form classes of grammar and lexicon must be accurately specified, so that automatic programming of morphemes into constructions is possible.

A generative grammar is a grammar that generates all the grammatical sentences of a language and none of the ungrammatical ones. A tagmemic grammar is generative in this sense. By programming concrete morphemes into the formulas of the grammar, the grammar will generate all and only the grammatical sequences of the language. In a limited corpus, all of the morphemes of this sublanguage can be programmed into all the appropriate slots, with the result that the maximum generation potential (MGP) of the grammar is realized. The MGP is the maximum number of utterances which can be generated by a finite grammar with a finite morpheme inventory. It includes all combinations, manifestations, and substitutions possible, but excludes permutation possibilities. It is calculated by programming the number of morphemes into the appropriate slots, and adding +1 for each optional slot to account for zero occurrence. The MGP of each construction is carried to the next higher level when the construction sequence occurs as a filler. The resulting total, under sentence, is the MGP of the grammar. The MGP answers the question: How many sentences can be generated by the grammar? It defines "all" numerically. Each sentence generated is grammatical; it has the right parts in the right order.

Morpheme Fillers: Restricted Generation Potential. The maximum generation potential of the grammar may generate nonsensible sentences as well as sensible ones. To restrict this output and to come closer to the "all and only" requirement, whatever formal restrictions necessary are imposed upon the grammar. Restrictions are of the form:

1. Morph of class A excludes morph of class B, or
2. Morph of class A requires morph of class B.

With these restrictions stated and built into the grammar, the MGP of the grammar is reduced. Certain sentences are not allowed, and the RGP (restricted generation potential) = MGP — restricted sentences. Restrictions are built in by concord ties, agreement markers, either/or notation, or by cover statements. The grammar is now a generative machine with a reduced potential and represents what the analyst considers to be the real grammatical output of the grammar. As long as the restrictions are formal, the sentences are grammatical, but still are not necessarily sensible sentences in the language (see also p. 83).

Morphemes Lexically Restricted. The tagmemic grammar as a generative machine is a formalized model which produces grammatical sequences automatically. Each of the sentences of the language now becomes grammatical because it is a product of the grammar. Nonsense sentences may occur; the only way to obviate this difficulty is to use a highly sophisticated lexicon, or semantic component, which will establish co-occurrence restrictions between various types of lexical items.

Current transformational theory approaches the lexical problem through the use of semantic features in much the same way as it approaches the phonological problem through features. But features occur in bundles; they can be programmed into the grammar as unit morphemes in classes cross-classified according to such features as:

animate	human	personal
inanimate	nonhuman	impersonal

Such features may be part of universal thought, but they are not manifest in every language. Whether the feature approach or the unit approach is used, attention must be paid to which features are grammatically pertinent. These lexical features with overt syntactic manifestation can then be used as a basis for subclassification of morpheme classes.

In an integrated theory of language, the fillers of various slots can be reclassified into subclasses for pertinent lexical features, whenever it is found that only items of one class, such as animate nouns, occur in this particular grammatical slot.

STRUCTURAL DESCRIPTIONS

The tagmemic grammar is also a generative grammar. By the use of programming techniques, the morphemes of the lexicon can be introduced into the formulas of the grammar to produce all and only the grammatical sentences of the language. But a generative grammar should also assign a structural description to each sentence generated by the grammar (Koutsoudas, 1966:4). How does the tagmemic grammar assign a structural description to each of the sentences generated?

Underlying Phrase Markers

A tagmemic grammar consists of a series of syntactic statements at the sentence, clause, phrase, and word levels. Each formula consists of a construction name, a rewrite or equals sign, and a string of tagmeme units marked as obligatory or optional to the construction. Such a grammar is not only a generative machine; it assigns a structural description, an underlying phrase-marker or tree diagram, to each sentence generated.

Patterns Generated. The tagmemic grammar with a finite morpheme inventory generates a well-defined set of grammatical sentences. We now ask the further question: How many patterns are generated by the grammar, and how many of the sentences generated fall into each of the generated patterns?

The tagmemic model is a closed system beginning with the symbol #Sent# and proceeding as far as the ultimate constituents or morphemes of the language. This closed system is an ordered set of rules, or formulas, stated from higher to lower at various levels of the grammar.

A *simple* formula is a formula that contains only obligatory units. A *conflated* formula is a formula that contains at least one optional unit. By definition, a conflated formula represents a set of simple formulas. When a series of formulas from sentence to morpheme is assembled in an ordered way, this series contains an underlying structural description or tree diagram. If any of the formulas are conflated formulas, then the resulting tree is a conflated tree, that is, it contains optional elements. Conflated trees represent a set of simple trees—a set which is determined by the exercise of each yes/no option in the tree. In the conflated tree, optional elements are enclosed in parentheses. Tagmemic models are normally of the conflated type, since they are designed to describe sets of sentences. A tagmemic grammar may be reduced to its underlying structural description by a rigid set of procedures.

Procedure for Generating Trees. Within the tagmemic model, we prefer to ignore the functional slots in the grammar and use only the form class symbols of the grammar in the representation of structural descriptions, or tree diagrams:[1]

1. Each equals sign in the grammar represents a branching node in the tree. Construction names are node labels,

---

[1] If function is included in the tree, the functions are inserted as labels on the branches. "A labeled branch (function) which terminates in a node (constituent) is not an inappropriate representation of the function-set notation" (Longacre, "Reply," 1967:327).

and the fillers in the construction string are the branches which spread out from the construction node.

2. In conflated trees optional elements are enclosed in parentheses; the relationships fixed by the functional grammar are then evident in the structural tree, represented in terms of form only.

$$Sent = +Base:tCl - Into:ICF$$

$$tCl = +S:N +P:tV \pm O:N$$

$$N = +H:n \pm Mod:aj$$

$$tV = \pm Mod:av +H:tv$$

Simple Trees from Conflated Trees. Conflated trees represent a set of simple trees. To determine how many simple trees are represented by a conflated tree diagram, simply program the numeral "one" into the formulas and calculate the MGP of the solution. The resulting "unitary manifestation," which supposes one and only one morpheme for each morpheme class, is equal to the number of underlying tree structures. To determine these structures in the concrete, redraw the tree as many times as required, exercising each yes/no option represented by the optional elements in the tree. The present tree diagram is reduced to 12 different simple tree diagrams, that is, the MGP of the grammar is realized in 12 grammatical patterns.

Once the trees are constructed the anatomy of the tagmemic model becomes apparent; it is different from other models. Branching is not binary, but multiple; and this branching occurs at a series of natural levels: the sentence, clause, phrase, word, and morpheme. The tagmemic tree is, as it were, overlaid on a structural grid, a functional grid. Any single horizontal line in the tree may be read as units at the same level in the grammar. It is the structure of this tagmemic tree, more than any other fact, that justifies Longacre's contention (1964:7) that tagmemic grammars represent a radical departure from former American structuralism.

In summary, the tagmemic grammar is an ordered set of rules which generates all and only the grammatical sentences of the language and assigns structural descriptions to the sentences generated. We must now inquire which patterns belong to which sentences.

Preterminal Strings of Grammar

Once the underlying phrase markers of the grammar have been established, first as a conflated tree, which is then reduced to a set of simple trees, this structure is mirrored in a set of preterminal strings. These preterminal strings are represented first by a single conflated string, for the conflated tree; then, each simple tree is reduced to a simple preterminal string. The strings and trees give the same information; they show relationships between morpheme classes.

Preterminal String Defined. A preterminal string is a string of morpheme classes which in a tagmemic grammar represents the correct morpheme classes in the correct order. The term is taken from Chomsky (*Aspects*, 1965:84), who defines preterminal string as a string that consists of "grammatical formatives and complex symbols," the result of applying the system of rewrite rules of the phrase structure grammar. This string, as we understand it, is an abstract string, derived from branching rules before the application of any of the lexical rules of the phrase structure grammar; it becomes concrete only when concrete morphemes are programmed into the string in place of the morpheme class symbols.

Just as there is one conflated tree representing many (here, 12) simple trees, so there is one preterminal conflated string, representing 12 simple preterminal strings. The conflated preterminal string is:

$$\text{Sentence} = +(n \pm aj) + (\pm av + tv) \pm (+n \pm aj)$$

The minimum preterminal string is the string formed when all of the optional elements are deleted from the formula, in this case:

$$\text{Minimum String} = n + tv$$

The maximum preterminal string is the string formed when all possible elements are included. In this case, the maximum string consists of:

$$\text{Maximum String} = n + aj + av + tv + n + aj$$

Between these two extremes are sentences of three, four, and five words. Simple strings are derived from the conflated string by patiently exercising each yes/no option until all simple strings are formed; or, the simple strings may be formed directly from simple tree diagrams. Once the set of simple trees is determined, the patterns of the language are clear in the abstract representation of preterminal strings.

To make these strings terminal, that is, to generate sentences with these patterns, simply program the morphemes of the lexicon into each of the preterminal strings, to obtain the terminal strings, which are the sentences of the language, each with its own pattern.

Simple Preterminal Strings. The patterns of the language are assigned to each sentence that is generated by the grammar. These patterns are called structural descriptions and are represented both by tree diagrams and formulas. The formulas or trees, if conflated, represent a set of simple formulas. Thus, in the present case, the set of underlying strings is as follows:

1. n + tv
2. n + tv + n
3. n + tv + n + aj
4. n + aj + tv
5. n + aj + tv + n
6. n + aj + tv + n + aj
7. n + av + tv
8. n + av + tv + n
9. n + av + tv + n + aj
10. n + aj + av + tv
11. n + aj + av + tv + n
12. n + aj + av + tv + n + aj

The grammar of the language, as formulated in tagmemics, generates these 12 patterns, and only these 12 patterns, for the language. The number of sentences formed in the language by each pattern depends upon the number of morphemes of each class in the lexicon of the language.

Terminal Strings of Morphemes. A terminal string is a string of morphemes in the correct order. The preterminal strings of language are reduced to terminal strings by substituting concrete morphemes for each of the morpheme class symbols in the preterminal string. The result is a terminal string, which is also a sentence in the language. This sentence, through morphophonemic and phonological rules, is reduced to a pronounceable sentence in the language.

The number of terminal strings produced by each single pattern can be calculated by programming the number of morphemes of each class into each pattern, to obtain the number of sentences. If these totals are added together, the sum of the sentences produced by each pattern will add up to the MGP of the solution, already calculated. Suppose, for example, that there were exactly two morphemes of each class in the above set of strings. Then the number of sentences produced is:

Type 1: $2 \times 2 = 4$
Type 2: $2 \times 2 \times 2 = 8$
Type 3: $2 \times 2 \times 2 \times 2 = 16$
Type 4: $2 \times 2 \times 2 = 8$
Type 5: $2 \times 2 \times 2 \times 2 = 16$
Type 6: $2 \times 2 \times 2 \times 2 \times 2 = 32$
Type 7: $2 \times 2 \times 2 = 8$
Type 8: $2 \times 2 \times 2 \times 2 = 16$
Type 9: $2 \times 2 \times 2 \times 2 \times 2 = 32$
Type 10: $2 \times 2 \times 2 \times 2 = 16$
Type 11: $2 \times 2 \times 2 \times 2 \times 2 = 32$
Type 12: $2 \times 2 \times 2 \times 2 \times 2 \times 2 = 64$

Total number of sentences generated by all patterns together would be equal to 252, which coincides with the MGP of the tagmemic grammar.

Sentence Generators

After the underlying tree markers have been established and the structure reduced to a set of preterminal strings, showing the same structure in formula form, the concrete sentences of the language can be generated by arranging the elements of sentences in a matrix form. These matrices, arrays of rows and columns, are called sentence generators.

Sentence Generator Defined. Preterminal strings represent the output of the grammar in an abstract way. When the concrete morphemes of the language are then programmed into the preterminal strings, the strings become terminal. In a tagmemic grammar, as opposed to a transformational grammar (Chomsky, 1965:84), the terminal strings are sentences of the language given in phonemic script. However, the terminal string here is analogous to that of Chomsky; the terminal string is formed from the preterminal string by insertion of lexical formatives. To generate the terminal strings of the grammar, we first set up a sentence generator.

A sentence generator is a matrix, or array of rows and columns. The columns represent the morpheme classes in the correct order and are labeled with a set of dummy indices, such as I, J, K, L, M, N, and so on. The elements in each row are numbered and represent the stock of morpheme fillers belonging to each morpheme class. When the same class occurs more than once in the string, it is entered completely into the generator as often as it occurs.

The generation of sentences from such a device is purely mechanical and is easily performed by a computer or other mechanical device. The morphs could, for example, be printed on the wheels of slot machines, so that each pull of the lever would generate, at random, a sentence of the language which is programmed into the machine. With digital computers, we enter the data, identify each morph by number and class, then call the pattern we desire, and give the command to execute the process. For example, the command DO I = 1,2, DO L = 1,2 would produce four different sentences of the I-L pattern. It is significant that, in the sample generation of the maximum pattern in which form classes are repeated, the computer refused to repeat operations on the noun and adjective classes, unless these classes were given a new dummy index. Telling the machine to generate the pattern I-J-K-L-I-J, produced the answer, "But I have already done I and J." However, after rewriting the program with the last two sets marked as M-N, the full output of the matrix was generated without further complicating the machine programming.

Method of Generation. Language problems solved by tagmemic methods have been run on an IBM 1620 computer, using Fortran II programming. The results have been the generation of the complete MGP of the problem as calculated by the methods already suggested. The method of generation of sentences from a sentence generator matrix is described below.

The computer works with a series of DO-loops, one for each morpheme class. To generate the complete output, each class is represented by a DO-loop, and all the morphemes of the sublanguage are read into the computer and identified as members of these classes. The first item in each category is chosen by the computer, beginning with the first morpheme in the sentence and proceeding from left to right. The computer picks the first morpheme of each group and prints the first sentence, using the top line of the matrix generator.

The second sentence is the same as the first, except that the morpheme at the end of the sentence is changed. For succeeding sentences all of the possibilities in the far right column are first exhausted, then the computer works on the possibilities in the next to last column, and so on, until every possible combination of these morphs in this order are completely exhausted. The printout then contains, in a definite fixed order, all of the sentences that can be generated by the solution.

Making Grammars Generative. Using all of the above procedures, it is possible to take a tagmemic grammar, determine the underlying structural descriptions, write out the preterminal strings, and generate the MGP of the grammar mechanically. This generative power results from the model as stated and is already implicit in that model. It is not dependent on the procedures by which the model was established as a tentative guess at the underlying grammar.

Longacre once suggested that future tagmemic grammars might well employ rewrite operations by "(a) stating them in the front of the grammar, (b) carrying them out in illustrative fashion here and there throughout the grammar, and (c) incorporating sections of rewrite exercises for the reader" (1964:32). We suggest, further, that future tagmemic manuals might carry mathematical answers to problems, the MGP and RGP of the solutions with structural descriptions, preterminal strings, and sentence generators illustrated here and there throughout the series of exercises.

After calculating the MGP for many language problems, determining the underlying phrase markers and the preterminal strings, and actually generating these solutions on computers with favorable results, it is difficult not to admit the generative power inherent in the tagmemic model.

GENERATIVE POSSIBILITIES OF THE MODEL

The generative possibilities of the tagmemic model are reduced to a series of operations by Longacre (*Grammar Discovery Procedures*, "Symbols and Rewrite Operations," 1964, 24–32). These operations, in order, are: (1) readings (or combinations), the number of combinations of elements in a fixed order; (2) permutations, the number of combinations possible where the order of elements is changeable; and (3) exponents (or manifestations), the number of fillers that may occur in each particular tagmemic slot.

Combinations: Elements in Fixed Order

The tagmemic formula is a formula made up of symbols, and these symbols are inherently mathematical. This formula, or any such formula which contains optional elements, may be read in a variety of ways. It represents, in summary form, many different formulas. Each concrete reading either includes or excludes each optional element.

Law of Combinations: $C = 2^n - 1$. In mathematics, the law of combinations states that the number of possible combinations of n elements in a fixed order is represented by the formula: $C = 2^n - 1$. In this formula, the numeral 2 is a binary base which represents the choice of occurrence or nonoccurrence for each element; the exponent n represents the number of times this choice is to be made; and the -1 excludes the possibility of choosing nonoccurrence for all elements, and thus producing a null string.

Problem: Given a string of 4 optional elements, $\pm A \pm B \pm C \pm D$, how many combinations are possible, with the elements in fixed order?

Solution: Let $n =$ the number of optional elements in the string, then:

$$C = 2^n - 1$$
$$C = 2^4 - 1 =$$
$$C = 16 - 1 = 15, \text{ Answer}$$

Check: Write the number of combinations of these elements.

ABCD
ABC, ABD, ACD, BCD
AB,   AC,   AD,   BC,   BD,   CD
A,   B,   C,   D   Total:15

This law of combinations and its applications may be found in any standard textbook for college mathematics. For example, in Schaum's Outline Series (*College Algebra*, Murray R. Spiegel, 1956, p. 231), it is suggested that a quarter, a dime, a nickel, and a penny may occur in 15 combinations.

Number of Combinations in a Formula. In tagmemics, each formula has one or more obligatory elements. Group all obligatory elements under one symbol, K = constant element. Let n = number of optional tagmemes in the string. Then the number of combinations possible, the number of ways the formula may be read, is $C = 2^n$. With a constant element (K) in the formula, there is no need to include the (-1) designation, as there is no possibility of a null string.

K $C = 2^0 = $ 1 combination
K $\pm$A $C = 2^1 = $ 2 combinations
K $\pm$A $\pm$B $C = 2^2 = $ 4 combinations
K $\pm$A $\pm$B $\pm$C $C = 2^3 = $ 8 combinations
K $\pm$A $\pm$B $\pm$C $\pm$D $C = 2^4 = 16$ combinations

The constant element, K, occurs in every combination, and n, in $C = 2^n$, represents the number of yes/no choices, the number of optional tagmemes.

Number of Elements in Each Combination. Not only the number of combinations, but the precise nature of each combination may be determined. If we consider our combination formula as a binomial expansion, then the kinds of combinations may be determined by the laws for finding the coefficients of binomial expansions. Thus $C = 2^n$ is considered as $C = (a + b)^n$, where a = yes, b = no. One method for determining the coefficients is known as Paschal's triangle.

Paschal's Triangle: Coefficients of Binomial Expansion

n = 0				1			$C = 2^0 = 1$
n = 1			1		1		$C = 2^1 = 2 = 1{+}1$
n = 2		1		2		1	$C = 2^2 = 4 = 1{+}2{+}1$
n = 3	1		3		3	1	$C = 2^3 = 8 = 1{+}3{+}3{+}1$
n = 4	1	4	6	4	1		$C = 2^4 = 16 = 1{+}4{+}6{+}4{+}1$

If, for example, the number of combinations is 16, the kinds of combinations are broken down into 1+4+6+4+1, that is, 1 C with five elements, KABCD, 4 C with four elements, 6 C with three elements, 4 C with two elements, and 1 combination with one element, K. These 16 combinations are: KABCD; KABC, KABD, KACD, KBCD; KAB, KAC, KAD, KBC, KBD, KCD; KA, KB, KC, KD, and the minimum string K.

Permutations: Elements Freely Movable

The Law of Combinations deals with elements of a formula independent of the order in which they occur. This may be understood simply by considering the elements in one fixed order. The Law of Permutations is then used for each single combination, if the order of elements in the formula is free. Given these freely movable elements, how many different permutations of each single formula are possible?

Law of Permutations: P = m! In mathematics, the law of permutations states that the number of possible permutations of a string of m elements, when the order of those elements is free, is represented by the formula:

P = m!

Read: The number of permutations equals the factorial of the number of elements. The symbol m! (m-factorial) means that the number m is the product of all of the integers from one to the number m; thus $3! = 3 \times 2 \times 1 = 6$.

Problem: Given a simple string of elements, such as KABC, with the elements freely movable, how many permutations will be possible?

Solution: Let m = the total number of elements in the string
Then
$$P = m!$$
$$P = 4 \times 3 \times 2 \times 1$$
$$P = 24, \text{Answer}$$

Check: Write the 24 permutations of the given formula.
KABC, KACB, KBAC, KBCA, KCAB, KCBA
AKBC, AKCB, ABKC, ABCK, ACKB, ACBK
BKAC, BKCA, BAKC, BACK, BCKA, BCAK
CKAB, CKBA, CAKB, CABK, CBKA, CBAK

In tagmemics, the Law of Combinations is first applied to all formulas which have optional elements (conflated or condensed formulas) to reduce these to many simple formulas with only obligatory elements. Second, the law of permutations is applied to any simple formula which has elements that are freely movable. Note that in applying the Law of Combinations, n = the number of optional elements, whereas in the Law of Permutations, m = the *total* number of elements present. This total includes the constant element K, as well as A, B, C, and so on.

This Law of Permutation may be found in the already cited *College Algebra* (Schaum's Outline Series, Murray R. Spiegel, 1956, p. 229), where the formula represents a special case of permutations—of m elements, taken m at a time, for example: 5 elements, taken 5 at a time.

Permutations of Each Combination. If the order is fixed, the number of combinations alone is to be calculated. If, however, the order of elements is freely movable, then the number of permutations must be calculated for each combination. Suppose for example, there are 4 optional elements, then $C = 2^4 = 16$. If the order of elements is freely movable, each of these 16 combinations has a definite number of permutations, calculated as follows:

Number of Combinations	Number of Elements	Number of Permutations
1	1	$1 \times 1! = 1 \times 1 = 1$
4	2	$4 \times 2! = 4 \times 2 = 8$
6	3	$6 \times 3! = 6 \times 6 = 36$
4	4	$4 \times 4! = 4 \times 24 = 96$
1	5	$1 \times 5! = 1 \times 120 = 120$
C = 16		P = 261

The formula, +K ±A ±B ±C ±D, will represent 16 combinations of elements if the elements are in a fixed order, but 261 permutations if the order of elements is freely movable. That is, the one tagmemic formula represents a maximum of 261 formulas.

Maximum Number of Permutations. The answers resulting from applying the Law of Permutations involve the maximum number of permutations if the order of optional elements is freely movable with the constant K. If some obligatory elements are movable with respect to each other, these elements must be counted separately in the calculation of permutations. If the order is not entirely, but only partially, free, the permutation formula will give only the *maximum* number of permutations. If some of these permutations do not occur, then restrictions must be imposed upon the permutations possible. Note that the maximum number of permutations is constant and may be calculated and tabulated as follows:

With no optional elements,	$C = 1$	$P = 1$	1
With 1 optional element,	$C = 2$	$P = 3$	$1 + 1$
With 2 optional elements,	$C = 4$	$P = 9$	$1 + 2 + 1$
With 3 optional elements,	$C = 8$	$P = 49$	$1 + 3 + 3 + 1$
With 4 optional elements,	$C = 16$	$P = 261$	$1 + 4 + 6 + 4 + 1$
With 5 optional elements,	$C = 32$	$P = 1631$	$1 + 5 + 10 + 10 + 5 + 1$

Manifestations: Strings Made Terminal

The law of manifestation deals with the fundamental principle underlying the mathematical theory of combinations and permutations. In tagmemic formulas, various manifestations of the formula are realized by programming the filler classes into the functional slots, whose combinations and permutations have already been calculated.

Law of Manifestation: $M = m \times n$. The fundamental principle of combination and permutation theory is: given an element that occurs m times, followed by an element that occurs n times, then the two elements in succession can occur $m \times n$ different ways. The total number of manifestations possible is equal to the product of each set in the string.

Problem: Given a string of Noun + Adjective + Adverb + Verb, with 2 nouns, 2 adjectives, 3 verbs, and 3 adverbs, what is the total number of manifestations possible of such a string?

Solution: Sentence = Noun + Adjective + Adverb + Verb
$$= 2 \times 2 \times 3 \times 3$$
$$= 36 \text{ possible manifestations, Answer}$$

Where the string contains optional elements, the number of manifestations and the number of combinations (excluding permutation possibilities) can be calculated at the same time. Each optional element has +1 added to account for the possibility of zero occurrence at that position.

Problem: Given the above string, in which the adjectives and adverbs are optional elements, how many manifestations of the string are possible?

Solution: Sentence $= +\text{Noun} \pm \text{Adjective} \pm \text{Adverb} + \text{Verb}$
$$= 2 \times (2 + 1) \times (3 + 1) \times 3$$
$$= 2 \times 3 \times 4 \times 3$$
$$= 72 \text{ possible manifestations, Answer}$$

Check: The number of manifestations when all elements were present has already been calculated: 36. With the adjective non-occurrent, the *noun + adverb + verb* manifestations $= 18$; with the adverb nonoccurrent, the *noun + adjective + verb* manifestations $= 12$; with both adjective and adverb nonoccurrent, *noun + verb* manifestations $= 6$. The total of all manifestations possible $= 36 + 18 + 12 + 6 = 72$, QED.

For manifestation of the preterminal strings of the grammar, program the numeral 1 into the formula to obtain the number of preterminal strings ($=$ number of structural descriptions). For the terminal strings, program the number of morphs of each class from the grammar into the formula to obtain the number of sentences.

Slots with Multiple Fillers. For the calculation of the preterminal strings or the terminal strings, of the grammar, manifestations that occur within the same slot must be added together; the resulting sum is the number of manifestations at that point of the pattern. This sum then enters into the product that gives the total number of manifestations in the string. For example: given a clause formula, with S:N/pn/np, read as a subject slot filled by either a noun phrase, or a pronoun, or a proper noun, the number entered as the "number of subjects" is $3 = 1 + 1 + 1$ for preterminal strings. If these elements are manifested by 240 noun phrases, 6 pronouns, and 2 proper nouns, then the sum $240 + 6 + 2 = 248$ is entered in this slot, in order to calculate the number of sentences that are generated.

Similarly, when two slots are tied by an either/or notation, these two slots are considered to be effectively the same slot for either one or the other must occur, but not both. In the formula $\pm t{:}tm_1 \mp t{:}tm_2$ tense must be expressed, but only once. In this case, the sum of the tense markers, tm_1 and tm_2 is entered as the manifestation of that slot. If, for example, $tm_1 = 3$ and $tm_2 = 1$, the number of manifestations is 4.

Calculations with Restrictions. When the formulas of the grammar express co-occurrence restrictions, the mathematical methods thus far described generate the maximum number of sentences, without taking restrictions into account. The only rule of thumb for calculating restrictions is to break down the manifesting number into subgroups and calculate the number of strings that are generated with each subgroup.

For example, given a restriction of gender-number concord on the formula for the noun phrase N = +Det:det +H:n ±Mod:aj in Spanish, with 4 articles, 4 adjectives, and 4 nouns (which are all different numbers and genders), the manifestation is not $4 \times 4 \times 4 = 64$, because not all of these elements combine in the phrase. Rather, calculations must be performed separately for masculine/feminine and for singular/plural groups. Each group has $1 \times 1 \times 1 = 1$ phrase, with a total of 4 phrases in all; the other 60 phrases are not generated, as they violate the concord restriction concerning gender and number.

In summary, the tagmemic model has definite generation possibilities, so that the exact number of patterns produced, the number of combinations, permutations, and manifestations that singly or together give us the full generation power of the grammar, can be accurately calculated. The solutions of concrete problems are reduced to mathematical answers.

PRACTICE 6: ASSIGNING STRUCTURAL DESCRIPTIONS

For the following sentences adapted from Problem #99, Vietnamese (*Laboratory Manual*, Merrifield, 1967):

1. Draw the conflated tree (structural description).
2. Generate the preterminal strings (sentence patterns).
3. Set up a sentence generator for computer generation.

VIETNAMESE

1. cho sem cum to
   'The dog sees the big bird.'
2. cho to xawng sem cho nyo
   'The big dog does not see the little dog.'
3. cho nyo thay chim nyo
   'The little dog perceives the little bird.'
4. chim ku?ng sem cho
   'The bird also sees the dog.'
5. chim ku?ng thay
   'The bird also perceives.'
6. chim xawng thay
   'The bird does not perceive.'
7. cho thay chim
   'The dog perceives the bird.'
8. cho sem
   'The dog sees.'

9.   chim to thay cho to
        'The big bird perceives the big dog.'
10. chim nyo ku?ng thay chim to
        'The little bird also perceives the big bird.'

GRAMMAR			LEXICON		
Sent = +Base:tCl −Into:ICF			chim	n.	'bird'
252	252	× 1	cho	n.	'dog'
tC1 = +S:N +P:tV ±O:N			nyo	aj.	'little'
252	6 × 6	× (6 + 1)	to	aj.	'big'
N = +H:n ±Mod:aj			ku?ng	av.	'also'
6	2 × (2 + 1)		xawng	av.	'not'
tV = ±Mod:av +H:tv			sem	tv.	'see'
6	(2 + 1)	× 2	thay	tv.	'perceive'

STRUCTURAL DESCRIPTION

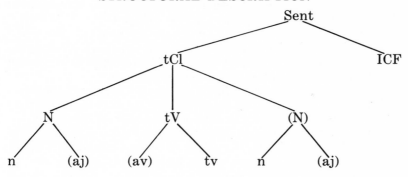

PRETERMINAL STRINGS

1.	n + tv	=	4 Sent, I L types
2.	n + tv + n	=	8 Sent, I L M
3.	n + tv + n + aj	=	16 Sent, I L M N
4.	n + aj + tv	=	8 Sent, I J L types
5.	n + aj + tv + n	=	16 Sent, I J L M
6.	n + aj + tv + n + aj	=	32 Sent, I J L M N
7.	n + av + tv	=	8 Sent, I K L types
8.	n + av + tv + n	=	16 Sent, I K L M
9.	n + av + tv + n + aj	=	32 Sent, I K L M N
10.	n + aj + av + tv	=	16 Sent, I J K L types
11.	n + aj + av + tv + n	=	32 Sent, I J K L M
12.	n + aj + av + tv + n + aj	=	64 Sent, I J K L M N

MGP = 252 Sent, 12 patterns

SENTENCE GENERATOR

	I	J	K	L	M	N
1.	chim	nyo	ku?ng	sem	chim	nyo
2.	cho	to	xawng	thay	cho	to

SUPPLEMENTARY READINGS 6

Chomsky, Noam, *Syntactic Structures*. The Hague, Mouton & Co., 1957. Grammar defined as generative, 13; all and only requirement, 18; phrase structure rules, derivations, and structural trees, 26–27.

, *Aspects of the Theory of Syntax*. The M.I.T. Press, 1965. Structural descriptions assigned, 9; branching vs. lexical rule, 68; terminal vs. preterminal string, 84; grammatical relations vs. grammatical category, 68. Extra-node tree, 69, not acceptable.

Cook, Walter A., S. J., *On Tagmemes and Transforms*. Washington, D.C., Georgetown University Press, 1964. Rules for generation, 53–56 developed from prepublication edition of Longacre, 1964 (infra).

, "The Generative Power of a Tagmemic Grammar," *Monograph Series on Languages and Linguistics, No. 20*, 27–41. Washington, D.C., Georgetown University Press, 1967. Methods for generating sentences and assigning structural descriptions.

Katz, Jerrold J., and Postal, Paul, *An Integrated Theory of Linguistic Description*. The M.I.T. Press, 1964. For semantic component restrictions on concurrence based on semantic features.

Koutsoudas, Andre, *Writing Transformational Grammars*. New York, McGraw-Hill, Inc., 1966. For notion of the conflated rule, 9 ff. and the construction of P-markers and PS rules, 14 ff.

Longacre, Robert E., *Grammar Discovery Procedures*. The Hague, Mouton & Co., 1964. "Introduction: Symbols and Rewrite Operations," 24–34, in terms of readings, permutations, and manifestations.

, "Some Fundamental Insights of Tagmemics." *Language*, 41: 65–76 (1965). Generative power of tagmemic grammar, 71, ff.

, "Reply to Postal's Review of Grammar Procedures," *IJAL*, 33:323–328 (1967), with sample tagmemic trees, 325.

Merrifield, William R., "On the Form of Rules in a Generative Grammar," *Monograph Series on Languages and Linguistics, No. 20*, 43–55. Washington, D.C., Georgetown University Press, 1967.

Postal, Paul M., "Constituent Structure: A Study of Contemporary Models of Syntactic Description," *IJAL*, vol. 39. no. 1, Part III, 33–51 (1964).

, "Review of Robert E. Longacre's *Grammar Discovery Procedures*," *IJAL*, 32: 93–98 (1966). For objections to the tagmemic system.

TABLE 7: LANGUAGE DESCRIPTION

LANGUAGE UNITS Trimodally Structured	VARIATION Manifestation Mode Wave-Dynamic	CONTRAST Feature Mode Particle-Static	SYSTEM Distribution Mode Field-Systematic
I PHONOLOGICAL COMPONENT (Phonology)	1 ALLOPHONES Set of etic sounds Phoneme variants	2 PHONEME Emic units of sound Differential function	3 PHONEMIC SYSTEM Paradigmatic Matrix of Phonemes
II LEXICAL COMPONENT (Lexicon)	4 ALLOMORPHS Set of etic forms Morpheme variants	5 MORPHEME Emic units of form Referential function	6 MORPHEMIC SYSTEM Paradigmatic Matrix of Morphemes
III SYNTACTIC COMPONENT (Grammar)	7 ALLOTAGMAS Set of etic patterns Tagmeme variants	8 TAGMEME Emic pattern units Syntactic function	9 TAGMEMIC SYSTEM Paradigmatic Matrix of Tagmemes

7 LANGUAGE DESCRIPTION

Language description has three basic requirements. It must deal with sounds, with forms, and with the arrangements of forms in sentences. "If language is a structure," says Sapir (1921:24), "and if the significant elements of language are the bricks of that structure, then the sounds of speech can only be compared to the unformed and unburnt clay of which the bricks are fashioned." The problem of language description is to isolate the units of sound, that are used to form the units of referential meaning, which then fit into the blueprints of language.

Phonology, Lexicon, and Grammar. The tagmemic model deals with sounds, forms, and arrangements in a triple grammatical hierarchy of phonology, lexicon, and grammar. These three hierarchies are systems that are "semi-autonomous but interlocking" (Longacre, 1964:7). The triple hierarchy, as explained by Pike (1958:275), is as follows:

1. *The phonological hierarchy*, with the phoneme as the minimum unit, and syllables, stress groups, and so on, as higher units in the hierarchy.
2. *The lexical hierarchy*, with the morpheme as the minimum unit, and with morpheme sequences or special collocations as higher units.
3. *The grammatical hierarchy*, with the tagmeme as the minimum unit, and various tagmemic constructions as higher units in the hierarchy.

Language description according to the tagmemic model has three components. The syntactic component, or tagmemic grammar, lists the arrangements of language in terms of basic tagmeme units; the lexical component, or tagmemic lexicon, lists the forms of language and their meanings; the phonological component lists the sound units of language and their allophonic realization in language utterances. The language description is in terms of "a phonological statement, a grammatical statement, and a highly sophisticated dictionary" (Longacre, 1964:8).

Particle, Wave, and Field. The units of language description may be considered as simultaneously particle, wave, and field, as explained by Pike (1959:37–54; 1967:510):

1. *Particle* refers to units in their feature mode. It is a static view of language, with units described as clear-cut particles, well defined.
2. *Wave* refers to units in their manifestation mode. It is a dynamic view of language, with variants subject to blurring and overlapping.
3. *Field* refers to units in their distribution mode. It is a systematic or functional view of language, with units as part of a set of oppositions.

The three different ways of viewing the unit are not contradictory but complementary. The unit is "structured three ways at once" (Pike, 1967:93). The unit is not divided into three parts, but considered from three different viewpoints: as a discrete unit, as manifested in variants, and as part of a set of oppositions within a matrix or field. Within this trimodal structuring, particle and wave are more closely related. In the formula $LS = (M/F)D$, the linguistic sign, or unit, is composed of a manifestation-feature complex, which is distributed in a field. The F mode corresponds to comprehension or definition, and the M mode to the extension or set of things defined. It is the comprehensive-extensive unit which is distributed as a single cell in a matrix of oppositions.

Contrast, Variation, and Distribution. The three modes of the unit may also be considered under the process titles of contrast, variation, and distribution. In an equivalence set up by Pike (1967:85, fn. 3):

1. *For feature mode*, one can read *contrast* (contrastive-identificational components). The feature mode is defined as composed of "simultaneously occurring identificational-contrastive components" (Pike, 1967:85).
2. *For manifestation mode*, one can read *variation* (range of free, conditioned, or complex variants with physical component obligatory). The manifestation mode is composed of "nonsimultaneously occurring physical variants" (Pike, 1967:85).

3. *For distribution mode*, one can read *distribution* (occurrence in a class as member of that class, in a sequence of segments organized hierarchically, and in cells of a matrix made up of intersecting dimensions). The distributional mode is defined as composed of "relational components" (Pike, 1967:85), and includes distribution in class, sequence, and matrix.

No justification is given for the three modes except the very practical justification of their usefulness in description. The basic modes seem to be linked to the discovery principles of (1) phonetic and semantic similarity; (2) contrast and complementation; and (3) pattern congruity. The contrast, variation, and distribution of units used in the discovery process appear as verified modes in the final language description.

THE PHONOLOGICAL COMPONENT

The first component of a language description deals with sounds—sounds as manifested in the forms of language, sounds grouped as units according to identifying-contrastive features, and sounds as part of a system. In the phonological component of a language description, we consider (1) the manifestation mode, (2) the feature mode, and (3) the distribution mode of the sound units of the language, the phonemes. The three modes of the phoneme are developed in Pike (1967, Chap. 8).

The Manifestation Mode: Phonetics

In the discovery process, we begin the study of the sound system with the study of phonetics—the isolation and classification of all of the sounds that occur in the given language. In the presentation of language descriptions, these sounds are listed as etic variants of the sound unit; they are grouped as allophones of the phonemes of the language.

Manifesting Set of Allophones. In a language description, we establish a phonemic inventory—a list of the essential sound units, or phonemes, of the language. Each phoneme has a well-defined set of manifesting forms, or allophones. Even if the phoneme has only one allophone, this one sound is considered as a set of manifesting forms. For example, in a partial description of the phoneme /p/ in English, defined as a "voiceless bilabial stop," the allophones may be listed as:

[p] unaspirated, in initial clusters, CCV-
     For example, *spot, spill, span*
[pʰ] aspirated, in initial position, CV-
     For example, *pot, pill, pan*

The phoneme is manifested at the concrete level of phonetic transcription. The allophones represented in that transcription are nonsimultaneously occurring physical variants of the phoneme. They are nonsimultaneous because in each "occurrence" of the phoneme, only one of these etic units occurs at a time. They are physical variants in the sense that they are an approximation of the physical event. Even in phonetic transcription, some of the physical sound is lost; but the features worth noting are based on wide experience with many languages and roughly correspond to the limits of transcription of the International Phonetic Alphabet. They are the variants of the same sound because they occur either in complementary distribution, or in partial complementation with some free variation, or in free variation; but they never occur in contrast with each other in the language. They are noncontrastive variants.

Allophones as Waves. The manifestation mode of an emic unit has wavelike features. It is a dynamic view of language, closer to the physical reality, and accounts for overlapping and blurring characteristics in language. In phonology, sounds are produced by a continuous movement, with the borders of individual sounds largely indeterminate. A word with a CVC pattern is not pronounced as a sequence of discrete sounds, but as a continuous wavelike movement in which the sounds overlap. The units are perceived as the peaks of sound, but the sound borders are indeterminate. For example, a word, such as /*pin*/, /pin/, might be represented by waves:

[pʰ]   [i]   [n]

The initial /p/ sound is aspirated and is in a forward position because of the following /i/ sound; the /i/, in turn, is partially prenasalized in anticipation of the following /n/. The overlapping of the sounds can be demonstrated in a phonetics laboratory by comparing the qualities of the vowels and consonants in different sequences. In recognizing the sounds as units, we recognize the peaks of the waves and ignore the overlapping indeterminate borders of the sounds.

Allophonic Variation. The manifestation mode of an emic unit is also characterized by the noncontrastive distribution of its variants. Allophones of the same phoneme may be in complementary distribution or in partial complementation with some free variation, but these allophones are never found in contrast with each other. The principles of phonemic analysis deal with possible variants:

1. *The Principle of Phonetic Similarity.* Similar sounds may belong to the same phoneme. Dissimilar sounds must belong to different phonemes. This principle deals with the form of the sound and declares that there must be some degree of similarity between two sounds before they can be considered as possible variants of the same phoneme.
2. *The Principle of Complementation.* Sounds not in contrast, which are either in complementary distribution in mutually exclusive environments or in partial complementation with some free variation, may belong to the same phoneme. Sounds in contrast must belong to different phonemes. This principle deals with the distribution of the sounds and declares that two sounds may be grouped as allophones of the same phoneme if they are never found in contrastive distribution.

According to these principles, allophonic variants are variants that are phonetically similar, suspicious pairs that are always found in noncontrastive distribution in the forms of the language.

The Feature Mode: Phonemics

The study of the sound system proceeds in two steps. First, the etic sounds which occur in the language are isolated and classified in the study of phonetics. Second, these etic sounds are grouped into emic units in the study of phonemics. In the presentation of the description, the essential sound units are listed as the phonemes of the language.

The *phoneme* is defined as a minimum unit of sound, which has the capacity for changing the meaning of a linguistic form. Sounds in contrast belong to different phonemes; sounds not in contrast belong to the same phoneme. The test for contrast is whether the sound change is capable of producing a change in the meanings of linguistic forms. For example, in testing for English consonants, use a test frame. Each consonant that forms a new word belongs to a new phoneme. Thus:

```
-ILL:        pill, bill; till, dill; chill, Jill; kill, gill
Phonemes:    /p, b/    /t, d/    /č, ǰ/    /k, g/
```

In testing for English vowel nuclei, use a test frame. Thus:

```
B___T:     bit, beat; bet, bait; bat, but; boot, bought
Phonemes: /i/, /iy/, /e/, /ey/, / æ /, /ʌ/, /uw/, / ɔ /
```

The use of many such frames would isolate all of the consonants and vowels of the English language as minimum essential units.

Distinctive Features of Phonemes. In a language description, all of the phonemes are listed with their identifying-contrastive features. If the description is based on articulatory phonetics, these features are articulatory. For consonants, the features are generally voicing, place of articulation, and manner of articulation; for vowels, the features are tongue height, tongue position, and lip rounding. In acoustic phonetics, the features are limited to 12 to 15 acoustic features universal in language.

The identifying-contrastive features, whether articulatory or acoustic, constitute the feature mode of the phoneme; these features are simultaneously occurring components of the unit. They are identificational because they positively identify the physical characteristics of the phoneme. They are at least implicitly contrastive, in that each feature used to identify a phoneme also sets it apart from other phonemes of the language.

Essential sound units, in this view, are not constituted merely by a set of oppositions. Each sound unit has positive identifying characteristics and because of these identificational characteristics, it is opposed to other units of the system which have positive characteristics. The /p/ phoneme, a voiceless bilabial stop, is opposed to nonvoiceless, nonbilabial, and nonstops. The features are first identificational; their contrastive nature only becomes apparent when the phoneme is viewed within the phonemic system.

Phonemes as Particles. The feature mode of an emic unit has particle-like features. The particle view is a static view of language, in which the essential units appear as clear-cut building blocks, out of which the meaningful forms of language are constructed. The sounds which actually occur may overlap, but these etic sounds are grouped under units called phonemes. A phoneme is said to "occur" when one of its manifesting forms occurs.

The phoneme is an abstraction. It is abstracted from the set of allophones in which it is realized. Because it is abstract, it is a clear-cut particle, defined by the features common to its allophones. It is part of organized language, belonging to language rather than speech, to competence rather than performance. In abstraction, essential features are retained, and nonessential features are ignored. Thus, the word /pin/, 'pin,' might be represented phonemically as made of particles:

$$\boxed{\text{/p/}} \quad + \quad \boxed{\text{/i/}} \quad + \quad \boxed{\text{/n/}}$$

In this representation, the overlapping characteristics of the sounds are ignored. /p/ is a voiceless bilabial stop. The feature of aspiration is ignored. /i/ is a high front unrounded vowel. Its prenasalization before /n/ is ignored. /n/ is a voiced alveolar nasal.

Phonemic Contrast. The feature mode of an emic unit is also characterized by the fact that in this mode the unit appears in contrast. Phonemes are in contrastive distribution. They are essential sound units which have the capacity for changing meaning. Because they can change meaning, they must be recognized, or the message can be distorted. The principles of phonemic analysis isolate the essential phonemes:

1. *The Principle of Phonetic Similarity* (Negative Norm). Sounds which are dissimilar are not grouped as allophones of the same phoneme. This principle prevents grouping of any sounds except those listed as suspicious pairs. Thus, the sound /h/ and the sound /ŋ/, despite their perfect complementary distribution, do not belong to the same phoneme.
2. *The Principle of Contrast.* Sounds in contrast in identical environments, where the sound difference is paralleled by a meaning difference, must belong to different phonemes. If two sounds occur in the same slot in a frame, in parallel distribution, and if, while occurring in this slot, they change the meaning of the form, they are different phonemes. Once the sound unit has demonstrated its capacity to change meaning, by actually changing meaning in at least one case, it is a phoneme. Once a phoneme, always a phoneme. Pairs of sounds occurring in identical frames, with parallel change in meaning, are called minimal pairs.

The Distribution Mode: Phonemic Systems

After the study of phonetics and phonemics, the results of the phonemic analysis are presented as a list of phonemes organized into a phonemic system. The consonants of the language are arranged in a contrastive chart of consonant phonemes; the vowels of the language are arranged in a contrastive chart of the vowel phonemes. In this mode, each phoneme is seen as part of the sound system of the language.

The phonemic system of a language is a list of all the phonemes of the language arranged in some systematic pattern. These sound systems generally range from 30 to 60 phonemes, segmental and suprasegmental. One standard analysis of English lists 24 consonants, 9 vowels, and 12 suprasegmentals, or 45 phonemes total (Dinneen, 1967:44). Hawaiian has only 13 segmental phonemes, 5 vowels, and 8 consonants, the least number of phonemes recorded for a language. The highest number estimated for any language is about 75.

The distribution mode of the phoneme may be interpreted as a set of syntagmatic relations, a set of paradigmatic relations, or both. The syntagmatic relations of the phoneme are its possibilities of occurrence in linear sequences and are sometimes referred to as phonotactics. For a clear understanding of phonemes as a system, it seems preferable to leave phonotactics aside and concentrate on paradigmatic relations.

Phonemic Systems. In a language description, phonemes are charted within a systematic framework, generally with separate charts for the consonants, the vowels, and possibly the suprasegmental phonemes. The distribution mode of the emic unit is the system of oppositions of which the emic unit is a part. It is only within this relational system that the unit, with its identifying features, is seen as contrasting with the other units of the system. The features, within the system, become explicitly contrastive. To completely understand the emic unit, we must know:

1. What is it? What are its identifying contrastive features?
2. How is it manifested? What comprises its existential set?
3. How does it fit into the system? What is it opposed to?

As in Gestalt psychology, the figure emerges more clearly when seen against the background of its immediate environment, within the system or matrix of which it is a part. Within the phonemic system, phonemes may differ by a minimal contrast of one feature, or they may differ by several features. The /p/ phoneme, in English, is seen as opposed to nonvoiceless, nonbilabial, and nonstops in a system where these sounds occur. The phoneme is partially determined by these contrasts. Likewise the range of allophones of the phoneme is limited by the sounds that surround it in its own phonemic matrix.

Phonemic Fields. The distribution mode of an emic unit has the characteristics of a matrix or field. The field view is a functional view of language, in which the emic units, already recognized as clear-cut units, are seen as functioning particles within a system. When the phoneme occurs, it occurs as part of a phonemic system. It brings with it a set of identifying features, seen within the system as explicitly contrastive.

Once the phonemic chart is established, the occurrences of the phonemes are easier to chart in linear sequence. First, the choice of essential units is limited to a concrete inventory. Second, the phonemes of the inventory are so closely interrelated that the choice of phoneme occurrence is limited by, and contrasts with, the nearest phonemes. Thus, in English, the phoneme /p/ is contrasted with other units in the following chart:

Like a navigator locating the position of his ship on the sea, the analyst uses two intersecting lines to get a fix on the position — on the one hand, the position of the sound in the linear string, a horizontal line, and on the other hand, the place of the phoneme in its paradigm, a vertical line. In this way, the sequence /pin/ is distinguished from /bin/ and /tin/.

Phonemic Symmetry. The distribution mode of the emic unit, seen as paradigmatic, places the phoneme in a symmetrical matrix, or at least in a matrix which tends towards symmetry. These essential units make up the total set of units of the language, arranged in a symmetrical system. They constitute a set of oppositions which is the sound system of the particular language. The principles of symmetry and economy are used to help isolate phonemic units:

1. *The Principle of Symmetry.* Phonemic systems tend towards symmetry or neatness of pattern. Asymmetrical solutions proposed for phonemic inventories are considered less likely. According to this principle, if a language shows a set of contrasts, such as /p,b/, /t,d/, and has the phoneme /k/, one would expect to find a corresponding phoneme /g/ to produce a balanced /p,t,k/ versus /b,d,g/ system of stops in the language.
2. *The Principle of Economy.* Interpretation of phonemic systems tends towards the least number of phonemes. However, as Hockett has pointed out (1958:110), the least number of phonemes per utterance is also part of economy. The principle of economy does not prevent the analysis of phoneme sequences as units, such as /č/ for [tš]. Such an analysis may add the new phoneme /č/ to the inventory, but it simplifies each of the phonemic utterances in which [tš] occurs in the language.

THE LEXICAL COMPONENT

The second component of a language description deals with forms — forms as they are manifested in language, forms in their identifying-contrastive features, forms as part of the lexical system. The minimum meaningful form unit is the morpheme. In the lexical component of a language description, we consider: (1) the manifestation mode, (2) the feature mode, and (3) the distribution mode of the form units of language, the morphemes. The three modes of the morpheme are developed by Pike (1967, Chap. 6).

The Manifestation Mode: Morphetics

In the discovery process, we begin the study of the lexical system of language with the study of morphetics, which is the study of forms that occur in language. In the presentation of language description, the results of the study of morphetics become the manifestation mode of the morpheme unit. Each etic morph discovered is listed as an allomorph of one of the emic units, the morphemes of the language.

Manifesting Set of Allomorphs. In a language description, we establish a lexicon for the language, which is an inventory of the "total stock of morphemes in a language" (Bloomfield, 1933:162). This listing may be extended to include other lexemes, such as polymorphic words and idiomatic expressions. Within the lexicon, each single morpheme is realized in a well-defined set of manifesting forms, which are called allomorphs of that morpheme. Even when the morpheme is invariant and is always manifested by the same form, the morpheme is realized in a set of allomorphs, which, in this case, is limited to a single member. These morphemes are realized on the concrete level of phonemic transcription as morphs, which are minimum meaningful forms. For example, in a description of English, the "plural" morpheme $\{Z_1\}$ is manifested by a concrete set of actually occurring plural forms, such as the forms:

/-ɨz/	after sibilants and fricatives, s, z, š, ž, č, ǰ as in, *horses, roses, churches, judges*
/-s/	after other voiceless sounds, (except s, š, č) as in, *cats, tacks, cliffs, myths*
/-z/	after other voiced sounds, (except z, ž, ǰ) as in, *dogs, pads, boys, girls*

The manifesting set of allomorphs corresponds to the manifestation mode of the emic unit. The morphs, in phonemic transcription, are the "nonsimultaneously occurring physical variants" (Pike, 1967:85) in the lexical component. They are nonsimultaneous because one and only one morph occurs at a given time. The selection of the proper morph depends upon the phonological, lexical, or grammatical environment of the form.

Allomorphs as Waves. The manifestation mode of an emic unit has wavelike features. In the dynamic view of language, in which forms are considered at the concrete level of occurrence, overlapping and blurring characteristics may be manifested. Forms in actual speech run together so that their occurrence appears like the overlapping of wave structures rather than as a continuous chain of discrete meaningful particles. For example:

| Did you enjoy it | sounds like | /djuwnjoyɨt/ |
| How did you like it | sounds like | /hawj ʌ/+/laykɨt/ |

To understand these phrases in which the borders of morphs are not well defined, we must revert to that level of analysis where the meaningful forms of language are abstracted and systematically grouped as well-defined lexical particles within the lexical system.

Allomorphic Variation. The manifestation mode of the emic unit is also characterized by the noncontrastive distribution of its variants. Morphophonemics is the study of the representation of alternate forms of a morpheme within different environments. Hockett (1958:273) distinguishes sporadic and systematic alternation:

1. *Sporadic alternation* is the nonpredictable variation of the forms of language, due to history, style, dialect, slips of the tongue, and so forth. Such alternates do not form part of systematic description.
2. *Systematic alternation* is predictable in terms of the environment in which the form occurs, either phonological, or morphological, or grammatical. This alternation is an essential part of description.

Allomorphs of the same morpheme may be in complementary distribution, or in partial complementation with some free variation, but not in full free variation (which would make them sporadic), and never in contrast in the language. The following principles are useful:

1. *The Principle of Phonetic-Semantic Similarity.* Invariant morphs with one form and one meaning in all occurrences are morphemes. Variant morphs with the same meaning must belong to the same morpheme. Semantic similarity is necessary and sufficient to establish morphs as allomorphs of a morpheme; phonetic similarity is generally found, but is not absolutely required. Where phonetic similarity is missing, as in the grouping of

go and *went* or *I* and *me*, strong arguments from pattern congruity are required to justify grouping these as allomorphs.
2. *The Principle of Complementation* (Negative Norm). Forms not in contrast, which are either in complementary distribution in mutually exclusive environments, or in partial complementation with some free variation, may belong to the same morpheme. This principle states that morphs may be grouped as allomorphs, provided they are never found in positive contrast in the language. It will in fact be the case that, if the morphs are to be grouped as allomorphs of a single morpheme, they will appear as noncontrastive variants, with well-defined environments for the occurrence of each variant of the morpheme.

The Feature Mode: Morphemics

Discovery of morphemes proceeds in two steps. First, in the study of morphetics, the minimum meaningful forms of the language are isolated with their proper meaning. Second, the etic morphs are grouped, in the study of morphemics, into minimum meaningful form units, which may be represented by one or more allomorphs. In the presentation of the lexical component, the morphemes are listed in the lexicon, together with their form, class, and gloss. Where these morphemes have more than one allomorph, the allomorphs are listed in a set of morphophonemic rules, which give the proper environment for each allomorph. These rules are appended to the lexicon.

The *morpheme* is defined as a minimum meaningful unit in the language. Forms with the same meaning belong to the same morpheme; forms with different meanings belong to different morphemes. The test for contrast is whether, given that the forms occur in identical environments, they have different meanings within the same environment. Thus, even homophonous forms, such as *pair/pare/pear*, are listed as different morphemes. If meanings are similar, an attempt should be made to set up a statement of complementary distribution, which describes the environment in which each form occurs. According to this test, so-called synonyms, such as *big/large*, fail to complement each other and are listed as different morphemes.

Distinctive Features of Morphemes. In the language description, the morphemes are listed in the lexicon together with their form, class, and gloss. For the form-meaning unit, the list of variant forms and their respective environments, the form class to which the morpheme belongs and the meaning carried by the morpheme, constitute its distinctive features. Meanings are often difficult to describe; morphemes are generally considered to have an "area of meaning" that is in contrast with the "areas of meanings" of other morphemes in the language.

The identifying-contrastive features of the morpheme correspond to the feature mode of the lexical unit. These features are the "simultaneously occurring identificational-contrastive features" (Pike, 1967:85). In the morpheme unit, the referential inward meaning occurs simultaneously with the outward form or set of forms of the morpheme. These forms, and the meaning they carry, contrast with other morphemes of the language. They constitute the morpheme as a form-meaning composite.

The features of the morpheme are first identificational and then contrastive. The morpheme of the language must be established as a form-meaning composite, with one meaning and the forms which carry this meaning; this unit is then seen as contrastive with the other form-meaning composites within the structure of the same language.

Morphemes as Particles. In the feature mode, the morphemes of the language are viewed as particles. This is the static view of language, in which units are seen as distinct and free of the overlapping characteristics that occur at the etic level. The form-meaning composites are the discrete building blocks of which utterances are made, independently of the concrete form which the morpheme assumes in a particular utterance.

The morpheme is an abstraction. It is abstracted from the set of allomorphs by which it is realized. Being abstract, it is a discrete type of particle, defined by the features of form and meaning common to its allomorphs. This abstract unit is part of organized language, belonging to competence rather than to performance. The essential features of the form-meaning composite are retained and the nonessential features ignored. Words may be blurred in actual speech, but the morphemes are distinct. Thus the sentence, which phonologically is /djuwnjoyɨt/, is represented:

$$\boxed{\text{do}} + \boxed{\text{past}} + \boxed{\text{you}} + \boxed{\text{en}} + \boxed{\text{joy}} + \boxed{\text{it}}$$

Each of the units is a morpheme, manifested in a particular allomorph. The morpheme sequence is particle-like, independent of the allomorphic representation chosen, and the phonological realization of the allomorphs.

Morphemic Contrast. In the feature mode of the emic unit, the unit is contrastive. Each form-meaning composite is opposed to all the other form-meaning composites of the language. Morphemes are essential form-meaning units. The message carried by each form must be recognized and the meanings behind forms are, in fact, recognized by the speech community, which enables them to communicate via language. The principles of morphemic analysis help isolate the morphemes:

1. *The Principle of Phonetic Similarity* (Negative Norm). Forms that are dissimilar phonetically normally are not grouped as allomorphs of the same morpheme. The presumption is that if two different forms occur with closely related meanings, they belong to different morphemes. We assume the so-called synonyms are different in the language. However, allomorphs differ from almost perfect identity of form to suppletion, in which the whole form is replaced. Without similarity, strong arguments are required from pattern congruity to establish morphemic identity.

2. *The Principle of Contrast.* Forms in contrast in identical environments, where the form difference is paralleled by a meaning difference, must belong to different morphemes. This is the positive principle of contrast. If two morphs occur in the same grammatical slot, in parallel distribution, and if, while occurring in this slot, they signal a change in meaning, then they belong to different morphemes, that is, the morphemes are in contrast.

The Distribution Mode: Morphemic Systems

In the discovery process, after the study of morphetics and the grouping of allomorphs in morphemics, the results of morphemic analysis are presented in a systematic arrangement in the lexicon. In this lexicon, morphemes are seen as part of a contrastive system, in which morphemes are grouped into morpheme class, system. The lexical units are separated into content classes are opposed to each other.

The lexical system of a language is a part-of-speech, or morpheme class, system. The lexical units are separated into content classes, such as noun, verb, adjective, and adverb; and function word classes, such as determiner, connector, relater, intensifier, negative, and auxiliary. In the form-class-gloss listing of the lexicon, the form class label sorts the morphemes according to classes; and within each class, the morpheme units differ according to their form and meaning.

The distribution mode of the morpheme considers the distribution of the morpheme units in sequence, class, and matrix. The distribution of morphemes in sequences is handled in the tagmemic grammar. The distribution of morpheme units into classes, and in matrices within the classes, belongs to the paradigmatic relations of the lexicon.

Morphemic Systems. Morphemes are grouped into classes, and the classes are opposed to each other in the morphology of the language. A morpheme marked as "noun" contrasts with all nonnouns in the language; it also contrasts with all other nouns within the noun class. This mode is "composed of relational components, including class membership" (see Pike, 1967:85).

The tagmemic lexicon is the semantic system of the language description; there is no semantic component divorced from the lexical (and grammatical) systems. Although this system has received little attention to date, Longacre suggests the need for a "highly-sophisticated lexicon" (1964:8) in order to generate both grammatical and sensible sentences. The detailing of semantic substrata need not be done by semantic features in isolation. Just as phonemes are units composed of a bundle of features, so the semantic features can be treated as bundles of features, and the morpheme classes broken down into subclasses. The semantic feature approach parallels the use of semantic subclasses:

± Count	± Human	± Common
count noun	human noun	common noun
mass noun	nonhuman noun	proper noun

The features chosen as norms for subdivision into classes would be only those which represent grammatical features of the language, and only those grammatical features which are not overtly marked by other formal means. The subclass categories must be selective, not inflective, categories.

Lexical Fields. The distribution mode of the emic unit of the lexicon may be viewed as the distribution of lexical units in classes within a lexical field. The total lexicon may be viewed as the network of relationships between the forms of language. The language system is like a net that casts its shadow upon a blank screen called the *purport* (Hjelmslev, 1963:57), which represents all of reality. It is the lexical system that divides up reality according to the mind of the native speakers. The lexical units are the functioning parts of a language system. In the field view, the morphemes of language are seen as explicitly contrastive.

Not only the whole lexicon, but individual parts of the lexicon, such as a single class, can be set up as a separate matrix. Some work has been done by lexicographers in establishing lexical fields: for example, within pronominal systems, kinship terms, tense-aspect contrasts, and so on. Languages with first person inclusive and exclusive, and with dual and plural numbers, have a different pronominal system from that used in English. For example, the Mundari language has a system of one inanimate and 11 animate pronouns. The pronoun *we* has four equivalents, using dual/plural, inclusive/exclusive features.

aling,	'we two, you (the hearer) and I'
alang,	'we two, he (not the hearer) and I'
abu,	'we plural, you (the hearers) and I'
ale,	'we plural, they (not the hearers) and I'

Once lexical systems are established for a language, the relations of class to class, and the associative relations within the class, are evident. The choice, for example, of one of the above pronouns in a grammatical slot, is the implicit exclusion of all the other pronouns of the language system.

Lexical Symmetry. The distribution mode of the lexical emic unit places each morpheme within a paradigmatic system which is generally symmetrical for the language. The lexical units constitute a system of oppositions, of class to class, and of units within each class. Forms are arranged in contrastive sets or within specific word class paradigms. The principle of symmetry is used to isolate morpheme units:

1. *The Principle of Symmetry.* Morphemic systems tend towards symmetry, or pattern congruity. The range of each morpheme should be nonunique (Hockett, 1958: 275); it should fit the emerging grammatical patterns of the language. According to this principle, we group /gow/ and /wen-/ as allomorphs of a single morpheme, for together they make a verb paradigm. Without this grouping, /gow/ would have no past, and /wen-/ would have no present.

2. *The Principle of Economy.* Morphemic systems tend to be as economical as possible. In applying this principle, simplicity of syntax takes precedence over morphological simplicity. For example, it is syntactically convenient to speak of one plural in English, even though this means grouping widely disparate forms. Likewise, the grouping of *I* and *me* as allomorphs fits the pronouns into the noun paradigm and eliminates the objective case from English.

THE SYNTACTIC COMPONENT

The third component of a language description deals with the patterns of arrangements — with arrangements as manifested in the forms of the language, arrangements in their identifying-contrastive features, and arrangements as part of a syntactic system. The minimum unit of this component is the tagmeme, considered in its manifestation mode, feature mode, and distribution mode. The tagmeme is treated under these three modes, by Pike (1967, Chap. 7).

The Manifestation Mode: Tagmatics

In the discovery process, we begin the study of grammar with the study of tagmatics, which is the isolation of the etic slot:class correlatives, the tagmas. These tagmas are then grouped as allotagmas of the emic units, the tagmemes. In the presentation of the results of analysis, the etic units constitute the manifesting set of function-form units and make up the manifestation mode of the tagmeme.

Manifesting Set of Allotagmas. In language description, we set up a series of tagmemic formulas at the natural levels of the sentence, the clause, the phrase, and the word. The formulas are composed of tagmeme units. Each tagmeme is manifested by a set, containing one or more slot:class correlatives, called tagmas. They may vary as follows (see also pp. 20–21):

1. *Form Variants.* Allotagmas of a tagmeme may differ from each other in form alone. Since the tagmeme is a slot:class correlation, the slot may remain constant but manifest different filler classes. Each filler class represents a different allotagma of the same tagmeme. Thus, the subject tagmeme S:N/pn has two variants, S:N and S:pn, with different fillers.

2. *Positional Variants.* Allotagmas of a tagmeme may differ from each other in position alone. Since the slot: class unit has a distribution in the language, any change of position, without corresponding change of form and without change in grammatical meaning, is a separate allotagma. In a language with SPO and POS order, the subject has two positions in the string, and these constitute two positional variants of the tagmeme.

3. *Meaning Variants.* Functional meaning of the tagmemic slot is the main identifying characteristic of the tagmeme and should be kept constant. In a formal analysis, where the generic meaning of the tagmeme is the same and the manifesting form and position of the tagmeme are constant, then there may be different shades of meaning within the same tagmeme. In order to avoid being misled by a priori categories, the analyst must consider the outward form, position, and type of construction as the main clues to the identity of the tagmeme.

Allotagmas as Waves. The manifestation mode of the tagmeme should show wavelike characteristics. However, in the syntactic part of the grammar, we are at a higher level of abstraction. The tagmeme is manifested by morpheme sequences; and the morphemes are, in turn, reduced via morphophonemics to phoneme sequences. Whenever the morpheme boundaries overlap, the tagmemes also overlap. But if we restrict tagmemic overlap to clear-cut sequences of morphemes, the only overlap is one of function, not of form. In those cases where the same morpheme sequence has more than one function, or where there is a portmanteau representation of two functions in one form, the wavelike characteristics of the grammatical unit are evident. In the sentence *John asked her to go to the dance tonight,* the form *her* simultaneously manifests the object tagmeme, with respect to the verb *ask,* and a subject tagmeme, with respect to the verb *go.* In a portmanteau representation, such as the verb form *won't = will not,* the auxiliary and the negative tagmeme are manifested in a single form. Grammatical constructions are represented as waves (Pike, 1967:1–14), with attention to an unchanged wave peak or nucleus, and with deletion or severe restrictions on form and meaning at the edges of the wavelike structure, occurring at all levels of the grammar.

Allotagmatic Variation. The manifestation mode of the tagmeme is characterized by the noncontrastive distribution of the allotagmas which are its manifesting set. A judgment must be made as to when two tagmas are the same (belong to one tagmeme) and when they are different (belong to different tagmemes). The main differences to be considered are: (1) differences in slot meaning, (2) differences in filler class, and (3) differences in position within a construction, or occurrence in different constructions.

1. *Grammatical Similarity.* Two tagmas with distinct slot meaning and distinct filler classes belong to different tagmemes, for example, S:N and P:tV. Tagmas with similar functional meaning and similar filler classes may belong to the same tagmeme, for example, S:N and S:pn.
2. *Complementation.* Two tagmas which never contrast, that is, which never occur within the same construction, may be in complementary distribution if one occurs in one construction and another in a different construction with similarity of slot meanings and some similarity of filler class.

Following this principle of complementation, it would seem that all subjects in English could be reduced to a single subject tagmeme, with the meanings subject-as-actor, subject-as-goal, and so on, depending upon the construction in which it stands. Pike, however, seems to prefer to call each different subject type a separate tagmeme in English (1967:196). In this view, the many subject tagmemes would constitute a class of subject tagmemes, which are analogously the same (see also, "Tagma," 1967:219; "Homophonous Tagmas," 1967:231).

The Feature Mode: Tagmemics

In the discovery process, we first isolate the etic slot:class units or tagmas; the next step is to group these into emic units, the tagmemes. Tagmatics is a cutting process, the isolation of the first approximations to the grammatical units. Tagmemics is a grouping process, which involves human judgment, an attempt to group tagmas into units essential to the language, as the language appears to the native speaker.

The *tagmeme* is defined as the correlation of a grammatical function, or slot, with the list of mutually substitutable items that fill that slot (Elson and Pickett, 1962:57). It is a slot:class correlation. The grammatical function is represented by the slot symbol and refers to the grammatical meaning attached to a functional position in a frame. The filler class refers to all the morphemes and morpheme sequences that may be used to fill that slot in the construction frame. Both form and function are explicit in the concept of the tagmeme.

Slot, or function, refers to such notions as subject, predicate, object, and agent, which, in transformational grammar, are called grammatical relationships. Filler class refers to such notions as noun, noun phrase, verb, transitive clause, and so on, which, in transformational grammar, are called grammatical categories (see Chomsky, 1965:64). In the complex notation of tagmemics, for example, S:N, function and form are never confused. Functional (relational) symbols are written to the left of the ratio mark (:); form (category) symbols are written to the right.

Distinctive Features of Tagmemes. The distinctive features of the tagmeme are the identifying-contrastive features of the unit. These are the features of meaning, form, and distribution, that is, (1) functional meaning of the slot, (2) the list of forms filling the slot, and (3) the position of the tagmeme within a given construction. We ask:

What is it?	a noun phrase	(filler class)
What does it do?	it acts as subject	(functional slot)
Where does it occur?	at clause level	(distribution)

All three of these features are used to identify the tagmeme, although within any one feature there may be variation. Each tagmeme will contrast with others in the system, according to these contrastive features.

The functional meaning of the tagmeme is vaguely defined, and this is an advantage in initial analysis. Subject is an intuitive notion; but it is opposed to predicate, object, location, and so on, which occur in the same construction. Subjects which occur in different constructions are only the same by analogy: active subjects are to active predicates as passive subjects are to passive predicates. The relation is the same; the meanings of the various subjects need not be univocal.

Tagmemes as Particles. The feature mode of the slot:class correlative establishes the tagmeme as a particle. Tagmemes are "structurally significant points within a given pattern" (Longacre, 1964:17). In this static view, there is no overlapping, but a clear-cut abstracted view of definite points in the construction pattern filled by definite filler classes. Further, the patterns occur at levels, so that we may speak of clause level tagmemes or phrase level tagmemes.

The points within the construction pattern are grammatically significant, in that they assign grammatical meaning to fillers of the slot. The grammatical meaning is determined by subtracting the lexical meaning of occurring items from the total linguistic meaning. This meaning is associated with the slot, not with the particular lexical item. By this method, we isolate such meanings as subject, predicate, object, and so on, at the clause level, or head and modifier at the phrase level.

There is correlativity between the slot meaning isolated and the meanings of the other slots in the same string. Point and pattern are correlatives; there is no construction without constituent tagmemes, and no tagmemes independent of the construction in which they occur. The "subject" is subject because it is opposed to the predicates, objects, and adverbial adjuncts within the same string.

Tagmemic Contrast. The feature mode of the tagmeme unit is also characterized by the fact that the tagmemes of the grammar are in contrast with each other. These are units of arrangement, which carry their own contrastive grammatical meanings in the language. These grammatical meanings must be understood by anyone using the particular language.

1. *Grammatical Similarity* (Negative Norm). Dissimilar tagmas are not grouped together into the same tagmeme. There must be some foundation of similarity, in form or function, before consideration is given to reducing two tagmas to the same tagmemic unit.

2. *Principle of Contrast.* Tagmemes contrast within the grammar. First, tagmemes at different levels are distinct, and not comparable. Second, within a given level, tagmemes are in contrast with each other within the same construction string. The fact of co-occurrence of two similar tagmas in the same string is prima facie evidence that there are two tagmemes present, although it is possible, in some languages, to have repetitions of a tagmeme within the string. Third, more subtle differences of meaning in the same tagmeme may require separation of one generic functional notion into two or more tagmemes, if there are other differences. If formal differences are minimal and the functional differences are analogous, the variants may remain as allotagmas of the one tagmeme.

The Distribution Mode: Tagmemic Systems

In the discovery process, the tagmas, or initial slot:class units, are first isolated. Then those tagmas which are functionally the same are grouped into tagmeme units. Finally, the tagmeme units are viewed as arranged in a systematic way within the grammar. This system involves: (1) the unit, the tagmeme, as a slot:class correlative; (2) the construction, or syntagmeme, which is a string of tagmemes; and (3) the levels of the grammar at which constructions occur.

The systematic distribution of the tagmeme occurs within the larger framework of grammatical space called the grammatical hierarchy. Each tagmeme is seen against the background of the total grammar. The tagmemes are arranged like the beads on an abacus, or counting board. The beads are the units. These units are arranged on wires to form strings. The strings are arranged from higher to lower within a frame. To locate a particular bead, one must specify which level, which string, which unit. Likewise, the tagmemic unit is part of a grammatical system in which the level, construction, and place within the construction determine its place in the total system.

Tagmemic Systems. The distribution mode of the tagmeme is its position within the tagmemic system. The system in which the tagmeme is distributed is the total grammar of the language. The tagmeme unit forms part of a set of oppositions which comprise the whole system. This set of oppositions is similar to phonemic and lexical systems, but there are differences:

1. The tagmeme unit is a correlation of function and set, and of slot and filler class. Just as phonemes differ by one or many distinctive features, so tagmemes may dif-

fer by function or form or both. Function and form are correlative and inseparable. Forms do not occur in grammar without having a specific grammatical function; and functions do not occur in grammar without forms to manifest that function.

2. The tagmeme construction is a string of tagmemes. The construction is a pattern; the tagmemes are the contrastive points in the pattern. This is a second correlativity. The tagmeme exists only in the string, and the string does not exist without its component tagmemes. The set of oppositions is between tagmemes within the same string.

3. Constructions occur at well-defined levels in the grammar; the level specifies the tagmeme as a clause level tagmeme, occurring in a clause level construction. Subject at word level and subject at clause level are distinct tagmemes, not by grammatical function, but according to the level of grammar at which they occur.

Tagmemic Fields. The distribution mode of an emic unit has the characteristics of a matrix, or field. The field view is functional and represents the units as functioning elements within the total system. When the tagmeme occurs, it occurs as part of a grammatical system, in explicit contrast with all other tagmemes of the system.

Once the tagmeme is clearly defined as part of a field, the actual occurrences of the unit are easier to recognize. The tagmeme will be clearly contrastive as to (1) the range of functional meaning allowable within the tagmeme unit; (2) the type of fillers allowable within the unit, including special case markings or recognizable sets of function words; and (3) the type of construction in which the unit occurs and the level at which the construction occurs.

To locate a specific tagmeme within the system, the tagmeme should be at a definite rank and depth within the system. Proceed to the proper level, go to the construction at the proper layer within that level, and follow the tagmemic string to the given tagmeme. It is fixed in position at a definite level in the hierarchy and at a special position within the level.

Tagmemic Symmetry. Language systems tend toward symmetry at the phonological and lexical levels. They also tend toward symmetry in grammar. Tagmemic constructions may be set up as matrix displays, showing elements of constructions as explicitly contrastive. Construction types may be charted in various dimensions, as was done at sentence and clause level, to determine whether there are gaps within the overall system.

The object of the language description is to reveal the facts of the grammatical structure of unknown languages in the simplest and most economical way. We have assumed five levels to be "natural" to language, but a particular language might require more or fewer levels. Within these levels we expect relational, coordinate and subordinate structures, yet all strata might not be represented. The language, for example, might lack an inflectional system. Finally, in the individual constructions, the order of elements is as we find it. The individual tagmemes are specified functionally according to the range of grammatical meaning allowed for the language under consideration; the filler classes that manifest these functions are those forms that actually occur fulfilling this function. In the overall language analysis, the symbols for function and form, the means for combining these in constructions, and the methods for ordering constructions at levels from higher to lower are present in the theory. It is up to the individual analyst to so use the techniques provided in tagmemics as to describe accurately a given language, and to so apply tagmemic theory as to reveal, in the simplest possible way, the structure of that language.

PRACTICE 7: WORKING FROM A GIVEN CORPUS

For the following sentences adapted from Problem #165, Sierra Popoluca, (*Laboratory Manual*, Merrifield, 1967):
1. Set up the grammar for the language, including formulas at the four levels of sentence, clause, phrase, and word. Include any transformation rules, restrictions, or assumptions that are necessary.
2. Set up the lexicon of the language, including all the morphemes which occur in the data. For morphemes which have variants, list the morpheme variants and summary rules for the morphophonemics of the language.

Procedures for the Grammar

1. *Sentence Level.* Final intonation assumed for each utterance #1-75.
2. *Clause Level.* The following clause level types occur:
   - a. Statements—transitive
        — intransitive
        — equational
   - b. Commands—transitive
        — intransitive

3. *Phrase Level.* The following phrase types occur:
   a. Head noun and modifiers
       {he?m} 'that,' {tu·m} 'a,' {ha?yang} 'much.'
   b. Head adjective and modifier
       {ca·m} 'very.'
4. *Word Level.* The following composite word types occur:
   a. Noun stem with possessive.
   b. Verb stem with subject, tense, and aspect.
   c. Imperative verb stem with mood marker.
   d. Noun stem with adverbializers expressing loca-
      tion or manner.

Restrictions and Assumptions

1. *Subject Permutability.* The subject is movable in tCl and
   iCl. It may occur before or after the predicate-object
   complex.
2. *Adjunct Permutability.* The adjuncts, LMT, are freely
   movable. They are optional and occur in any order after
   the SPO complex.
3. *Negative Transformation.* Affirmative statements become negative by the addition of {dʸa} 'not'; negative
   commands take {odoy} 'don't.'
4. *Cross-Functional Usage.* Some words have two uses:
   a. Indeclinable nouns are used as locationals
      {playa} 'beach' and {a·tebet} 'Soteapan.'
   b. The locational adverb {huuma} 'far away' is
      used in the predicate attribute position with
      the adjective class.

Lexicon and Morphophonemics

1. *The Lexicon* may be set up as a classified lexicon.
   a. The noun system, including nouns, pronouns,
      determiners, adjectives, intensifiers, and noun
      suffixes.
   b. The verb system, including verb stems, tense,
      aspect, and mood; and subject pronouns, nega-
      tives, introducers, locatives, and temporals.
2. *Morphophonemics.* Some of the morphemes have variant
   forms.
   a. Morphemes with variants are listed in the lexi-
      con in braces{ }.
   b. Allomorphs are listed for each of these in the
      lexicon, with a statement of the conditioning
      environment.

3. *Summary Rules.* The principal changes can be summarized in the following rules:
   a. Assimilation of prefix-final nasals, except palatal
      nasals.
   b. Loss of stem final vowel in nouns, loss of prefix
      initial /h-/.
   c. Palatalization of initial consonants, /t,n/ after
      prefixes with high front vowels.
   d. Vowel changes in the imperative form of the
      verb stem.

Maximum Generative Potential

The maximum generative potential (MGP) can be reduced by
these restrictions:

1. Subject and predicate have person and number concord.
2. Equational clauses require a noun phrase which includes {he?m}, 'that.'
3. Manner adverbs in {-yukma}, and {-ma}, are in complementary distribution, with one form for transitives,
   one for intransitives.

Even with these restrictions, the restricted generation potential
(RGP) is over 280 billion sentences, excluding all permutations.
The combinations of the adjuncts, LMT, alone account for
40,000 possibilities with each transitive and intransitive verb
form, whether statement or command. Since the subject and
object slots are filled by almost 250 forms, the output is necessarily large.

Conclusion. The modes of procedure are given for one particular problem to indicate the information which is sought in a
particular language corpus. *First,* sort the corpus according to
sentence and clause types. This reduces the present problem of
75 sentences to a set of five different problems dealing with tCl,
iCl, eqCl, C-tCl, and C-iCl. *Second,* each of these 5 isolated sets of
data is solved for grammar and lexicon, then the grammars and
lexicons are grouped in one solution. Restrictions across clause
types, for example {he?m} above, should be noted. *Third,* morphemes with variants are checked, and summary rules are constructed to account for all the morphophonemic changes.

SUPPLEMENTARY READINGS 7

Cook, Walter A., S.J., *On Tagmemes and Transforms.* Washington, D.C.,
    Georgetown University Press, 1964. For grammatical hierarchy,
    10–12; particle, wave, and field, 12–14; and discussion, 27–39.

Conklin, Harold C., "Lexicographical Treatment of Folk Taxonomies." *IJAL*, 28, Part IV (1962). Problems in Lexicography, 119–141. Methods for establishing distribution mode for lexical units.

Longacre, Robert E., *Grammar Discovery Procedures*. The Hague, Mouton & Co., 1964. "Introduction: The Notion of Grammar," for the triple hierarchy of "semiautonomous and interlocking" systems.

, "Prolegomena to Lexical Structure." *Linguistics, An International Review*, 5:5–24. The Hague, Mouton & Co., 1964. For a different viewpoint on field structure, with a matrix showing phonology, lexicon, and grammar, opposed to particle, string, field.

Pike, Kenneth L., *Language in Relation to a Unified Theory of the Structure of Human Behaviour:* The Hague, Mouton & Co., 1967. Language unit, with feature, manifestation, distribution modes.

Chap. 6, Morpheme 6.4 (154)   6.5 (163)   6.6 (169)
Chap. 7, Tagmeme 7.3 (196)   7.4 (228)   7.5 (236)
Chap. 8, Phoneme 8.3 (293)   8.4 (306)   8.5 (318)

, "Language as Particle, Wave, and Field," *The Texas Quarterly*, 2:37–54 (1959). Original presentation of particle, wave, field theory showing that the three views may be reconciled in single units.

, "Grammar as Wave." *Monograph Series on Languages and Linquistics, No. 20*, 1–14. Washington, D.C., Georgetown University Press, 1967. Applied to Kasem language of Ghana.

, "Non-linear Order and Anti-Redundancy in German Morphological Matrices." *Journal of Dialectology*, 32 (1965), Wiesbaden. For application of matrix theory in the lexical component.

, "Tagmemic and Matrix Linguistics Applied to Selected African Languages." *HEW Contract No. OE–5–14–065 Report* (1966).

Sapir, Edward, *Language: An Introduction to the Study of Speech*. New York, Harcourt, Brace and World, Inc., 1921. Chap. 2, "The Elements of Speech (Lexicon)," and Chap. 3, "The Sounds of Language (Phonology)."

SUPPLEMENTARY EXERCISES

The problems suggested as supplementary exercises are from the *Laboratory Manual for Morphology and Syntax* by William R. Merrifield, Constance M. Naish, Calvin R. Rensch and Gillian Story, published by the Summer Institute of Linguistics, Santa Ana, California, 1967 Revision.

chapter 2: Sentence Level

This is best illustrated by problems involving all levels of structure, with some mixed clause types, commands, and nested constructions (to follow Chapters 3, 4, and 5).

#96. Mezquital Otomi
#97. Michoacan Aztec
#106. Coatlan Mixe
#107. Turkish

chapter 3: Clause Level

This is best illustrated by problems that require sentence and clause level formulas, but require no formulas at the level of the phrase or word.

#92. Mixtec of San Miguel
#93. Awa of New Guinea
#94. Lotuko of Africa
#95. Palantla Chinantec

chapter 4: Phrase Level

This is best illustrated by problems that require sentence, clause, and phrase level formulas, but require no formulas at the word level.

#98. Palantla Chinantec
#99. Vietnamese

#100. Apinaye of Brazil
#102. N. Puebla Totonac

chapter 5: Word Level

This is best illustrated by problems that require sentence, clause, phrase, and word level formulas. Introduction of concord ties in formulas.

#101. Chontal of Oaxaca
#103. Otomi of Mexico
#104. Western Warburton
#105. Hausa of Africa

chapter 6: Morpheme Level

This is best illustrated by problems that require sentence, clause, phrase, and word level formulas. Introduction of relater-axis phrases.

#108. Mixtec of San Miguel
#109. Pocomchi
#110. Guajarara
#111. Mezquital Otomi

chapter 7: Language Description

This is best illustrated by problems with 75 or more sentences, involving many clause types; this is suggested as a review of all the tagmemic procedures.

#164. Cashinahua
#165. Sierra Popoluca

TAGMEMIC SYMBOLS

aj	adjective	word class 3
Aj	adjective phrase	group with adjective head
ajzr	adjectivizer	derivational affix
App:	appositive slot	in item-appositive phrase
asp:	aspect slot	at word level, verbs
aspm	aspect marker	word level affix
aux	auxiliary verb	subclass of verbs
Aux:	auxiliary slot	at phrase level, verb phrase
av	adverb	word class 4
Av	adverb phrase	group with adverb head
avzr	adverbializer	derivational affix
Ax:	axis slot	in relater-axis phrase
Base:	base slot	at sentence level
c	connector	function word
C:	connector slot	at levels above the word
core:	core slot	at word level
det	determiner	function word
Det:	determiner slot	at phrase level, noun phrase
eqCl	equational clause	clause type, equational verb
eqv	equational verb	subclass of verbs
H:	head slot	in head-modifier phrase
i	introducer	function word
I:	introducer slot	at clause level
IA	item-appositive phrase	multiple head, one referent
ICF	final intonation contour	suprasegmental
iCl	intransitive clause	clause type, intransitive verb
Id:	identifier slot	at phrase level, for clauses

197

int	intensifier	function word
Int:	intensifier slot	at phrase level
Into:	intonation slot	at sentence level
It:	item slot	in item-appositive phrase
iv	intransitive verb	subclass of verbs
iV	intransitive verb phrase	group with intransitive verb head
ivs	intransitive verb stem	stem of intransitive verb
L:	location slot	at clause level, adjunct
loc	locational adverb	subclass of adverbs, place
M:	manner slot	at clause level, adjunct
Marg:	margin slot	at sentence level
md:	mood slot	at word level, verbs
mdm	mood marker	word level affix
Mod:	modifier slot	in head-modifier phrase
n	noun	word class 1
N	noun phrase	group with noun head
N_{co}	coordinate noun phrase	multiple head, many referents
ns	noun stem	stem of nouns
neg	negative	function word
Neg:	negative slot	at phrase level, verbs
nnuc:	noun nuclear slot	at word level, nouns
nom	nominalizer	derivational affix
np	proper noun	subclass of nouns
num	numeral	subclass of adjectives
num:	number slot	at word level, sg/pl
numm	number marker	word level affix
o:	object slot	at word level
O:	object slot	at clause level
om	object marker	word level affix
P:	predicate slot	at clause level
PA:	predicate attribute slot	at clause level, equational clause
pn	pronoun	substitute, bound or free
pos:	possessive slot	at word level
Pos:	possessive slot	at phrase level
posm	possessive marker	word level afflx
Qn:	quantifier slot	at phrase level, nouns
R:	relater slot	in relater-axis phrase
RA	relater-axis phrase	exocentric phrase type
rel	relater	function word
s:	subject slot	at word level
S:	subject slot	at clause level
Sent	sentence	utterance with final intonation
sm	subject marker	word level affix
t:	tense slot	at word level, verbs
T:	temporal slot	at clause level, adjunct
tCl	transitive clause	clause type, transitive verb
tem	temporal adverb	subclass of adverbs

tm	tense marker	word level affix
tv	transitive verb	subclass of verbs
tV	transitive verb phrase	group with transitive verb head
tvs	transitive verb stem	stem of transitive verb
vbzr	verbalizer	derivational affix
vnuc:	verb nuclear slot	at word level, verbs

SELECTED BIBLIOGRAPHY

Allen, Robert Livingston, *The Verb System of Present-Day American English*. The Hague, Mouton & Co., 1966.
, "Sector Analysis: From Sentence to Morpheme in English." *Monograph Series on Languages and Linguistics No. 20*, 159–174. Washington, D.C., Georgetown University Press, 1967.

Becker, Alton L., "Conjoining in a Tagmemic Grammar of English." *Monograph Series on Languages and Linguistics No. 20*, 109–121. Washington, D.C., Georgetown University Press, 1967.

Belasco, Simon, "Tagmemics and Transformational Grammar in Linguistic Analysis." *Linguistics*, 10:5–15 (1964).
, "The Role of Transformational Grammar and Tagmemes in the Analysis of an Old French Text." *Lingua*, 10:375–390 (1961).

Blansitt, Edward Lee, *The Verb Phrase in Spanish: Classes and Relations*. Ph.D. Dissertation, University of Texas, 1963.

Bloomfield, Leonard, *Language*. New York, Holt, Rinehart and Winston, Inc., 1933.

Boas, Franz, *Introduction to the Handbook of American Indian Languages*. Washington, D.C., Georgetown University Press, 1963.

Bochenski, J. M., *The Methods of Contemporary Thought*. Dordrecht, Holland, D. Reidel Publishing Co., 1965.

Brend, Ruth M., *A Tagmemic Analysis of Mexican Spanish Clauses*. The Hague, Mouton & Co., 1968.

Chafe, Wallace L., "Review of Longacre's Grammar Discovery Procedures 1964." *Language*, 41:640–647 (1965).

Chomsky, Noam, *Syntactic Structures*. The Hague, Mouton & Co., 1957.
, *Aspects of the Theory of Syntax*. Cambridge, Mass., The M.I.T. Press, 1965.

Conklin, Harold C., "Lexicographical Treatment of Folk Taxonomies." *IJAL*, 28:2, IV: *Problems in Lexicography*, 119–141 (1962).

Cook, Walter A., *On Tagmemes and Transforms*. Washington, D.C., Georgetown University Press, 1964.

———, *A Descriptive Analysis of Mundari*. Ph.D. Dissertation, Georgetown University, 1965.

———, "The Generative Power of a Tagmemic Grammar." *Monograph Series on Languages and Linguistics*, No. *20*, 27–41. Washington, D.C., Georgetown University Press, 1967.

DeSaussure, Ferdinand, *Course in General Linguistics*, trans. by Wade Baskin. Geneva, 1916. New York, Philosophical Library, Inc., 1959.

Dinneen, Francis P., S.J., *An Introduction to General Linguistics*. New York, Holt, Rinehart and Winston, Inc., 1967.

Elson, Benjamin, and Pickett, Velma, *An Introduction to Morphology and Syntax*. Santa Ana, Summer Institute of Linguistics, 1964.

Fillmore, Charles J., "The Case for Case." *Universals in Linguistic Theory*, eds. Emmon Bach and Robert Harms. New York, Holt, Rinehart and Winston, Inc., 1968.

Fodor, Jerry A., and Katz, Jerrold J., *The Structure of Language: Readings in the Philosophy of Language*. Englewood Cliffs, N.J., Prentice-Hall, Inc., 1964.

Fries, Charles C., *The Structure of English*. New York, Harcourt, Brace and World, Inc., 1952.

———, *Linguistics and Reading*. New York, Holt, Rinehart and Winston, Inc., 1962.

Gleason, Henry A., Jr., *An Introduction to Descriptive Linguistics*. New York, Holt, Rinehart and Winston, Inc., 1955; revised, 1961.

———, *Linguistics and English Grammar*. New York, Holt, Rinehart and Winston, Inc., 1962.

———, "Contrastive Analysis in Discourse Structure." *Monograph Series on Languages and Linguistics*, No. *21*, 39–63. Washington, D.C., Georgetown University Press, 1968.

Greenberg, Joseph H., *Universals of Language*. Cambridge, Mass., The M.I.T. Press, 1963.

Halliday, M. A. K., "Categories of the Theory of Grammar." *Word*, vol. 17 (1961).

———, McIntosh, Angus, and Strevens, Peter, *The Linguistic Sciences and Language Teaching*. London, Longmans Green, Ltd., 1964.

———, "Syntax and the Consumer." *Monograph Series on Languages and Linguistics*, No. *17*, 11–14. Washington, D.C., Georgetown University Press, 1964.

Harris, Zellig, *String Analysis of Sentence Structure*. The Hague, Mouton & Co., 1962.

Hjelmslev, Louis, *Prolegomena to a Theory of Language*, trans. by Francis J. Whitfield. Madison, Wisc., The University of Wisconsin Press, 1963.

Hockett, Charles F., "Problems of Morphemic Analysis." *Language*, 23:321–343 (1947).

, "Two Models of Grammatical Description." *Word*, 10:210–231 (1954).

, *A Course in Modern Linguistics*. New York, The Macmillan Company, 1958.

, "Linguistic Elements and Their Relations." *Language*, 37: 29–53 (1961).

Huddleston, R. D., "Rank and Depth (in Scale-and-Category Grammar)." *Language*, 41:574–586 (1965).

Joos, Martin, *The English Verb: Form and Meanings*. Madison, Wisc., University of Wisconsin Press, 1964.

Katz, Jerrold J., and Postal, Paul M., *An Integrated Theory of Linguistic Description*. Cambridge, Mass., The M.I.T. Press, 1964.

Kemeny, John G., *A Philosopher Looks at Science*. Princeton, N.J., D. Van Nostrand Company, Inc., 1959.

Koutsoudas, Andre, *Writing Transformational Grammars*. New York, McGraw-Hill, Inc., 1966.

Lado, Robert, *Linguistics Across Cultures*. Ann Arbor, Mich., University of Michigan Press, 1957.

, *Language Teaching: A Scientific Approach*. New York, McGraw-Hill, Inc., 1963.

Law, Howard W., "The Use of Function-Set in English Adverbial Classification." *Monograph Series on Languages and Linguistics, No. 20*, 93–102. Washington, D.C., Georgetown University Press, 1967.

Lees, Robert B., "The Grammar of English Nominalizations." *IJAL*, 26:3, II:3, 1–205 (1960); fourth printing, The Hague, Mouton & Co., 1966.

Liem, Nguyen Dang, *English Grammar: A Combined Tagmemic and Transformational Approach, A Contrastive Analysis of Vietnamese and English*. Vol. I, Linguistic Circle of Canberra, 1966.

Lonergan, Bernard J., S.J., *Insight: A Study of Human Understanding*. New York, The Philosophical Library, Inc., 1958, reprint, 1961.

Longacre, Robert E., "String Constituent Analysis." *Language*, 36: 63–88, (1960).

, *Grammar Discovery Procedures*. The Hague, Mouton & Co., 1964.

, "Prolegomena to Lexical Structure." *Linguistics*, 5:5–24, (1964 b).

, "Some Fundamental Insights of Tagmemics." *Language*, 41: 65–76 (1965).

, "The Notion of Sentence." *Monograph Series on Languages and Linguistics, No. 20*, 15–25. Washington, D.C., Georgetown University Press, 1967.

, "Reply to Postal's Review of Grammar Procedures." *IJAL*, 33:323–328 (1967).

, and Williams, Ann F., "Popoloca Clause Types," *Acta Linguistica Hafniensia*, 10:161–186 (Copenhagen, 1967).

Marchand, Hans, *The Categories and Types of Present-Day English Word Formation*. Wiesbaden, Otto Harrassowitz, 1960.

Matson, Dan M., "Tagmemic Description of Agreement." *Monograph Series on Languages and Linguistics, No. 20*, 103–108. Washington, D.C., Georgetown University Press, 1967.

Merrifield, William R., *Laboratory Manual for Morphology and Syntax*, with Constance M. Naish, Calvin R. Rensch, and Gillian Story. Santa Ana, Summer Institute of Linguistics, 1962; revised, 1967.

――, "On the Form of Rules in a Generative Grammar." *Monograph Series on Languages and Linguistics, No. 20*, 43–55. Washington, D.C., Georgetown University Press, 1967.

Morgan, James O., "English Structure above the Sentence Level." *Monograph Series on Languages and Linguistics, No. 20*, 123–132. Washington, D.C., Georgetown University Press, 1967.

Nida, Eugene A., "The Identification of Morphemes." *Language*, 24: 414–441 (1948).

――, *Morphology: A Descriptive Analysis of Words*. Ann Arbor, Mich., University of Michigan Press, 1949.

――, *Learning a Foreign Language*. New York, Friendship Press, National Council of Churches, 1957.

――, *A Synopsis of English Syntax*. Norman, Okla., Summer Institute of Linguistics, 1959; 5th edition, 1964.

O'Brien, Richard J., S.J., *A Descriptive Grammar of Ecclesiastical Latin*. Chicago, Loyola Press, 1965.

Pickett, Velma, *The Grammatical Hierarchy of Isthmus Zapotec*. Language Dissertation 56. Baltimore, Waverly Press, 1960.

Pike, Kenneth L., *Language in Relation to a Unified Theory of the Structure of Human Behaviour*. Glendale, Calif., Summer Institute of Linguistics, Part I(1954), Part II(1955), Part III(1960); reprinted in one volume, The Hague, Mouton & Co., 1967.

――, "On Tagmemes nee Gramemes." *IJAL*, 24:273–278 (1958).

――, "Language as Particle, Wave and Field." *The Texas Quarterly*, 2:37–54, (1959).

――, "Dimensions of Grammatical Structure." *Language*, 38:221–244, (1962).

――, "A Syntactic Paradigm." *Language*, 39:216–230 (1963).

――, "Discourse Analysis and Tagmemic Matrices." *Oceanic Linguistics*, 3:5–25 (1964).

――, "Non-linear Order and Anti-Redundancy in German Morphological Matrices." *Journal of Dialectology*, 32: 193–221 (1965).

――, *Tagmemic and Matrix Linguistics Applied to Selected African Languages*. HEW Report, No. OE 5-14-065 (November, 1966).

――, "A Guide to Publications Related to Tagmemic Theory." *Current Trends in Linguistics*, Vol. III, ed. Thomas A. Sebeok, 365–394. The Hague, Mouton & Co., 1966.

――, "Grammar as Wave." *Monograph Series on Languages and Linguistics, No. 20*, 1–14. Washington, D.C., Georgetown University Press, 1967.

Postal, Paul M., "Constituent Structure: A Study of Contemporary Models of Syntactic Description." *IJAL*, 30:2, III (1964).

, "Review of Robert E. Longacre's Grammar Discovery Procedures." *IJAL*, 32:93–98 (1966).

Sapir, Edward, *Language: An Introduction to the Study of Speech*. New York, Harcourt, Brace and World, Inc., 1921.

Stageberg, Norman C., *An Introductory English Grammar*. New York, Holt, Rinehart and Winston, Inc., 1965.

Thorndike, Edward, and Lorge, Irving, *The Teacher's Word Book of 10,000 Words*. New York, Columbia University Press, 1944.

Trager, George L., and Smith, Henry Lee, Jr., *An Outline of English Structure*. Studies in Linguistics, Occasional Papers No. 3. Washington, D.C., American Council of Learned Societies, 1957.

Waterhouse, Viola, "Independent and Dependent Sentences." *IJAL*, 29:45–54 (1963).

Warriner, John E., *English Grammar and Composition*. New York, Harcourt, Brace and World, Inc. 1951; revised, 1965.

Weinreich, Uriel, *Languages in Contact: Findings and Problems*. Linguistic Circle of New York, 1953; reprinted The Hague, Mouton & Co., 1963.

, "Lexicographic Definition in Descriptive Semantics." *IJAL*, 28:2, IV: *Problems in Lexicography*, 25–43 (1962).

INDEX

abbreviated language, 59
active voice, 41–42, 47, 49, 51, 58, 66, 72, 80
addition sentence, 56–57
adjectival, 6–7, 69, 76, 96
adjective, 122–124, 197
adjective compound, 135
adjective phrase, 107–108, 197
adjectivizer, 128–131, 197
adverb, 124, 197
adverb compound, 135
adverb phrase, 107–108, 197
adverbial, 6–7, 69, 76, 95
adverbializer, 128–131, 197
affirmative, 41–42, 47, 49, 51, 58, 66, 72, 80
affix, 118
agent, 27, 72
agreement, 68, 70, 105, 109–110, 149
-AL designation, 6, 69
allomorph, 19, 85, 168, 178–180
allophone, 19, 168, 171–172
allotagma, 19–20, 168, 185–187
appositive, 92, 100–101, 103, 105–106
aspect, 112, 125, 197
assumption, 82–83
auxiliary, 107, 111–112, 123, 197
axis, 74–78, 93–99, 197

base, 12, 38, 40, 44–47, 52–54, 56–57, 61, 86, 113, 138, 165, 197
Becker, A. L., 45, 100, 114, 200
Bloomfield, L., 39, 40, 48, 57, 62, 83, 117, 118, 139, 178, 200

Bochenski, J. M., 3, 200

calls, 38, 58
case, 16, 94, 99, 103, 106, 109–110, 121–122, 125, 148–149
case grammar, 69
Chomsky, N., 1, 5, 24, 41, 43, 60, 62, 100, 112, 145, 146, 147, 148, 154, 166, 187, 200
clause, 65–66
clause analysis, 79–86
clause level, 65–86
clitic, 30, 98
closure, 4, 23–24
combinations, 5, 144, 158–160
command, 42, 49, 50, 51, 52, 71–72
competence, 1–3
complex sentence, 39–46
complex stem, 130
component, 169–170
compound sentence, 39–46
compound word, 131–138
computation, 82, 158–164
computer generation, 156–158
concord, 68, 83, 99, 103, 105, 109, 149
conflated tree, 152–153
conjoining, 44, 99–100
connector, 45, 100, 197
construction, 21–26
contrast, 168, 175, 181, 188
contrast, variation, and distribution, 170–171
coordinate phrase, 99–106
coordinate strata, 31–32
core slot, 129, 135, 197